Fiddler's CURSE

The Untold Story of Ervin T. Rouse, Chubby Wise, Johnny Cash, and the *Orange Blossom Special*

By Randy Noles

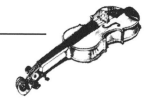

ISBN-13: 978-1-57424-214-0
ISBN-10: 1-57424-214-8

Cover Design: Ray Kilinski
Interior Layout/Design: Gisele Marasca and Susan Pagán

Dedicated to Hattie Whitehurst Rouse Miscowich, Carrie White Rouse, Geneva Kirby Wise Meeks and Rossi Truell Case Wise, who married fiddlers and lived to tell the tale.

Contents

Preface

Let's Get Vapor-Locked

The violin, or the fiddle, is the ancient grandfather of all musical instruments. Essentially, it's no more than string strung over a box, and can be played using a bow fashioned from a stick and some hair—or anything else rough enough to produce friction. Rubbing the bow across the strings produces sounds not unlike human and animal voices in excitement, pain, or flagro delecto.

If you're clever enough, you might even get someone to give you money in return for your waltzes and breakdowns. Sometimes, however, it seems that the fiddle is the most difficult instrument with which to earn a living—especially playing hillbilly style, or whatever you want to call it.

One way to survive is by performing on a cash-and-carry basis—a practice called "busking"—in taverns, on streetcorners, or wherever else people might stop and listen.

Ervin T. Rouse worked this way most of his life, even after *Orange Blossom Special* had become one of the most familiar fiddle tunes of all time. Chubby Wise also did his share of busking, both before and after he hooked up with Bill Monroe and hit the big time.

Why? Well, there are those who claim that fiddlers behave strangely because they continually breathe in rosin dust that accumulates under the strings and between the f-holes, thereby affecting the brain.

For example, my friend Vassar Clements, the great fiddler who hails from Kissimmee, Florida, says that all he ever wanted to do was to get "vapor-locked," drink black coffee, smoke his pipe, and play music. He simply hoped that the rest of the world would bring him what he needed—food, a little money, a good rhythm section (or none at all)—and carry him from place to place as needed. Luckily for Vassar, that's pretty much how things worked out.

As musicians, we have a tendency to spend a lot of time contemplating the mysterious problem of why one melody that you don't care for is so popular, while another one that you love nobody else seems much to like. We're always trying to play somewhere close to what we hear in our heads, and we're never satisfied—unless we stay drunk all the time, and even then it's hard. As a result, our dreams are flooded with the little triangles and parallelograms of fingering, sometimes to where we can't sleep at all.

Some, however, contend that the act of fiddling is fairly simple because, at its very essence, there are only four choices to be made; two choices each on which way to go with your fingers and with the bow. In other words, if you pull and it ain't right, then you push.

Ervin and Chubby knew when to push and when to pull. I knew and admired both men, and am glad that they're finally getting their due.

Vassar once met Ervin at the Nashville bus station, and recalls that the Old Man from the Everglades was wearing an overcoat despite the summer heat. The first thing he did upon his arrival was to go out in front of the depot, "unveil that antique," and start to play. What a great Rouse Brother thing to do.

Fiddlin' in Florida, to me, is Vassar, Chubby, Ervin, and *Orange Blossom Special*. I like this book. Let's get vapor locked.

John Hartford
Nashville, Tennessee
May, 2000

John Hartford was a Nashville-based singer-songwriter whose compositions included Gentle On My Mind, *one of the most recorded songs in popular music history. In 1976, his solo album* Mark Twang *(Flying Fish Records) won a Grammy for Best Ethnic or Traditional Recording. He played banjo, fiddle, guitar, and mandolin, and has released numerous critically acclaimed collections of acoustic music. Hartford died after a long battle with cancer in 2002.*

Foreword

Shaking Hands With a Ghost

O*range Blossom Special* is the definitive fiddle tune, used by fiddlers worldwide as a showpiece. It's a standard, performed at every bluegrass festival or fiddle event.

In fact, some musicians feel that this seventy-year-old crowd-pleaser has been played to death. Requesting it of an accomplished fiddler, for example, is not unlike asking a great mariachi band to play *La Bamba*. The weight of the tune's own popularity has crushed it into becoming a kind of musical tourist trap.

However, if you go back and listen to Ervin and Gordon Rouse's original 1939 recording, it's easy to hear the *Special's* beauty, elegance, and power. It bonds the romance of rambling around on trains through the Everglades with the mystique of a far away land known as Florida. It is pure country music; it is pure Americana.

The Rouse Brothers, say old-timers, were colorful characters whose legend was built around traveling up and down the Eastern Seaboard, playing their music along the way. Vassar Clements once told me that Ervin would "unveil" that fiddle for a quarter, perform until the hat was full, and then move on.

The *Special* made him the most money. But good as it was, he also wrote another classic, *Sweeter Than the Flowers*, and is credited with at least some connection to the bluegrass standard *Some Old Day* (although it now appears that another Rouse Brother, Earl, was the composer of that chain-gang ballad).

I met Ervin in Miami at a bluegrass festival in 1973, when I was working in Lester Flatt's band. We had an enjoyable conversation, and I had my picture made with him. The thing I remember most is the briefcase he was carrying; it was filled with pictures of swamp buggies he claimed to have built, and an uncashed royalty check for twenty-five thousand dollars. I was honored to meet him. I knew I was in the presence of where greatness had lived. When I look back on it, it was like shaking hands with a ghost.

Now, Ervin's story is finally being told—along with that of Chubby Wise, another Florida fiddler strongly associated with the *Special*. It's a strange story, but like the song, it's unforgettable. Knowing its origins will enable us to hear this old tune in a new way, and to appreciate its magnificence all over again.

Marty Stuart
Nashville, Tennessee
May, 2000

Marty Stuart has been a professional musician since the age of 13, when he joined Lester Flatt's band, the Nashville Grass. He later backed Johnny Cash before embarking on a successful solo career. He is also one of country music's most articulate scholars, and has authored numerous articles and published a book of photography.

Introduction

In Case of *Orange Blossom Special,*
Break Glass

For many years, Orange Blossom Special *has been not only a train imitation piece, but also a vehicle to exhibit the bluegrass fiddler's pyrotechnic virtuosity. Performed at breakneck tempos and with imitative embellishments that evoke train wheels and whistles, OBS is guaranteed to bring the blood of all but the most jaded listeners to a quick, rolling boil.*
 Norm Cohen, author,
  Long Steel Rail: The Railroad in American Folksong

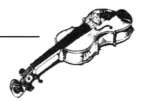

When folklorist Alan Lomax described bluegrass music as "folk music in overdrive," he could have had in mind arguably the most recognizable fiddle tune in the history of popular song, *Orange Blossom Special*. Played at a frantic pace and enlivened by showy instrumental breaks and exuberant—if ultimately superfluous—lyrics, this feel-good composition has for three generations inspired audiences in symphony halls, hay fields, and honky-tonks to stand up and shout. Written in 1938, the *Special* salutes Seaboard Air Line's luxurious, all-Pullman passenger train, which carried wealthy visitors between New York and Miami during railroading's romantic golden era.

This musical evergreen has been recorded by an astonishingly eclectic array of artists, from Bill Monroe to Englebert Humperdink; from Johnny Cash to Al Hirt. Others who have immortalized the *Special* include Alabama, Chet Atkins (with Arthur Fiedler and the Boston Pops), Box Car Willie, Glen Campbell, Roy Clark, the Charlie Daniels Band (on its 1975 album *Fire on the Mountain*), Johnny Darrell (whose 1974 version reached No. 63 on *Billboard's* country singles chart), Flatt

& Scruggs, the Flying Burrito Brothers (featuring country-rock pioneer Gram Parsons), Kinky Friedman, Mickey Gilley (on the 1981 soundtrack album for the film *Urban Cowboy*), Guy and Ralna (the pseudo country duo featured in Lawrence Welk's musical entourage), Sonny James, Doug Kershaw, Allison Kraus, Charlie McCoy (whose 1973 harmonica instrumental reached No. 26 on *Billboard's* country singles chart), Willie Nelson, the Nitty Gritty Dirt Band (on its Grammy-winning 1972 album *Will the Circle Be Unbroken*, featuring Vassar Clements on the fiddle and a who's who of traditional and contemporary country artists), the Ozark Mountain Daredevils, Ray Price, Marty Robbins, Jerry Reed (on the 1977 soundtrack album for the film *Smokey and the Bandit*), Scott Stoneman and the Stoneman Family, Marty Stuart (on his 2006 album *Live at the Grand Ole Opry*), Mel Tillis, Hank Williams Jr., and bandleader Billy Vaughn (on his 1961 album *Orange Blossom Special and Wheels*).

Musical evangelist Donna Stoneman incorporated the *Special's* melody into a gospel song called *The Glory Bound Train*, while the fusion band Seatrain concocted a searing hybrid arrangement featuring Bill Monroe disciple Richard Greene on the fiddle. The first internationally known Swedish rock band, The Spotnicks, took the *Special* to No. 1 in Australia in 1963. Twelve years later, an Irish acoustic combo called The Cotton Mill Boys made the tune a hit in England and throughout Europe. The *Special* remains a staple in the repertoires of Asia's top country and bluegrass artists. Indeed, Japanese-born fiddler Soji Tabuchi, who now has a theater in Branson, Missouri, learned the tune as a child and still performs it as the rousing centerpiece of his popular revue.

Charlie Daniels, the bearded fiddler who fronts the Charlie Daniels Band, calls *Orange Blossom Special* an undisputed classic, and "as much a part of Americana as anything Aaron Copeland ever wrote." It is ideally performed as the last song of the evening, says Daniels, because "you always want to leave everyone screaming for more."

Charlie McCoy, the renowned Nashville session musician who played harmonica on Cash's unorthodox but effective 1965 release, says he always closes his solo performances with the timeless train tune. "It just plain excites people," McCoy says. "I think anybody with even the slightest sense of music can hear it being played and realize how difficult it is to pull off. I've played it all over the world, and I can tell you that wherever I am, ninety-nine times out of a hundred, the *Special* will get you an encore."

Riders in the Sky, a popular retro-cowboy trio, would certainly attest to the composition's enduring audience appeal after a memorable 1998 concert at Tweetsie Railroad, a wild-west theme park located near Blowing Rock, North Carolina. Unfortunately for visiting musicians, the attraction's centerpiece is a vintage steam locomotive that emits long, piercing bellows at unwelcome intervals. After several such interruptions, fiddler Woody Paul vowed that, each time the offending whistle sounded, he would halt whatever song was in progress and launch into the *Special*; consequently, assembled fans heard the familiar melody no less than seven times during a single, one-hour show. "It was quite a bonus, actually," said one attendee.

Indeed, so pervasive has the *Special* become that some old-time fiddling organizations have banned it from competitions—along with the similarly ubiquitous *Black Mountain Rag*—reasoning that, if left to their own devices, just about everyone would attempt to dazzle the judges by trotting out this rollicking old war-horse. For example, at a 1972 fiddling contest in Athens, Alabama, contestants waiting backstage were amused to discover a fire-alarm case, containing the requisite extinguisher and ax, along with a note affixed to the front which read: "In case of *Orange Blossom Special*, break glass."

Small wonder. An instruction book by Stacy Philips called *Hot Licks For Bluegrass Fiddle* (Oak Publications) contains sections on double stops, upper positions, connecting licks, kickoffs, tags, fills—and an entire chapter devoted to the *Special*, appropriately subtitled "Crowd Manipulation and Riot Control for the Bluegrass Fiddler." Philips, who has also written instruction books for advanced dobro players and is himself an accomplished bluegrass fiddler, affectionately calls the *Special* "an orgy of acoustical overindulgence," and contends that playing it— even playing it badly, but with enthusiasm—virtually ensures a standing ovation. "The tavern goes wild with applause," Philips says. "Adulation showers on you for a few moments. Then, the audience slowly settles back into their seats, the jukebox is turned on, you are left alone. Welcome to the manic-depressive world of bluegrass fiddling."

Largely because of its visceral appeal, student fiddlers still regard mastery of this single tune as perhaps the most telling indicator of their progress. Among them is a Michigan fourth-grader, who at her English teacher's behest, wrote an essay regarding her violin lessons. The youngster first praises her teacher—a member of the Lansing Symphony Orchestra—and then offers a detailed exposition on the differences between a violin and a viola. She declares that her favorite note is E, "because it has the highest pitch and it is the most joyous sound," and concludes by stating: "Sometime, I don't know when, after many, many lessons and a lot of practice, I will be able to play my favorite song on the violin—*Orange Blossom Special.*"

Since classically trained musicians rank among the *Special's* most ardent boosters, the child should have no difficulty finding similarly inclined violinists among her peers. Symphony orchestra conductors, in particular, seem to delight in using the tune to elicit whoops and hollers from their highbrow patrons—while compelling their string sections to work up a healthy sweat. In 1996 alone, the *Special* was performed in concert by more than thirty orchestras, including those in Asheville, Boston, Baltimore, Columbus, Dallas, Fort Worth, Greenville, Jacksonville, Oklahoma City, San Antonio, Toledo, Washington, D.C., and Winston-Salem. When the Rapid City Symphony added the tune to its repertoire and performed it in concert, a reviewer for local newspaper opined: "I believe the hit of the evening was *Orange Blossom Special*, featuring the country music style of the 'fiddle section' of the orchestra."

Additionally, the *Special* continues to make unexpected and decidedly bizarre whistle-stops. In 1998, for example, members of the Lone Star Ballet in Amarillo, Texas, pirouetted as western-swing pioneers the Light Crust Doughboys performed the tune during an arts appreciation function held at the Amarillo Civic Center. And in 1997, a unique rendition of the fiddle classic ignited sedate scholars of ancient acoustic instruments gathered for the Sixth Annual North American Jew's Harp Festival, held in Richland, Oregon. (The Jew's harp is a small devise that is held against the teeth or lips and plucked with the fingers, creating a distinctive, twangy sound.)

Particularly in the South, high-school marching bands blare brass-heavy arrangements during half-time shows, while at the other extreme aficionados of the spoons—yes, the spoons—rank the *Special* alongside such stainless-steel standards as *You Are My Sunshine, Sweet Sue, Alley Cat, Liechtensteiner Polka,* and *Missouri Waltz*. The hoary old scorcher has likewise been performed on the piano, the banjo, the vibraphone, the trumpet, the sitar, the kazoo, the flute, and the flugelhorn. The *Special* has even been tamed for Muzak, and has been piped innocuously into department stores and elevators around the world.

Writer Tom Wolfe, a bluegrass music fan and an amateur musician, was so delighted at hearing the *Special* at a bar in Nairobi, Kenya, that in 1997 he wrote a letter to the editor of *Bluegrass Unlimited* about the experience: "I walked into the bar area of a big hotel here in Nairobi, and [Bill Monroe's] 1939 version of *Orange Blossom Special*...was playing on the P.A. I asked one of the African waiters, 'Where in the world did that tape come from?' He smiled and said, 'It's the bar man's personal tape, not the hotel's.'"

As a result of its undiminished popularity, in October 1999 Universal Music Publishing Group named *Orange Blossom Special* one of ten "Songs of the Century" during its annual Country Music Awards gala in Nashville. (Universal, an entertainment colossus, is the parent company of MCA Music Publishing Inc., which administers the *Special's* copyright). Other honorees, which were selected based in part upon the number of performances licensed, included *Don't It Make My Brown Eyes Blue, The Gambler, Honey, Little Green Apples, Rhinestone Cowboy, Take Me Home Country Roads, Wind Beneath My Wings*, and *Wichita Lineman*. With the notable exception of the *Special*, which was written as Franklin D. Roosevelt began his first term in the White House, the winners are relatively contemporary. None appear likely to match the *Special's* staying power.

Undoubtedly, one reason for the tune's longevity is that no two performances are exactly alike. In his 1997 book *The Devil's Box: Masters of Southern Fiddling* (Vanderbilt University Press and the Country Music Foundation Press), the late musicologist Charles K. Wolfe noted that the *Special*, like other fiddle favorites such as *Train 45* and *Going Down the Lee Highway*, employs an open-ended C-part to which measures can be added at the fiddler's discretion. Wrote Wolfe: "The C part gives the fiddler a chance to improvise around the sketchy melody, gradually building tension in the manner of a jazz soloist, until he decides to 'release' by returning to the A part. This last technique might be the most uniquely American [of all Southern fiddle styles]. It is a favorite of professional show-off fiddlers even today, and its basic technique has been borrowed by rock guitarists."

Even the *Special's* formulaic lyrics, drawn largely from traditional folk sources, invite improvisation—particularly during a freewheeling dialogue linking the second and third verses. In Cash's version, for example, a record company custodian named Ed Grizzard, who is not identified on session logs, assumes the role of an inquisitive friend, asking the singer when he plans to return to Florida:

Cash: *When am I goin' back to Florida? I don't know; I don't reckon I ever will.*
Grizzard: *Ain't you worried about gettin' your nourishment in New York?"*
Cash: *Well, I don't care if I do-die-do-die-do-die-do...*

Other embellishments have been more off-the-wall. When the *Special* was performed by Lester Flatt and the Nashville Grass, fiddler Clarence "Tater" Tate often launched into a deadpan monologue about a curious puppy unfortunate enough to stumble over a cross-tie, thereby causing his tail to be severed by the wheels of a passing train. Then, in grand trick-fiddling fashion, the versatile Tate convulsed audiences by coaxing frantic canine yelping and howling sounds from his instrument.

Granted, neither Cash's nor Tate's additions make much sense within the context of the song as it was written. Such unabashed playfulness does, however, illustrate a key point: The *Special* mandates no set form or exact structure; consequently, around the core fiddle melody, performers are afforded the freedom to cavort in sometimes outrageous fashion. "The possibilities are endless," says Phillips, who encourages young fiddlers to ignore the *Special's* lyrics. "Pick out a couple of likely double stops that at least vaguely fit the desired chord. Then shuffle off to your heart's content."

Although the *Special* is loved worldwide, it is particularly revered in the Sunshine State, where a member of the Florida Legislature once attempted to have it designated as the official state song, replacing *Old Folks at Home*, Stephen Foster's dreary and arguably racist 1850 dirge. In 1983, Democratic State Senator John Hill of Miami argued that Foster, a Pennsylvanian, had never set foot in Florida, and had written *Old Folks* only after spotting the bucolic-sounding Suwannee River on a map of the United States. Although Hill's proposal went nowhere, it captured still more media attention for a tune that had long been regarded as the unofficial Bluegrass National Anthem—an honorary status which, luckily, required no legislative approval.

Yet, the compelling and often tragic story behind this instrumental tour d force has, until now, remained a matter of conjecture and speculation. The two men most closely associated with its composition, Ervin Thomas Lidel Rouse and Robert Russell "Chubby" Wise, were unpolished but deceptively complex characters whose lives were marked by poverty, by mental and physical illness, and by self-destructive behavior on a grand scale.

Rouse, long considered by musicologists as one of the genre's most intriguing enigmas, lived his final years at the edge of the Florida Everglades, sleeping in a plywood shack and fiddling for tips in rough-and-tumble bars along the Tamiami Trail. Wise, generally acknowledged as bluegrass music's seminal fiddler, traveled the world as a sideman to legends, but remained emotionally scarred by childhood abandonment and abuse. More than anything else, this tune—which is often mistakenly thought to be a traditional folk melody—shaped their lives and defined their legacies.

I became interested in Rouse and Wise—and in the song that inexorably bound them—when writing an article for *Jacksonville Magazine* entitled, "The Fastest Train on the Line: The Untold Story of Ervin T. Rouse, Chubby Wise and the *Orange Blossom Special*." Rouse and Wise were said to have composed the tune after viewing the sleek, diesel-electric locomotive at Union Station, where it had stopped during a much-ballyhooed east coast exhibition tour.

The magazine piece was intended to celebrate the song's sixtieth anniversary, and to emphasize its reputed connection to the northeast Florida port city. However, this seemingly straightforward assignment proved far more elusive and complex than I had imagined. So, with deadlines approaching and lose ends remaining, I settled for a painfully inadequate fifteen-hundred-word essay employing what little information could be readily uncovered regarding the reclusive Rouse, whose heirs held the tune's copyright, and the loquacious Wise, who was widely regarded as an uncredited co-author.

Still, I knew that I was far from finished with these musically brilliant but deeply flawed men. Ultimately, I was able to spend a year immersing myself in Rouse and Wise lore, piecing together their lives through archival sources and lengthy interviews with friends and family members from coast to coast.

I also received invaluable help from academicians, musicians and recording industry insiders, all of whom shared my curiosity and tolerated my zeal. Notable among them was Wolfe, who had long contended that the tale behind *Orange Blossom Special* was one of the genre's "great untold stories." Pleased that a book on the topic was forthcoming, he met with me at his home and graciously shared some preliminary research he had done regarding Rouse's ill-fated career. Wolfe, more than anyone else, made it acceptable to take a scholarly approach to writing about country music and analyzing its impact on our culture. It is my hope that he will someday be inducted into the Country Music Hall of Fame as a non-performing member.

Two modern-day artists with a genuine reverence for their musical forebears, John Hartford and Marty Stuart, not only offered their memories of Rouse and Wise, but also penned a preface and a foreword. Hartford, who was far more ill than I realized when I began imposing upon his time, was nonetheless enthusiastic and hospitable, and generously agreed to critique my manuscript prior to publication. Stuart, who maintains a heavy performing schedule, actually called my office from the road to dictate his contribution. "This is important," he said when I thanked him for his interest.

What follows, then, is essentially several stories in one. There are biographies of Rouse and Wise, whose lives run parallel and intersect—or perhaps "collide" would be a better word—at pivotal moments. Also, for the sake of context, there are chapters on the origins of old-time fiddle music, and on the locomotive that inspired the immortal song.

That said, let's get the fiddle off the mantle, rosin up the bow and take a musical journey through seven decades of history. But we'll have to hurry; Ervin and Chubby are already on board, and this train always departs on time.

Randy Noles
Orlando, Florida
August 27, 2006

I

For the Record, They
Never Rode the Train

My name is Rouse, ma'am. I used to sing a little, and play the Special—Orange Blossom Special, that is. [The song] belongs to everybody by now, I guess, but it used to be my best number.
Ervin T. Rouse to
Mother Maybelle Carter

That was just the melody I helped write, not the lyrics. I gave Ervin my half of the song. But it didn't hurt my stature any. I've made a lot of money, not directly but indirectly, on the Orange Blossom Special. *It has got me a lot of jobs and, in sense, a lot of dollars.*
Chubby Wise to
the Associated Press

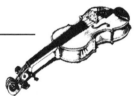

At a godforsaken tavern made of plywood and pecky cypress, a wizened, toothless old man clutching a battered fiddle stands before a boisterous, beer-guzzling throng that includes day laborers, dope smugglers, and gator poachers. Despite the oppressive heat, he wears a multicolored Seminole Indian jacket over a stained white dress shirt; a fishing cap sits atop a tangle of wiry gray hair. His ruddy face is creased, his jowls are stubbly and his narrow, his wide-set eyes appear filmy and unfocused.

"Hello, folks," he rasps in a mush-mouthed, all but undistinguishable Deep South brogue. "The first number we'd like to do for you is one we wrote back in 1938 about a mighty fine train that used to run between New York and Miami—and we're so proud that people all over the world still love it and play it."

Then, as he holds the fiddle to his chin and slides the bow across the strings, the unmistakable blast of a train whistle pierces the noxious haze. Abruptly, conversations cease, fights are interrupted, and drinks are set aside. The old man is Ervin T.

Rouse, author of *Orange Blossom Special*, and his presence commands respect—even here, even now.

***

At a bluegrass festival somewhere in the Midwest, a pudgy, white-bearded elf of a man stands beside a makeshift stage overlooking several thousand people—families, mostly—lounging on blankets and lawn chairs. Beyond the crowd are rows of campers and motor homes sporting license plates from Maine to Montana. The autumn evening is cool; in the distance, campfires flicker and string music wafts in the breeze.

The man, who looks for all the world like St. Nicholas himself, patiently demonstrates a few basic fiddle techniques to a group of admirers gathered around him. His manner is kindly, and his laugh—hearty and deep from the belly—is infectious. Onstage, an emcee recites his lengthy professional resume. "He's the king of the bluegrass fiddlers and writer of *Orange Blossom Special*, the most played fiddle tune in the world," the announcer intones. "And what a treat for us to have him here, playing the song that made him famous. Ladies and gentlemen, please welcome the great Chubby Wise!"

YET, IT IS NOT CHUBBY WISE but Ervin T. Rouse, a native of Craven County, North Carolina, who is the credited author of *Orange Blossom Special*. Rouse, who ranks as one of country music's most mysterious figures, began his professional career at the age of eight, fiddling popular songs on the nation's most prestigious vaudeville stages. But he spent his final years in southern Florida, sick in body and mind, plying his trade at remote roadhouses frequented by swamp denizens. "Ervin just loved playing for those people down there," says Rouse's widow, Hattie Whitehurst Rouse Miscowich, known to friends and family as "Louallie." Now living quietly with her second husband in Bowie, Maryland, Louallie remains Ervin's most staunch defender—despite the fact that she left the unstable, frequently abrasive musician in 1954. "And the people loved him. He was the most talented person you can imagine, and he once played with the best. But if you met him, you never would have known it."

Robert Russell "Chubby" Wise, a product of Lake City by way of St. Augustine, Florida, has long been cited as the *Special's* uncredited co-author. Chubby himself always ruefully maintained that he had collaborated with Ervin during a boozy, late-night jam session in Jacksonville, after which he had impulsively—but voluntarily—given his friend and colleague all rights to what would become a substantial money-maker for decades to come. "That was my first mistake," he said in 1982. "About a hundred thousand dollar mistake."

Nonetheless, the portly, white-bearded fiddler spent his final years performing before large and enthusiastic audiences at bluegrass festivals, where he was adored by fans as a peerless entertainer and respected by fellow performers as a groundbreaking musical pioneer. "Chubby always got standing ovations wherever he played," says the musician's widow, Rossi Truell Case Wise. "People always crowded around him, and wanted to talk to him or to shake his hand. And I'll tell you this: He never forgot his fans, and he never refused to give an autograph or pose for a picture, no matter how long it took."

Still, Wise's contribution to *Orange Blossom Special*—or his lack thereof—has for years been a subject of discussion and debate among bluegrass scholars, and a source of hard feelings between family members, friends, and fans of both men. "Ervin wrote that song, and nobody else," says Louallie. "I once asked him, 'Ervin, did Chubby have anything to do with writing *Orange Blossom Special?*' And he said, 'Hell, no.'" But Rossi, now living near her children in Upper Marlboro, Maryland, contends that "everyone knows Chubby contributed to *Orange Blossom Special*; in fact, Chubby and Ervin used to get together and talk about how poor they were when they wrote that song."

Yet, beyond hardcore bluegrass fans, the song remains most strongly identified with the late Johnny Cash, an entertainment icon and arguably the biggest international star the country music industry has ever produced. Cash, the only person to be inducted into the Country Music Hall of Fame, the Rock 'n' Roll Hall of Fame, and the Songwriters Hall of Fame, adopted the *Special* and made it his own by eschewing fiddles and using a harmonica and a saxophone on his landmark 1965 recording.

Cash's release scaled the charts, thereby guaranteeing a measure of financial security for Rouse, who had by then virtually abandoned his suburban Miami home for Collier County's sprawling Big Cypress Swamp, where he shared a makeshift shelter with a succession of pet dogs and poignant mementos of a career gone awry. "I'd never leave now," Rouse said in 1976, seemingly unburdened by bitterness over his descent into obscurity. "Out here, you're in the wilds. When night falls, it's so dark. Oh, it's wild!"

Musicologist Charles K. Wolfe contributed a biographical sketch of the Rouse Brothers to the *1998 Encyclopedia of Country Music* (Oxford University Press). "The Rouse Brothers are receding more and more into legend," said Wolfe, who died in 2006. "So it seemed an appropriate time to try and piece together their story." The brief entry marked the first, and thus far the only, significant acknowledgment of Rouse in any country-music reference book. And sadly, even this well-meaning nod is marred by the usually reliable Wolfe's erroneous references to Rouse as "Erwin" instead of "Ervin." Inexplicably, the error has not been corrected in subsequent editions. Thus, nearly a quarter-century after his death, the luckless musician remains all but forgotten.

Still, if academicians have given up on the elusive Rouse, at least one fiction writer has not. The old fiddler appears as himself in Randy Wayne White's inventive 1993 mystery novel, *The Man Who Invented Florida* (St. Martin's Press). The well-reviewed volume, the third in a series featuring marine biologist Doc Ford, introduces Doc's conniving uncle, Tuck Gatrell, who discovers that spring water from his Big Cypress property causes testicles to regrow on his gelded horse, Roscoe, and rejuvenates the sexual prowess of his elderly Calusa Indian friend, Joseph Egret. The intricate plot encompasses kidnapping, shady development deals, and Tuck's outrageous schemes to market the miraculous elixir nationwide—assisted by his curmudgeonly neighbor, one Ervin T. Rouse.

White, who befriended the flesh-and-blood Rouse in the late 1970s, notes that the book is a work of fiction. However, he effectively laces the fast-paced narrative with amusing personal anecdotes that the loquacious but seemingly destitute swamp rat had related as being factual. "Ervin had such great vitality and humor," says White. "I may have paraphrased in places, but I tried to repeat his stories pretty much as they were told to me."

Yet, unfortunately for biographers, much of what Rouse told White and other journalists, while entertaining, was at best only partially true and at worst pure nonsense. Indeed, the fiddler appeared remarkably heedless of his legacy, and apparently took pleasure in exasperating those who sought to tell his story in a straightforward manner.

Toward the end of his days, Miami newspapers would, on occasion, send young reporters out to what Rouse deemed "God's country" to extract a few colorful bromides from this irascible, hard-drinking hillbilly who claimed to have composed a famous song. And, while the ailing iconoclast always obliged by providing pithy copy, he avoided revealing anything substantive about his life or about his career. For example, after "interviewing" Rouse in 1977, a *Miami News* correspondent wrote that "the toothless, craggy-faced man…is vague about dates and places, about when [Johnny] Cash first recorded his song, about what he did to make a living in the lean years besides play small clubs. At one time, he apparently pumped gas in a Hialeah station, but he does not talk about that, saying: 'You hear all kinds of things, you know; people say all kinds of things.'"

So, the question lingers: Why did Rouse consciously portray himself as nothing more than a dissipated ne'er do well; a tragic figure who debased his magnificent gift? Granted, this disheartening depiction is not altogether inaccurate; but it is incomplete.

Had he chosen to do so, Rouse could just as easily have expounded upon ornate vaudeville theaters in New York and Boston, posh nightclubs in Miami Beach, the outlandish Village Barn in Greenwich Village, the venerable *Grand Ole Opry* in Nashville, RCA Victor recording sessions, and network radio broadcasts. He could have dropped names such as Roy Acuff, Moon Mullican, Grandpa Jones, Mother Maybelle Carter, and even his buddy the Man in Black. He accentuated the negative, say his friends and family, because Ervin was Ervin; a lifelong nonconformist, always uncomfortable with self-promotion, who had simply ceased giving a damn.

Further complicating matters is the fact that many of the people who knew Rouse best—including all of his siblings—have died. Likewise, Rouse's travels were poorly documented and, apart from his music, he left behind little of a tangible nature from which a personal history might be readily reconstructed; just a tattered scrapbook containing a few publicity photographs, a handful of performance contracts, a smattering of yellowed newspaper clippings, and a simple business card which reads:

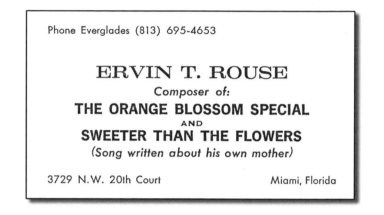

Phone Everglades (813) 695-4653

ERVIN T. ROUSE

Composer of:

THE ORANGE BLOSSOM SPECIAL

AND

SWEETER THAN THE FLOWERS

(Song written about his own mother)

3729 N.W. 20th Court   Miami, Florida

Conversely, Wise's legendary career, although not his turbulent personal life, has been fairly well documented. He was, after all, an entertainer for more than sixty years, and remained notoriously garrulous—if not always factually precise—with writers, fans, and friends. His abiding musical contributions are respectfully reviewed in encyclopedias of country and bluegrass music, where he is often granted such lofty titles as "Dean of the Bluegrass Fiddlers."

Unlike Rouse, Wise generally enjoyed a sweet and active old age, booking to seventy-five to eighty performances per year—a workload that undoubtedly became excessive as his health began to decline—and, after embracing religion, mesmerizing star-struck parishioners at the Macclenny (Florida) Christian Fellowship Church with spine-tingling fiddle renditions of *How Great Thou Art* and other spirituals. Although the facts do not bear him out, Wise's version of the story behind *Orange Blossom Special* has become generally accepted as gospel.

In truth, like many stories behind early folk, country, and bluegrass songs, the saga of the *Special* is at times a convoluted one, involving the principles, Rouse and Wise, as well as an eclectic cast of peripheral players—singers and songwriters; pickers and publishers—who run the gamut from the famed to the forgotten; from the scrupulous to the scurrilous. And, across the length and breadth of the tale rolls the ghost of a plush, diesel-powered streamliner on which, ironically, neither Rouse nor Wise ever rode—except in their imaginations.

"I never rode [the train], and I'm so sorry to say that I didn't," said Rouse to writer Dorothy Horstman for her 1978 book, *Sing Your Heart Out, Country Boy* (Country Music Foundation Press), which contains two brief, first-person statements provided by Rouse to introduce lyrics from *Orange Blossom Special* and *Sweeter Than the Flowers*, his only other commercially successful song. "Because our train from Miami to New York, I've been told by engineers, was without a doubt the most powerful train in the entire world."

So it was. But interstate highways and airplanes ultimately rendered the *Special* obsolete—and only the most fervent railroad nostalgia buffs seemed to care when it pulled into Miami for the last time on April 12, 1953.

II

'You'd Have Thought That Jesus Christ Hisself Was Comin' Down the Line'

Country music...confers a kind of honorary natural status on certain machine-manufactured objects, like trains and trucks.
Cecelia Tichi, author
High Lonesome: The American Culture of Country Music
(University of North Carolina Press)

Of all the sounds of the Industrial Revolution, those of trains seem across time to have taken on the most attractive sentimental associations.
R. Murray Scafer, composer

At his Walden retreat in 1846, Henry David Thoreau summed up the railroad's power to inspire: "When I hear the iron horse make the hills echo with his snort like thunder, shaking the earth with his feet and breathing fire and smoke from his nostrils (what kind of winged horse or fiery dragon they will put into the new mythology I don't know), it seems to me as if the earth had got a race now worthy to inhabit it."

Thoreau was not alone in his fascination with trains. Since the mid-nineteenth century, railroads have captured the imagination of Americans, and have inspired countless stories and songs. By 1850, slightly more than nine thousand miles of track had been laid in the United States, primarily in the South and the East. But on May 10, 1869, just twenty-one years after the *New York Herald* had pronounced the concept of a transcontinental railroad "ridiculous and absurd," and just sixty-five years after Lewis and Clark had begun their epic journey across an uncharted continent, the western-based Central Pacific and eastern-based Union Pacific lines were joined at Promontory Point, Utah. The driving of a ceremonial golden spike into the final tie added an exclamation point to this remarkable and widely celebrated achievement, which had been dubbed by a contemporary journalist as "the grandest enterprise under God."

Still, there was more to running a railroad than merely laying track. In 1842, Charles Dickens, traveling by train on a lecture tour of America, had not been complimentary of the experience:

> There is a great deal of jolting, a great deal of noise, a great deal of wall, not much window, a locomotive engine, a shriek and a bell; the cars are like shabby omnibuses, but larger, holding thirty, forty, or fifty people. In the centre of the carriage there is usually a stove, fed with charcoal or anthracite coal, which is for the most part red-hot. It is insufferably close; and you see the hot air fluttering between yourself and any other object you happen to look at, like the ghost of smoke.

Many Europeans were also appalled at the concept of "one-class travel," which compelled them to share uncomfortably snug quarters with common riffraff—an indignity that would never have occurred aboard properly segregated continental coaches. Even democratically inclined Americans, while they were generally more sociable and less class-conscious, yearned for a modicum of comfort and privacy, particularly during long journeys.

Fortunately for put-upon travelers, by 1865 George M. Pullman and others had introduced passenger car accommodations that rivaled those found in the most lavish steamboats. The first Pullman sleeping coaches, which the inventive Chicago-based designer dubbed "hotel-cars," featured plush window curtains, rich carpeting, black walnut woodwork, and chandeliers. The upper berth was akin to a fold-out bunk, while the lower berth was designed so that facing seats could slide together to form a bed.

In May 1870, ever the promoter, Pullman invited members of the Boston Board of Trade on what proved to be a highly productive junket—the first ever uninterrupted coast-to-coast train trip. While enroute to California, the influential passengers were so impressed with the pleasing ambiance that, while puffing cigars in the smoking car, they approved a resolution vowing that "there will be no delay in placing these elegant and homelike carriages upon the principal routes in the New England states, and we will do all in our power to accomplish this end."

In short order, then, Pullman-style luxury became a competitive necessity for the country's railroads. By the late nineteenth century, *The New York Times* was reporting that rail passengers were able to sip champagne—without spilling a single drop— while steaming across the nation's vast interior at an unheard-of sixty miles per hour.

Wrote one satisfied customer: "[The train], with its great, glaring, Polyphemous eye, lighting up long vistas of the prairie, rushed into the night and the wild. Then to bed in luxurious coaches, where we slept the sleep of the just and awoke the next morning to find ourselves crossing the North Platte, three hundred miles from Omaha—fifteen hours and forty minutes out."

By 1900, the United States boasted more miles of track than all the countries of Europe combined, much to the dismay of Mark Twain, who watched grumpily as ever-expanding ribbons of steel rendered his beloved sternwheelers obsolete. Observing the Eads Bridge, which traversed the Mississippi River at St. Louis, Twain lamented the dearth of steamboats navigating the muddy water, writing that "former steamboatmen told me that the bridge doesn't pay; still, it can be no sufficient compensation to a corpse to know that the dynamite that laid him out was not of as good quality as it had been supposed to be."

Sentimental humorists notwithstanding, railroads powered a transportation revolution, and altered long-held concepts of time and distance. The ramifications of this sea change were immense, but nowhere was the emotional impact more bittersweet than on isolated farms and in small, cheerless towns, where a train whistle in the night became an almost irresistible siren song for young people longing to escape the drudgery of their daily lives.

"There was an aura approaching spiritualism surrounding trains in the old days," says George Custer, a fifth-generation fiddler whose maternal uncles were legendary old-time fiddlers Robert Hugh "Georgia Slim" Rutland and Slim's older brother, Henry. "Trains sent a lonesome, distant sound through the valleys and the mountains. Yet, it was also comforting. It was a link to that wonderland that was supposed to be off in the distance somewhere. I remember as a child running through the woods barefoot when I heard the train coming so I could wave at the engineer. He'd always wave back and blow the whistle for me."

Some would answer the call, and later write about their experiences. As an adolescent, novelist Jack London (*Call of the Wild, White Fang*) fell in with a gang of "road kids," adopted the moniker "Sailor Jack," and hopped a freight train leaving Oakland, California, to join legions of hoboes—a quarter-million of whom where teenagers at the height of the Great Depression—roaming the countryside and haunting the railyards. Cowboy singer Harry "Haywire Mac" McClintock was a hobo-turned-composer whose name may be unfamiliar, but whose songs about the rambling life are classics: the defiant *Hallelujah, I'm a Bum* and the immortal *Big Rock Candy Mountain.*

However, most aspiring adventurers stayed safely home, tended to their responsibilities, and later drew upon their suppressed wanderlust when contributing to the vast repertoire of railroad songs that enliven American music. Indeed, trains have inspired music since the first tracks were laid, and countless railroading compositions populate the classical, jazz, blues, folk, and popular idioms.

Viennese composer Johann Strauss wrote one of the first imitative train songs for full orchestra, *Eisenbahn-Lust (Railway Delight)* in 1836. Celebrating the first public railway line between Vienna and Breclav, *Eisenbahn-Lust* begins and ends with the sounds of a steam locomotive. Hungarian composer Joseph Gungl wrote a piano piece inspired by train sounds called *Railroad Steam Engine Gallop*. Instructions on the circa-1844 sheet music suggest that "the noise which the smoke makes in the chimney of the locomotive steam engine may be very naturally imitated by clapping the door of the tunnel of a stove."

Throughout Europe, in fact, new rail lines were celebrated in music, much of which incorporated effects such as train whistles, bells, and the clickity-clack of steel-on-steel.

Concurrently, American composers saluted trains with no less fervor and ingenuity. The Library of Congress American Memory Project has preserved dozens upon dozens of pieces of sheet music in which railroading is evoked, including now-forgotten works such as *The Underground Railroad March, The Charming Young Widow I Met in the Train, The Pacific Railroad Polka, The Union Pacific Grand March, The Gospel Railroad,* and *The C.B.& O. (Chicago, Burlington and Quincy Railroad) Waltz*. Some are bouncy piano solos written for music-hall audiences, while others are orchestral extravaganzas aimed at highbrow listeners. One song, *The D.O.R.A. Railroad Polonaise*, is specifically written "for piano and sandpaper," with blocks of the latter material intended to simulate train sounds.

Likewise, immortals such as Irving Berlin (*When That Midnight Choo-Choo Leaves for Alabam'*), W.C. Handy (*The Yellow Dog Rag*), and Scott Joplin (*The Great Crush Collision March*) are listed among the composers who contributed railroad songs to early American popular music. And, while George Gershwin's 1924 masterpiece *Rhapsody in Blue* is not overtly related to train travel, the composer insisted that railroad sounds inspired the unforgettable jazz concerto. "The *Rhapsody* began as a purpose, not a plan," Gershwin said. "I worked out a few themes, but just at this time I had to appear in Boston. It was on the train, with its steely rhythms, its rattle bang that is often so stimulating to the composer—I frequently hear music in the very heart of noise—that I suddenly heard, even saw on paper, the complete construction of the *Rhapsody* from beginning to end." (Gershwin later included train themes and locomotive sounds in *Leavin' for the Promised Land*, a song from his musical *Porgy and Bess*.)

Aaron Copeland also adopted railroad sounds in his version of *John Henry,* a four-minute chamber orchestra composition commissioned in 1940 by CBS radio for its "School of the Air" series. Said Copeland: "A clarinet introduces the theme, and to add to the excitement and help achieve the sound of a train and John Henry's hammer, the scoring calls for a triangle, anvil, sandpaper blocks, a train whistle, and a piano in addition to the chamber orchestra."

Perhaps the most elaborate railroad composition is *U.S. Highball: A Musical*

Account of a Transcontinental Hobo Trip, written in 1943 by Harry Partch. The epic, twenty-five-minute work is based on Partch's experience hopping freights between San Francisco and Chicago, and includes voices of hoboes and train sounds emanating from instruments designed and constructed by the composer.

Duke Ellington (*Across the Track Blues*), Louis Jordon (*Choo-Choo Ch'Boogie*), Glenn Miller (*Chattanooga Choo-Choo*), and Thelonious Monk (*Locomotive*) also popularized train songs, as did Roy Acuff and the Carter Family (*Wabash Cannonball*), and rockabilly Elvis Presley, who in 1954 covered "Little" Junior Parker's *Mystery Train*. In the 1960s, Bob Dylan called upon his folk and blues influences for *It Takes a Lot to Laugh, It Takes a Train to Cry*, while the Monkees incited teenyboppers with *Last Train to Clarksville*. Crosby, Stills & Nash immortalized *Marrakesh Express*, while Steve Goodman, via Arlo Guthrie's recording, did the same for *City of New Orleans*.

Train songs have been—and still are—being written as metaphors for salvation and damnation (*Devil's Train, Down There By the Train, Last Train for Glory, Light at the End of the Tunnel, Heaven Bound Train, This Train, Life's Railway to Heaven*), as sources of heartbreak (*My Baby Thinks He's a Train, Lonesome Whistle, Trainwreck of Emotion*), and celebrations of homecoming (*Going Home Train, Hey Porter, Night Train to Memphis, Put Me On a Train Back to Texas*).

Other songs glorify specific trains or routes (*Atchison, Topeka & the Santa Fe, Canadian Pacific, The Diplomat, Rock Island Line*), or eulogize railroading folk heroes (*Casey Jones, The Legend of John Henry's Hammer*). Still others document disasters (*Wreck of the Old 97, Wreck of the Royal Palm, Wreck of the Number 9, Wreck of the FFV, Wreck of the 1262*) or venerate hoboes (*Dying Hobo, Great American Bum, Hobo Bill's Last Ride, Hobo Heaven, Waiting For a Train*).

Country hitmaker Tom T. Hall even places the Almighty aboard a train, rambling "across the hills and valleys, through the prairies, through the skies," in *God Came Through Bellville, Georgia*. (Ominously, however, God chooses not to disembark.)

So, where does *Orange Blossom Special* fit in the pantheon of great train tunes? Aside from the fact that it lionizes a legendary train, the *Special* differs from many popular railroad songs in at least one important respect: It was originally written as an instrumental; "a little ol' fiddlin' piece we thought was a little crazy," as the self-deprecating Rouse once described it. Words were added almost as an afterthought. Therefore, a case can be made that the *Special* is nothing more than an amusing trifle; a novelty number composed by an erstwhile vaudevillian solely to facilitate the separating of nightclub patrons from their dollar bills—no small consideration for a musician dependent upon tips. Admittedly, this assessment would not be entirely off the mark.

Yet, *Orange Blossom Special* still ranks among the best in its genre, if only because of the unbridled response it evokes when performed live, in virtually any setting, in front of virtually any crowd. Adults and children alike hoot and holler when the *Special* is played by bluegrass combos at outdoor festivals, while typically staid, formally clad patrons of the arts leap to their feet and cheer when it is performed at ornate concert halls by full orchestras. If for no other reason, the *Special* is deserving of immortality because its gut-level appeal crosses every imaginable musical and cultural boundary.

"Also, it's widely assumed that *Orange Blossom Special* is a traditional melody," added Charles Wolfe. "Any time a contemporary writer composes something that becomes so popular during his or her lifetime that it's thought to be a folk tune, then that's about the greatest possible compliment a writer can receive." In fact, the *Special* was originally copyrighted on October 20, 1938 does not lapse into the public domain until December 31, 2013.

By the time the song was written, the Great Depression had damaged the national psyche, rendering those who had once considered themselves impervious to disaster frightened and uncertain of the future. As families struggled to survive and war clouds gathered over Europe, the debut of this magnificent train was an affirmation that the country was still strong, free, and capable of greatness.

Indeed, viewing the gleaming diesel streamliner as it powered through Florida on an east coast exhibition tour, tens of thousands of breathless spectators—including, as fate would have it, a couple of itinerate Florida fiddlers—instinctively realized that they were privy to something far more profound than a faster, more comfortable way to transport moneyed Yankee snowbirds to their Florida vacation homes. Those feelings were eloquently expressed through the *Special's* soaring and optimistic melody.

Ironically, however, the distinctive whistle and the rhythmic chug-a-lug that power the tune are indicative of a steam locomotive, not a diesel streamliner. Still, it is appropriate to allow some artistic license in this case; despite their many advantages, no one ever claimed that diesel engines made musical sounds.

THE ORANGE BLOSSOM SPECIAL, inaugurated in November 1925, was Seaboard Air Lines' premier passenger train, operating during Florida's busy winter tourist season—from mid-December to mid-April—between New York's chilly Pennsylvania Station and sunny West Palm Beach. In 1927, the east coast run was extended to Miami, while a separate west coast run terminated in St. Petersburg.

By 1929, however, Florida's land boom had gone bust, compelling Seaboard officials to operate the Special as a single New York-to-Miami train—the journey took roughly twenty-nine hours, assuming there were no unanticipated delays—with a Wildwood-to-St. Petersburg connection offering access to resort communities on the Gulf Coast. The west coast Special would be restored in 1936.

Certainly, in the mid-1920s, there was no scarcity of New Yorkers wishing to migrate south. Typical among them was journalist T.H. Weigall, set out for Florida in the summer of 1925 because he became "convinced that if I didn't get down there soon, the whole of America would be there before me." Weigall, who would later write about his journey in *Boom in Paradise* (Alfred H. King), vividly described, albeit with tongue in cheek, the anticipation as he climbed aboard a stifling and crowded Pennsylvania Railroad day coach bound for the Miami:

> I had begun to feel, even already, some remote infection of the almost holy exaltation characteristic of the true Floridian. I felt moved, almost ready to defend the claims of Florida with my fists. Florida was the finest country in the world—the freest, the most wonderful, the most opportunity giving. And there I was, on an August afternoon, bound to make my fortune.

Weigall, unfortunately, was unable to ride the Orange Blossom Special, which would not debut until four months later, and his scathing account of the grueling, forty-seven-hour trip demonstrates the timeliness of Seaboard Air Line's all-Pullman concept:

> The seat which I had managed to secure for myself turned out to be extraordinarily uncomfortable, and apparently almost on fire from the heat of the sun that had been beating down on it all day in the shunting yards. The interior of the day coach is designed along the lines of the seating accommodation of the Inner Circle; and I, for one, never want to travel fifteen hundred miles on the Inner Circle again.
>
> From time to time, a depressed-looking porter wandered down the compartment with a basket of chocolate and pink lemonade, occasionally saying, 'Good eats, gents!' in a low voice of which nobody took the slightest notice. A small child at the end of the carriage was vigorously sick, and was being just as vigorously reprimanded in voluble Italian. Ever since we had started, its parents had been eating sausages out of a greasy newspaper.
>
> I came to the conclusion that if this were "The Most Luxurious Manner of Travel Yet Devised by the Human Race," then the human race had not progressed very far.

The Orange Blossom Special, however, promised an altogether different sort of experience. "The passengers, they couldn't get over it," recalled former flagman Richard Rector in a 1983 interview. Rector worked on the Special in the 1940s, and served as mayor of Wildwood, Florida, following his retirement. "They'd smell the orange blossoms and they'd see the oranges hanging on the trees, and the oranges were so close to the track that you could almost touch them. That really excited all those tourists from up North."

Certainly, time passed pleasantly aboard this "beautiful and commodious moving hotel," as George Pullman once described the first trains featuring his sumptuously appointed cars. A barber, a valet, and a manicurist were on call, as was a lady's maid. Passengers not snoozing in the sleeping berths could socialize in the club-library car, or soak up the scenery from an observation car at the rear.

The dining car, offering fare comparable to that found in most fine restaurants, featured polished walnut walls, mosaic tile floors, and gleaming brass fixtures. Up to sixty passengers per sitting could enjoy exquisite cuisine—and, with the repeal of Prohibition in 1933, an after-dinner toddy—at tables set with white linen and silver-plated flatware.

In 1934, the Special became one of the first trains in the country to be "fully air-conditioned"—via an electric fan rigged to blow over ice containers—and this low-tech but decidedly marketable advance was heralded during an elaborate re-christening ceremony at Penn Station.

However, the most significant improvement to the Special came in 1938, when the class M-2 4-8-2 steam locomotives on its east coast run were replaced by nine sleek and powerful diesel, or diesel-electric, locomotives. (The west coast Special would not be dieselized until the following winter). Manufactured by the Electro-Motive Corporation, a division of General Motors, these streamlined, stainless-steel marvels of modern engineering were massive, three-unit outfits, 210 feet long, weighing 450 tons, and packing a total of 6,000 horsepower. "The world's largest and mightiest locomotives" promised to shear two hours and fifty minutes off the New York to Miami run and, according to colorful promotional brochures, "will provide sustained, high-speed transportation with the utmost in safety and comfort at economical fares."

Aside from being faster and more powerful, diesels offered additional advantages. Steam locomotives required servicing after only a few hours of operation, while a diesel could complete a two thousand-mile journey without tinkering. Also, fewer people were needed to operate diesels—a plus for railroad management if not railroad workers—and standby costs were reduced because diesels, unlike steam locomotives, could be completely shut down when parked in a roundhouse.

Passengers, though, were particularly grateful for the elimination of a long-standing inconvenience that Weigall had so pungently addressed:

> Within a half a minute [of opening a window in the day coach], I was covered with a peculiarly filthy soot. I banged down the window, but with another half-minute discovered that the heat was so unbearable that it had to be opened

> again. Another deluge of grime convinced me that it would
> have to be closed again; and this opening and closing
> process continued during the whole interminable distance
> between the respective paradises of North and South."

The new locomotives were, of course, smokeless. Plus they were quite literally breathtaking works of art—shaped by the era's finest industrial designers using clean, sweeping lines. On the Special, bright, daring stripes of orange and green accented the gleaming silver. Indeed, these modern streamliners were as starkly different in appearance from traditional steam locomotives as Dusenbergs were from Model Ts.

"One cannot view these new locomotives without realizing that here is a symbol of progress," said Legh R. Powell Jr., co-receiver for Seaboard Air Line in a self-congratulatory 1938 interview with Jacksonville's morning daily newspaper, *The Florida Times-Union*. "The largest and most powerful diesel-electric locomotives ever built, they bespeak more clearly and emphatically than any words that I can utter our firm confidence in the future."

To showcase the mighty diesels, Seaboard Air Line officials planned a highly publicized exhibition tour that would begin in Washington, D.C., on Monday, October 31, 1938. Florida First Lady Mrs. Fred P. Cone was invited to the Capitol to christen one of the locomotives with a bottle of water taken from Biscayne Bay. Following the ceremonies, the massive contrivance would pull seven generously outfitted Pullman cars down the coast, stopping along the way to give the citizenry a peek at what progress had wrought.

The tour was slated to roll into Jacksonville from Savannah on Monday evening, November 7, and to depart the River City on Wednesday morning, November 9, enroute to Lake City, Live Oak, Madison, Tallahassee, Gainesville, Leesburg, Tavares, Orlando, Wildwood, Bushnell, Dade City, Plant City, Tampa, Clearwater, St. Petersburg, Sarasota, Bradenton, Manatee, Bartow, Lake Wales, West Palm Beach, Ft. Lauderdale, Hollywood, and Miami; then north to Seabring, Avon Park, Winter Haven, Ocala, and Starke before leaving the state on Thursday, November 17.

In each city along the route, the railroad purchased newspaper advertisements featuring dramatic line drawings of a locomotive seeming to barrel headlong off the page. The high-minded copy reads, in part:

> Through its progressive policies, the Seaboard has kept
> pace with the advance of the South during its one hundred
> and six years of service—service that has been inseparably
> linked with the development of this great empire.
>
> As always, the Seaboard gives its utmost to boost the
> communities it humanely serves. Of each it considers itself
> a citizen, with the same civic pride; gives employment to

vast numbers of men and women; helps support govern-
ments and educate children through its taxes; and aids in
development of new industries and localities.

Again, the Seaboard evidences its faith in the South. It is
serving the present and building for the future. In return, the
Seaboard asks only fair treatment and the support of the
people in the further promotion of our mutual interests.

However, no such advance politicking was required in Jacksonville, where a warm
welcome had been all but assured. The train had rolled into Union Station (now the
Prime Osborn Convention Center) on Monday evening, and hundreds of citizens had
been on hand to watch its arrival. But on Tuesday morning, when official welcoming
ceremonies were scheduled, a throng of perhaps ten thousand—including schoolchildren, who had been excused from their lessons to watch history in the making—
braved chilly weather to cheer the spectacle.

In part, the public fascination was a result of extensive and fawning coverage in
The Times-Union and its sister publication, the evening *Jacksonville Journal*. Such
boosterism would not be unexpected, since railroad interests—including the Atlantic
Coast Line Railroad, Flagler Systems Incorporated, and Seaboard Air Line—held
most of the stock in the Florida Publishing Company, owners of both local dailies.
Therefore, many Jacksonvillians were preconditioned to accept the notion that what
was good for the railroad was good for the city.

William J. Kenealy, the railroad's general passenger agent in Florida, acted as
master of ceremonies during a brief program that preceded opening the potent locomotive—which had achieved speeds of one hundred miles per hour enroute from
Savannah with scarcely a sway or a rattle—and its Pullman cars for public inspec-
tion. Kenealy was joined on the platform by Powell, railroad attorney Francis P.
Fleming, and Jacksonville Mayor George C. Blume.

The Times-Union reported that "little Hester Williams, daughter of Mr. And Mrs.
Herbert Williams, and granddaughter of Mr. and Mrs. Fleming, presented Powell
with a handsome basket of flowers decorated with orange and white ribbons symbolic of the Seaboard's famous Orange Blossom Special. 'Mr. Powell, I thought you
would like these flowers,' the little girl said to the railway executive amid applause."

Powell then delivered a lofty speech affirming the railroad's commitment to
Florida and adding, "We have tried not only to keep abreast of the times, but also to
search the future and, so far as is within our power, to bring to you all the benefits
that modern research has proved to be worthwhile in transportation."

Fleming and Blume contributed further platitudes, and the mayor introduced
seventeen "pioneer citizens," who had been tapped as guests of honor, as well as
ten of the season's pretty young debutantes, who had apparently been invited to the
platform for purely decorative purposes.

Later, during the twelve-hour span that the train was open and accessible, ecstatic railroad officials declared that some 33,526 people had come aboard—a record for the tour—while hundreds more were unable to gain admission because of time constraints.

To a modern reader, the fact that more than thirty thousand people would show up to see a locomotive—highly touted diesel streamliner or not—seems difficult to accept. But, like rocket ships at the dawn of the Space Age, this train and others of its ilk were viewed as much more than machines. "The diesel locomotives on the Orange Blossom Special represented the world of the future," says Seth Bramson, a Miami-based author and lecturer on Florida railroad history. "People understood that they were witnessing the birth of a new era."

One of the most evocative railroad songs of the twentieth century was written in the early 1970s by Guy Clark, and later recorded by Johnny Cash. The autobiographical *Texas 1947* describes as vividly as any newspaper account the excitement and awe generated by the advent of the diesels, which by the 1950s would entirely supplant the sooty, stream-age engines that had powered the nation's westward expansion. The song is set in a small Texas town, where "fifty or sixty people, all sittin' on their cars," are waiting to catch a glimpse of the first diesel streamliner to speed through their community:

> *Trains are big and black and smokin',*
> *Louder'n July Four.*
> *But everybody's actin' like this might be something more,*
> *than just pickin' up the mail,*
> *or the soldiers from the war.*
> *Somethin' even old man Wyman's never seen before.*
> *So it's a late afternoon, on a hot Texas day.*
> *Somethin' strange is goin' on, and we're all in the way.*

The train does not stop, but its passing leaves speechless spectators "wonderin' what it's comin' to, and how it got this far." Certainly, the multitudes who viewed the Special on its 1938 exhibition tour must have felt similar emotions. Unquestionably, even those who never expected to join the well-to-do passengers on an excursion were enthralled, and hailed the Special and all it represented with unbridled enthusiasm.

As Clark wrote, with only a touch of artistic license, "you'd have thought that Jesus Christ hisself was a-rollin' down the line."

III

Ervin Rouse, Chubby Wise,
and the Devil's Box

*And one night Jeremiah noted a fiddle hanging on the wall and said,
"Granddaddy, what is that?" and Pink took it down and played it
fer him. And Jeremiah loved it! He took to the fiddle like a duck to
water, and when they got back home, hit was the first thing he told
his daddy about the trip. "Now you hark me," Moses said, his voice
deep and terrible. "The fiddle is an instrument of the Devil, and iffen
you ever take it up you will have to leave home. Fer you won't be my
boy no more, you'll be the Devil's boy." And then he put both hands
on Jeremiah's head and prayed on him.*

The Devil's Dream
by Lee Smith
(G.P. Putnam's Sons)

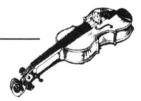

T he modern violin probably emerged in the mid-sixteenth century, and was
brought to America by Anglo- and Scots-Irish settlers because, unlike bulky
bagpipes, it was an easy-to-transport form of entertainment. References to
fiddling contests have been found in Virginia newspapers from as early as 1736,
and the fiddle held sway among both rural whites and slaves throughout the nineteenth century.

But, just as certain segments of the clergy would later denounce jazz and rock 'n'
roll, pioneer preachers railed against the fiddle as "the devil's box," and dark tales
were told of fiddlers who had sold their souls to Old Scratch in exchange for greater
musical prowess. Charlie Daniels would resurrect these eerie folk yarns for his 1979
hit, *The Devil Went Down to Georgia*, in which a young hot-shot named Johnny bets
his soul against Satan's gold fiddle in a winner-take-all fiddling showdown.

This disdain for fiddling was prompted by the assumption that playing an instrument left useful work undone. In colonial America, there was little tolerance for frivolity; hard labor was a Christian virtue, idleness was a sin, and the concept of guilt-free leisure time was all but unknown. At Merry Mount, for example, in the early days of the Plymouth Colony, Governor William Bradford harshly criticized settlers for "dancing and frisking togither, like so many fairies."

Frightened of damnation, some fair-weather fiddlers destroyed their instruments, while others, penitent but not given to extremism, simply hid them away. Charles Wolfe wrote that "people tearing down log cabins to get at the logs would find hidden in the wall an old, beat up fiddle...[it was explained that] the man who lived there was once a fine old-time fiddler, but that in later years he had gotten religion [and] in his zeal, he became convinced that he must turn his back on his old life, and especially the devil's instrument."

George Custer, who performed at the 1984 World's Fair in New Orleans and has been a judge at the Grand Masters Fiddle Championships in Nashville, recalls that the Primitive Baptists among whom he was reared had warned him repeatedly of the fiddle's dangerous allure. "They'd say, 'Son, stay away from that fiddle, because it leads to the bottle and loose women,'" Custer recalls. "But, although my grandmother wouldn't have a fiddle in the house, she'd come over and visit my uncles and say, 'Henry, could you please play a tune before I go?'

Americans, however, were not the first to ascribe Mephistophelean characteristics to fiddlers and to fiddling. Niccolo Paganini (1782-1840), the flamboyant Italian virtuoso, was widely rumored to have entered into a pact with the devil; some attendees at Paganini's recitals swore that they saw apparitions hovering above the musician as he performed. Perhaps because it enhanced his mystique, Paganini seemed to encourage such speculation by publicly indulging his many vices, which included predilections toward gaming and promiscuous sex.

Yet, even those who were certain that he was evil incarnate were forced to admit that Niccolo Paganini was a showman of the first order; indeed, he may have been the first prominent trick fiddler, augmenting his technical mastery with stunts such as playing complex melodies uninterrupted while intentionally severing several violin strings.

Hell's instrument? Perhaps; but it certainly produced heavenly sounds. Consequently, this diabolical music survived its New World detractors, and unrepentant fiddlers, without apparent damage to community morals and standards, entertained neighbors with melodies such as *Fisher's Hornpipe, Arkansas Traveler, Sallie Gooden,* and *The Eighth of January.* "Dancing and frisking" likewise continued unabated, although the informal character of early American dance was often puzzling to outsiders.

Andrew Burnaby, a British clergyman, wrote that the dancing he observed in pre-Revolutionary War Virginia "was without method and regularity; a gentleman and a lady stand up and dance about the room, one of them retiring, the other pursuing, then perhaps meeting, in a fantastical manner. After some time, another lady gets up, then the first lady must sit down, she being, as they term it, 'cut out.' The second lady acts the same part as the first did, 'till somebody cuts her out, while the gentlemen perform in the same manner."

Among America's finest fiddlers was no less a personage than Thomas Jefferson, who was considered to be perhaps the country's first great amateur violinist. In 1760, the seventeen-year-old Jefferson, enroute to William and Mary College, is said to have stopped in Hanover County, Virginia, where he was offered shelter for the night at a private home. Following dinner, the grateful young man fiddled an Irish jig while his host, one Patrick Henry, leapt from his seat and danced about the room.

Throughout most of his life, Jefferson practiced the fiddle daily; yet he still found time to author the Declaration of Independence, to invent the revolving chair and the weather vane, to master paleontology and architecture, and to serve as the third President of the United States. Clearly, had he not succumbed to the lure the devil's box, the squire of Monticello might truly have made something of himself.

Jefferson, however, was not the only early American notable to take up a fiddle bow. Frontiersman Davy Crockett was also an accomplished fiddler and buck dancer, and his song, *Col. Crockett's Reel*, is sometimes played today under the name *The Route*.

Yet, aside from icons, thousands of anonymous fiddlers populate American history. Diaries left behind by members of the doomed Donner Party, many of whom perished or resorted to cannibalism after being trapped by snowstorms in the Sierra Nevada mountains, refer to an unnamed fiddler who entertained the California-bound settlers before tragedy struck. (The musician's ultimate fate is unknown.) And dozens of Civil War photographs show soldiers posing stiffly with their prized fiddles.

Some fiddlers have even enjoyed successful political careers. In the 1880s, a pair of musically inclined brothers, Alf and Bob Taylor, ran against one another for the governorship of Tennessee. Contemporary newspapers feature engravings of the siblings performing before large crowds at joint political rallies. (Alf, who lost the election, went on to make recordings in the 1920s, and helped to popularize a tune called *The Fox Chase*.)

In the 1940s, *Grand Ole Opry* star Roy Acuff, who began his career as a fiddler, likewise ran for governor of the Volunteer State. Voters, however, seemed to prefer Acuff's music to his politics; the King of Country Music lost badly. Albert Gore Sr., father of the Clinton-era vice president, fared better in the 1960s, fiddling *Soldiers Joy* at campaign stops and winning election to the United States Senate.

Still, perhaps the best-known performing politician remains Gore's courtly colleague, Robert Byrd. The West Virginian, who was known as "Fiddlin' Bob

Byrd" in his youth, recorded an album in 1978 called *U.S. Senator Robert Byrd: Mountain Fiddler* (County). Byrd has also sawed traditional country tunes on the television show *Hee Haw* and on the stage of the Kennedy Center for the Performing Arts.

By the late nineteenth century, fiddlers had become staples in minstrel shows, during which blackface performers presented barn-dance favorites such as *Turkey in the Straw* and *Old Dan Tucker*. Later, fiddlers led string bands that consisted of guitars, banjos, and eventually mandolins—elements that would come to comprise "old-time" or "hillbilly" music when groups sporting such colorful names as the Skillet-Lickers, the Hoss-Hair Pullers, the Fruit Jar Drinkers, the Dixie Clodhoppers, the Possum Hunters, and the Buckle Busters were first recorded commercially.

In the aftermath of World War I, fiddlers found themselves in greater demand than ever, in part because fiddling and square-dancing competitions were being heavily promoted nationwide by Henry Ford, who believed that the traditional values he cherished were being trampled by flappers and jazz. "I'm trying in a small way," Ford told the *New York Times*, "to help America take a step, even if it is a little one, toward the saner and sweeter idea of life that prevailed in the [pre-war] days."

In 1925, the eccentric automaker and amateur social engineer launched an annual search for "The King of the Fiddlers," and sponsored well-attended fiddling contests at Ford dealerships throughout the South and Midwest. A Northeast regional winner, seventy-two-year-old Mellie Dunham of Norway, Maine, became a Ford favorite. In fact, Ford invited the flinty old snowshoe maker to Dearborn and helped him launch a wildly successful—if highly improbable—second career as a vaudevillian.

Ford's fervor also led him to painstakingly construct an idealized historic town called Greenfield Village, where he hosted hoedowns in a barn salvaged from his birthplace. In his weekly magazine, *The Dearborn Independent*, Ford published stories about fiddle music, and on his half-hour radio program, *Early American Dance Music*, he showcased old-time fiddle tunes. Under the tutelage of a full-time instructor, puzzled but compliant company executives were required to attend country dance lessons at Ford's Dearborn research facility.

Concurrently, radios and phonographs were becoming increasingly commonplace in rural homes, where farmers disillusioned by the rampant immorality of the Jazz Age echoed Ford's wistful longing for simpler times, when communal work activities—hog-killings, bean-stringings, flax-scrutchings, barn-raisings, house-raisings, and quilting bees—were also social functions, at which both camaraderie and traditional music were enjoyed. "Lassy-making tunes," for example, referred to folk songs shared when the coming of autumn marked molasses-making time.

"Americans of all ages, all conditions and all dispositions constantly form associations," Tocqueville had written in the 1830s, "to give entertainments, to found seminaries, to build inns, to construct churches, to diffuse books...I met with several kinds of which I had no previous notion."

From Tocqueville's time through the mid-twentieth century, virtually all of these diverse "associations" featured a fiddler.

Novelist Harry Crews, reflecting upon his southern Georgia upbringing in *A Childhood: The Biography of a Place* (University of Georgia Press), recalled how fiddle music enlivened wood-sawings and peanut poppings:

> Families gathered all over Bacon County to saw logs that would be used to cook tobacco the following summer and to shell peanuts for seed. A farmer snaked up as many logs as he could cut, and then the night of the party all the men and the young bucks sipped a little moonshine and sawed themselves into a sweat. Sometimes, eight or ten crosscut saws would be working at the same time, steam rising off the men's bodies in the cold air, their faces lighted by an enormous bonfire. Sometime later in the evening, a fiddler started and the sawing stopped.
>
> Peanut poppings were the same kind of party. A farmer would have saved back sacks of peanuts from the year before. If he wanted to plant ten or fifteen acres, an incredible number of peanuts had to be shelled by hand. Thirty-five or forty people, men, women and children, sat around for three or four hours with peanuts in their laps, shelling as fast as they could. Finally, somebody began pushing the furniture back, and the first tentative squawks of the fiddle cut through the cold night air.

Renowned fiddlers, plucked from obscurity by record company executives eager to exploit nostalgia pangs, included Uncle Jimmy Thompson, a moonshine-guzzling, seventy-eight-year-old farmer who, on November 28, 1925, became the first performer to appear on WSM's *Barn Dance* radio program—the precursor of the *Grand Ole Opry*. "Never took a music lesson in my life," Uncle Jimmy told a Nashville reporter in 1926. "I'd jest as soon look a mule in the face (actually, he probably said 'look a mule in the ass') as look at a sheet of music."

Other fiddlers making records and appearing on radio programs were Fiddlin' John Carson, Curly Fox, Henry Gilliland, Fiddlin' Sid Harkreader, Clark Kessinger, Clayton "Pappy" McMichen, Doc Roberts, Eck Robertson, Arthur Smith, and Uncle Bunt Stevens.

Robertson and Gilliland, in fact, are widely credited with making the first true country records. In June 1922, the pair had completed a series of performances at an Old Confederate Soldiers Reunion in Virginia—Gilliland was a bonified Confederate veteran—when they decided, somewhat audaciously, to board a train for New York City and, upon their arrival, to audition for the Victor Talking Machine Company.

Wearing either Confederate attire, cowboy outfits or a combination of the two, Robertson and Gilliland certainly would have made a sartorially vivid first impression on Victor executives, who agreed to hear them play and were impressed enough to record ten sides, including four duets and six solo turns by Roberts. (Among them was the definitive version of *Sally Goodin*).

However, it was the Georgia-born Carson who cut what are acknowledged to be the first commercially successful country recordings—*The Little Old Log Cabin in the Lane* and *The Old Hen Cackled and the Rooster's Going to Crow*—for the Okeh (pronounced "okay") label in June 1923. The unexpected popularity of these records persuaded Okeh's artist and repitore (A&R) man, Ralph Peer—a sophisticate who privately opined that Carson's singing was "terrible"—that that there was actually money to be made selling unadorned folk tunes in rural markets.

Peer, who left Okeh for Victor Records in 1926, would soon thereafter discover and record Jimmie Rodgers and the Carter Family, among others, thereby launching the modern country-music industry.

The early recordings of old-time fiddlers also influenced mainstream superstars of the 1940s. In fact, it is safe to surmise that most second-generation country musicians would have been weaned on fiddle music, and that many learned from older friends and relatives how to play traditional melodies on the accessible instrument, which could be ordered through the 1900 Sears Roebuck catalog for a relatively affordable four dollars, including bow and case.

"The soprano voice in the family was provided by the fiddle," says George Custer. "And, if the player was truly an artist, then the fiddle could also express the broadest range of emotions of any musical instrument."

Boosted in large part by exposure on the vaudeville stage, the sub- genre of trick fiddling also began to gain in popularity, reaching its apex at colorful, old-time fiddling contests held throughout the country in the 1920s and 1930s.

Some competitions, such as those sponsored by Ford, were relatively authentic, and were scrupulously judged by panelists who possessed appropriate credentials and expertise. By the early 1930s, however, many fiddling contests had become purely commercial ventures staged by promoters, with winners chosen based upon audience response. Therefore, savvy fiddlers, many of whom supplemented their incomes by competing at such gatherings, came to realize that showmanship was as important as musicianship—perhaps even more so—in winning over spectators.

Perhaps the first widely known American trick fiddler was James Gideon "Gid" Tanner, a north Georgia chicken farmer who fronted the influential Skillet Lickers, and whose comedic antics, if not his technical skills, made him a perennial favorite at fiddlers' conventions held following World War I. (Tanner, it was said, "could turn his head all the way around like an owl" while playing.) Other performers, such as

"Natchee the Indian" (real name: Lester Storer) even went so far as to don costumes and assume "good" or "evil" personas, not unlike those employed by modern-day professional wrestlers.

Mellie Dunham, for one, wasn't above talking trash to boost interest in a potential showdown. When Uncle Jimmy Thompson won a high-profile fiddling contest against some eighty competitors in Dallas, Texas, Dunham told reporters that Thompson's victory was hollow because his foes were mostly Southerners. Therefore, Dunham said, he would happily travel to Tennessee to meet Thompson, one-on-one, and conclusively demonstrate the musical superiority of New Englanders. Thompson replied in kind, saying that if Dunham set foot in the state, "I'll lay with him like a bulldog."

The contest was never held, and the animosity may well have been manufactured. "There was a spirit of competition among [contest] fiddlers that was unusual in its intensity, but there was a great mutual respect as well," says Custer, whose uncles entered and won their share of such musical showdowns. "They listened to one another and learned."

Trick fiddlers were also among the first solo performers on the *Opry*. Charles Wolfe, in his 1999 book *A Good Natured Riot: The Birth of the Grand Ole Opry* (Vanderbilt University Press and the Country Music Foundation Press), wrote:

> Theirs was a fancy show-off music, music designed to display fiddle techniques and effects. It was the kind of performance that won contests, delighted audiences and reeked of nineteenth-century vaudeville and medicine shows. It ranged from the dense variations of Uncle Bunt Stephens to the chicken imitations of Whit Gaydon, and from the ornate Italian waltzes of Uncle Joe Mangrum to the rowdy gyrations of Henry Bandy...The display fiddlers were mostly veterans, some with birth dates reaching back before the Civil War.
>
> Though much of their appeal was visual, these musicians soon learned to translate their acts to radio and to earn the highest compliment an old-timer could give their performance: 'It was a regular monkey show.'

The late John Hartford, the eclectic musician-composer perhaps best known for writing the country-pop evergreen *Gentle on My Mind*, was an aficionado of old-time fiddling, and an admirer of great trick fiddlers. "It's all a matter of trying to get attention," said Hartford, who was also a Rouse Brothers and Chubby Wise enthusiast. "If you put a cup down (for tips), then you'd better be good and have tricks, or they'll walk right past you. They might even walk right past you and kick your cup over."

Added Wolfe: "Some people tend to dismiss trick fiddling. It may have gotten something of a bad rap. But there's a whole tradition of trick fiddling in this country, and it's a legitimate art form."

By the early 1940s, however, juke boxes had become the most important conduits for dissemination of country records, leading to a surge in amplified honky-tonk music of the type pioneered by gravel-voiced Ernest Tubb. Concurrently, fiddler Bob Wills and his Texas Playboys had popularized western swing—rollicking dance-hall arrangements that added drums, brasses, and reeds to the mix.

String bands, too, were evolving; Kentuckian Bill Monroe, a master of the mandolin, had combined traditional folk stylings with elements of blues, jazz, and his trademark piercing vocals to create bluegrass—a genre that Alan Lomax described in 1959 as "a sort of mountain Dixieland combo."

Consequently, back-porch bands—and old-time fiddlers—had become vaguely embarrassing anachronisms to an industry determined to move into the commercial mainstream. Fiddles remained acceptable—even desirable—in country combos, but a more sophisticated, polished style was mandated so as not to alienate audiences beyond Appalachia. "When you call me hillbilly, smile," warned Tubb—and the Texas Troubadour meant it.

Chubby Wise admitted that he was not a bluegrass fiddler, per se, when he joined Bill Monroe in 1942—but he learned. "I was a country fiddler player," he said in 1977. "Bill Monroe taught me how to play bluegrass. He taught me the long, blue notes. Many a day—in motels and hotels—him with that mandolin and I'd have my fiddle—he'd say, 'Now, do it this way,' and I'd try. And he'd say, 'No, that's not what I want.' And he'd show me how on the mandolin. And, finally, when I'd get it, he'd say, 'Yep, that's what I want.'"

Later, Chubby easily navigated bluegrass and mainstream country music—with occasional forays into the blues, jazz and even light classics—employing a smooth, refined sound that was described by one critic as "the sweetest fiddle this side of Heaven."

Ervin Rouse, conversely, would have described himself simply as a showman. "He could play the damn fiddle better between his legs and behind his back than most fiddlers could under their chins," says musician Gene Christian, a musician with whom Rouse shared both stages and streetcorners.

No doubt, this was true; but by stubbornly adhering to his vaudeville-tinged hillbilly routine, entertaining as it may have been, Rouse never moved beyond novelty-act status as a live performer, and failed altogether as a recording artist. Consequently, it could be said that Rouse inexplicably squandered his monumental talent; or, perhaps he simply came to understand that he was emotionally ill equipped to pursue fame in Nashville, New York, or Hollywood, thereby negating the necessity for artistic growth.

Certainly, Rouse and Wise were alike in many ways: Both were raised on farms; both were prodigies who endured strange, truncated childhoods; and both became heavy drinkers seemingly bent on self-destruction. But Wise was adaptable and ambitious—driven, perhaps, by his abandonment as a child to seek approval and to demonstrate his worth as both a musician and as a human being.

Rouse, however, was neither adaptable nor ambitious—"It just seemed like Ervin didn't care sometimes," opines Gene—and was furthermore cursed by bouts of mental illness and just plain buzzard's luck on an almost cosmic scale.

ERVIN THOMAS LIDEL ROUSE was born on an eastern North Carolina cotton and tobacco farm near the tiny settlement of Dover (population six hundred) in Craven County, on September 18, 1917. "We were all poor people," he recalled in 1976. "We hardly knew where our next meal was comin' from. I was raised on a farm. Fifteen head 'o children to one mother and father."

As was his wont, Ervin was exaggerating the humble circumstances of his upbringing for dramatic effect—although not by much. Ernest Hayward Rouse (born in 1878) and Eloise Coriene Chadwick Rouse (born in 1880) may indeed have produced fifteen children, but just twelve survived past infancy: brothers James Joshua (born in 1898), Paul Lumas (born in 1901), Leslie Hayward (born in 1906), Herbert Webster (born in either 1907 or 1908), Guy Humble (born in 1909), Earl Bryan (born in 1911), Ernest Gordon (born in 1914), and Durwood Thurlow (born in 1921); and sisters Mable (born in 1902), Bettie Mae (born in 1905), Hattie (born in 1916), and Durwood's twin, Ida Coe.

As a teenager, Hattie was horribly burned when, during the Christmas holidays, an errant fireplace spark ignited a cotton robe she was wearing. After lingering for several weeks, she died. Additionally, at least one Rouse family miscarriage—an unnamed boy—is documented, although there may have been others. In any case, the Rouse family had deep roots in eastern North Carolina; Ernest's ancestors had settled there in the early 1730s.

In 1920, there were 2,598 farms in Craven County, half of which were occupied by sharecroppers. The Rouses, however, owned the fifty-eight acres on which they grew tobacco, cotton, and corn. And, like many small-time farmers, they were relatively self-sufficient and adequately fed. "We've had some awful hard times [in Craven County]," says Tull Jackson, a seventy-six-year-old farmer whose family once lived about a quarter-mile from the Rouses. "But we had our own meat, and what we produced, we consumed. We were poor, but so was everybody else."

Carrie White Rouse, widow of Gordon, Ervin's most consistent performing partner, still lives in the small, northwestern Miami home that she and her husband built and shared for fifty-seven years. She says that Gordon's childhood memories "were very fond, and he certainly didn't think of his family as poverty stricken. I'm sure it was a struggle, but none of those dozen children ever went hungry."

The old Rouse homestead is still standing, although additions and renovations have significantly altered its original appearance. In the 1920s, however, it was a simple but spacious white frame structure with two stories and a wrap-around front porch; hardly a mansion, but a respectable farmhouse nonetheless.

The Rouses were a musical clan; virtually everyone played an instrument and sang. Ernest, in addition to being a farmer, was an ordained Methodist minister who loved traditional gospel songs. He did not pastor his own church, but carted his brood to services at nearby Lane's Chapel, where he would sometimes be called upon as a substitute preacher. "I remember that Mr. Rouse didn't seem to be much for workin' too hard," says Jackson. "My daddy and I would drive by their house in an old Model T Ford, and we'd see the old man leaned back in a chair on the front porch, readin' the Bible. My daddy wanted to point him out as a good example to me. He'd say, 'Son, do you see what Mr. Rouse is doin'?' And I'd say, 'Well, it looks to me like he's takin' a rest.'"

Matriarch Eloise, known to friends and neighbors as "Miss Ella," played the fiddle, although it was apparently eldest brother James Joshua, also known as Jimmy, who was Ervin's musical tutor. "My daddy, I'm told, was the only member of the family who could read music," says Elizabeth Walters, Jimmy's daughter. "He taught Uncle Ervin to play the violin, and was very rigid about music lessons. Uncle Ervin would slip off into a dream world, and my daddy would whip him with a stick." According to Elizabeth, Jimmy also showed his six-year-old brother the rudiments of trick fiddling and crowd-pleasing showmanship.

In large part because performing generated income for the family, Ernest and Eloise encouraged their children to hone their skills. "My father would always lead the church singing, and my mama would sing, too," said Gordon in 1992. "But my daddy is where we got our good singing from. There was only one brother [Paul, who later operated a service station and died of a heart attack in 1948] who couldn't carry a tune. We started out in the music business playing school houses and tobacco warehouses all over North Carolina."

In fact, it was a tobacco warehouse in Kinston, just northwest of Dover in Lenoir County, at which Jackson first saw the Rouse Brothers—"We called 'em the Rouse Boys back then"—captivate a crowd. "In the fall of the year [during the tobacco harvest] the farmers and their families would all come into town to bring in their crops," Jackson recalls. "It was always quite a time. The stores were open late, and the streets were full of people. Mr. Rouse would come in with the boys—maybe four or five of 'em—and they'd play while the old man passed the hat. If they got done and the collection wasn't what it should have been, then he'd say, 'Boys, we need to do another number.'"

But of all the siblings, Ervin displayed the most versatility, mastering the guitar, the banjo, and the mandolin as well as the fiddle. Therefore, while playing popular tunes, gospel songs, and folk melodies for appreciative locals, he came to realize that a musician's life was infinitely preferable to that of a tobacco farmer. Moreover, he came to understand that he was the family band's star attraction, and successfully leveraged this knowledge at every opportunity. "Ervin was the second-youngest brother, but in that family, whatever he said, that was it," says Carrie. "I loved Ervin, and unless you knew him, you just couldn't imagine his talent. But he was a spoiled child and a spoiled adult, and just had to have his way."

Elon Smith Scheifer, who befriended Ervin as an adolescent, also recalls that the young fiddler could be temperamental, even obstinate, when it came time to perform. "You had to beg him to play," she says. "He wouldn't outright refuse, but he'd just change the subject and talk about something else entirely. Still, he was the headliner, so the other brothers had to really pamper him."

Ervin was, by any definition, a child prodigy. While some youthful musicians attain superior levels of performance through formal training, Ervin never received instruction from anyone outside his immediate family, and was able to compose original melodies before he could read. Like Mozart, Schubert, Mendelssohn, and Chopin—heady company, to be sure—Ervin clearly was born with a type of cognitive excellence that cannot be taught.

Yet, his genius was narrowly focused; as an adult, he often gave the impression of being slow-witted, and one acquaintance even believed him to be mildly retarded. In fact, although Ervin was unschooled and unsophisticated, his intelligence was probably average. If he later appeared to be a borderline idiot savant, it was because alcoholism and mental illness accentuated an already pronounced intellectual laziness.

Still, although Ervin's talent was innate, his musical mastery was not achieved in a vacuum. Aside from his parents and older siblings, early influences likely included hillbilly musicians who made records or performed on the radio. By 1927, the newly established Federal Radio Commission (later the Federal Communications Commission) had licensed 732 stations—there had been only twenty-two stations on the air five years earlier—some of which featured live performances of old-time music. Assuming they owned a receiver, on a clear evening the Rouses could have picked up such programming on WSB in Atlanta, WBT in Charlotte, and WSM in Nashville.

Minstrel shows, vaudevilles, and burlesque troupes also found receptive audiences in eastern North Carolina. Minstrel shows, featuring burnt-cork comedians who combined unrefined humor and vivacious music, were considered to be family entertainment, while burlesque performances, featuring companies of spectacularly costumed females who sang and danced, offered somewhat more risqué fare. Fundamentalists, of course, railed that such entertainment was inherently sinful and detrimental to public morality. Perhaps so, opined a columnist in a local newspaper, the New Bern *Journal*, but "it does not follow that we should be bad people because we go there and enjoy it."

How much of this local color Ervin absorbed is unknown, although it is probably safe to assume that the rustic Rouses could not have afforded to attend theatrical or musical performances en masse. Yet, it is difficult to imagine that at least some members of a clan so immersed in music would not have made the relatively short trip into New Bern for an occasional vaudeville performance at the Masonic Opera House, the Athens Show Shop, or the Kehoe Theater. At the very least, they would have attended medicine shows—then commonplace in the rural South—during which purveyors of allegedly medicinal elixirs and tonics employed comedians and musicians to attract crowds.

Although Ernest Rouse may have been a deeply religious man, his "stage father" behavior on behalf of Ervin and his brothers indicates that he did not regard popular entertainment as evil. So, it may have been during a vaudeville performance, a community shindig, a revival meeting, a medicine show, or even a fiddling contest when Ernest came to the conclusion that Ervin, in combination with one or more of his siblings, had a bright, and hopefully lucrative, future in show business.Certainly, at least for the boys, formal education was not a priority; none of the brothers appear to have advanced beyond the eighth grade, while the sisters all benefited from at least some college. "Mr. Rouse was always looking for ways to make money," says Louallie, "and he could be easily talked into sending Ervin [and his brothers] out on tour."

Money was understandably a concern with the deepening of the Great Depression, during which the Rouses, like many others, struggled to keep the banker at bay before ultimately losing their heavily mortgaged farm around 1929.

But for Ernest, a slumping economy was not the only obstacle to solvency. Tobacco was a delicate, labor-intensive crop that demanded considerable skill and vigilance, and the Rouse patriarch—who seemed far more interested in squiring his musical progeny to performances than in sowing, transplanting, suckering, worming, cropping, stringing, and curing his leafy yield—was likely a sorry excuse for a farmer, even in the best of times.

In any case, financial hardships, combined with Hattie's death, apparently caused Ernest to suffer a nervous breakdown, during which he was institutionalized at the North Carolina State Hospital in Raleigh. Once he was released, Ernest, along with Eloise and whichever children were still in their care (probably only Durwood and Ida Coe), lived at various times with one or the other of Ernest's two sisters in Pollocksville.

Inexplicably, this scripture-quoting stalwart, whom his neighbors had described as a "full-blooded Methodist," had emerged from the hospital as an equally devout Jehovah's Witness. So, for the remainder of his long life, Ernest enjoyed vehemently arguing the merits of his new faith—which departs from most Christian denominations by holding that Jesus is not equal to Almighty God—as unconvinced family members listened politely.

Still, if his misfortunes and his eccentricities diminished the old man in the eyes of his children, they never let on. "All the brothers and sisters respected their parents," says Carrie. "That's how they were raised."

VAUDEVILLE IS AN AMERICAN term dating from the 1840s, although the origin of vaudeville as a specific type of entertainment may be traced to nineteenth century pastoral plays in France, which featured musical interludes.

In the United States, the term became commonly used to describe an eclectic program of brief acts with no connecting theme. Until the 1930s, when moving pictures became the distraction of choice, vaudeville showcased the country's most popular performers, and routinely drew packed houses.

A typical vaudeville package featured eight to fourteen acts, or "turns," which might include magicians, singers, dancers, acrobats, jugglers, comedians, female impersonators, trained animals, and even non-show business celebrities, such as athletes or prominent newsmakers. Vaudevillians who went on to fame in film and television included Fred and Adele Astaire, Jack Benny, Joe E. Brown, Milton Berle, George Burns and Gracie Allen, W.C. Fields, Ted Healy and the Three Stooges, Al Jolson, Buster Keaton, Laurel and Hardy, the Marx Brothers, Will Rogers, and Lillian Russell. Helen Keller also appeared in vaudeville shows, as did temperance crusader Carrie Nation, illusionist Harry Houdini, and baseball great Babe Ruth.

"Rube" acts were also vaudeville staples, and some of country music's earliest luminaries—including Jimmie Rodgers, the tubercular blue yodeler who is considered to be the father of the genre, and Uncle Dave Macon, the banjo-playing comedian who emerged as the first true star of the *Grand Ole Opry*—played vaudeville circuits.

The natty Rodgers, once he became phenomenally popular, did not feel compelled to wear overalls; he generally sported stylish, tailor-made suits. However, with the notable exception of the Singing Brakeman, impresarios required their fiddlers, old-time string bands, and hayseed comedy combos to outfit and comport themselves as though they had just ridden into town on a mule-drawn wagon.

Even the Brooklyn-born Three Stooges once billed themselves, along with their manager, as "Ted Healy and Three Gentlemen from the South." (It should be noted, however, that rustics were not the only ones to be ill-treated by vaudeville; racial and religious groups—particularly blacks and Jews—were also portrayed in stereotypical fashion.)

Vaudeville was controlled by owners of theater chains, or "circuits," among the most powerful of which was Keith-Albee-Orpheum (KAO), which in 1928 would be acquired by the Radio Corporation of America (RCA) and become Radio-Keith-Orpheum (RKO). The Keith organization was considered to be "big-time" vaudeville, meaning that theaters were in larger cities, talent was better-paid, and fewer shows—usually three instead of five—were required per day.

It is certainly easy to understand how a diminutive, dark-haired moppet with Ervin's skills would have made an ideal addition to any vaudeville bill, but it is unknown how his initial connection with KOA was made. Since New Bern was the region's entertainment mecca, it seems likely that Ernest simply picked a theater where a show was booked, showed up with Ervin in tow, and persuaded someone in authority to give the boy an audition. Whatever the case, eight-year-old Ervin, chaperoned by his father, was soon playing KAO's premier theaters, including the Palace in New York City and the Colonial in Boston, as well as the Lowe's circuit venues, including the Capitol, the Palace, and the Columbia, all in Washington, D.C.

On the Lowe's engagements, and perhaps others, Ervin was joined onstage by guitarist Gordon, who had by then assumed what was to become a long and often frustrating role as his mercurial brother's primary accompanist and duet partner.

At various times, according to Carrie, additional older brothers also may have been part of the troupe; but it was precocious Ervin, who was so small that he was often placed atop a wooden crate in order to be seen, who was again the star attraction. "I'd be trembling at the microphone," Ervin said in 1979. "You get hundreds of people, and you can feel them out there. You'd be lying if you said you can't, and half the time I thought I was out of my cotton-pickin' mind for being there. How I made it through some of my numbers the Lord knows."

Unfortunately, little more is known of Ervin's first vaudeville stint. It is unclear exactly how much time he spent on the road—although it was probably not more than two years—or with whom he appeared. However, vaudeville is undoubtedly where Ervin perfected the art of trick fiddling; learning to play his instrument behind his head, between his legs, and while lying down.

Yet, the only specific statement about vaudeville that Ervin made for the record was in a 1976 interview with the *Miami Herald*, during which he claimed to have once played a show with Will Rogers, although he did not specify where or when. This is possible, since the cowboy-philosopher was also a Keith attraction during the early 1920s.

As for tangible souvenirs of this heady time, little remains. The family scrapbook holds an eight-by-ten-inch publicity photograph of a grinning Ervin, clad in knickers and a cap, playing his fiddle by holding the instrument upside down and rubbing it back and forth over a bow protruding from between his knees. On the back of the tattered relic, in a childlike scrawl, the youngster has written a note from New York City to his older brother, Jimmy, which reads: "To the old fisherman J.J. Rouse—Oh was I killing the people in the audience, 1,000 people in the Keith [probably the Colonial] theater in Boston!"

In the same scrapbook is preserved a letter of recommendation written by a Lowe's executive in 1944, when Ervin and Gordon apparently planned to audition for a USO troupe traveling to Europe. The complimentary missive ("I think the GIs would go for this act in a big way!") confirms the Rouses' earlier affiliation with the circuit, and also makes reference to their having appeared in vaudeville units headed by Broadway musical comedy stars Harry Richman and Ted Lewis, among unspecified others. (The proposed overseas trip never materialized, perhaps due to Ervin's terror of flying.)

Carrie says that the brothers' vaudeville stint was cut short when an under-aged Ervin was removed from the Capitol Theater's stage by police. Although there were no federal child labor regulations until the Fair Labor Standards Act was passed in 1938, many individual states had adopted their own statutes. Enforcement was spotty, but local authorities would sometimes act when enough pressure was applied by crusading social service agencies. Given such laxity, a single such incident need not have permanently scuttled Ervin's vaudeville career. Nonetheless, says Carrie, the experience frightened Ernest enough that he felt it prudent to take the boys home.

However, the musical siblings soon experienced another run-in with the law that Louallie believes may have traumatized Ervin, and instilled in him a lifelong fear—bordering on a full-blown phobia—of uniformed authority figures. It seems that the brothers, this time including Earl, were playing for tips on the streets of Kinston when a woman accused them of stealing her purse, occasioning their arrest. "They definitely didn't do it," Louallie says. "But Ervin was scared to death. When the police told him they'd go easier on him if he confessed, then that's just what Ervin did. Earl and Gordon were so mad that they gave him a whipping for it."

As an adult, the anxiety-riddled fiddler always insisted upon driving well under posted speed limits—much to the annoyance of his passengers and of other motorists—simply to lessen the possibility of being pulled over. (Ironically, he was sometimes stopped for driving too slowly; a ruse commonly employed by drunken drivers.)

Still, claims Tull Jackson, the young Rouses—although they generally complied with their father's wishes—sometimes displayed a collective rebellious streak.

For example, he says, around 1927, Buck and Violet Jackson, Tull's parents, were visiting Rouse daughter Bettie, who lived in Greenville with her first husband, a well-to-do real estate investor named William E. McGowan. That same evening, Ernest and a retinue of boys showed up unexpectedly. "I reckon they were in town to play somewhere," Jackson recalls. "Bettie said, 'I'd love to have you stay, but I don't have any room.' The old man [Ernest] said, 'Well, you've got a whole floor right here.'" As the evening wore on, the brothers became restless, and asked Ernest to let them use the car; a request that was denied. "So, they just waited until their daddy was asleep, snuck out the back door and pushed the car down the hill before they started it," Jackson continues. "The boys, they went out and had a party until two or three in the mornin', and when they got back, the old man was still asleep, and never knew a thing had happened."

Ervin later said that he was nine years old—although he was probably closer to twelve—when he, Gordon, and Earl were taken off the farm by an itinerant evangelist and longtime family friend, who used the boys to energize the faithful at tent revivals. All that is known of the preacher is that his surname, Lidel, was bestowed upon Ervin at birth—which indicates that he was held in high esteem by Ernest and Eloise. Also, Louallie recalls, Lidel had been Jewish before abandoning his religious heritage to preach the gospel of Jesus Christ. (Decades later, in fact, Ervin told writer Randy Wayne White about having traveled with "a Jew preacher" and "a Greek Jew.")

"We come down to Florida and we played the beaches and all over," Ervin said in 1976. "The preacher would get the people to listening and then we'd run them out with our playing. We knowed one song. I think it was *Under the Double Eagle*. Like to drove everybody crazy, playing it over and over. But that preacher taught us some manners that we didn't learn from Momma and Poppa, and we got prayed for a lot."

Ervin may well have been the recipient of Lidel's prayers, but his money was another matter; following an Orlando-area service, the brothers abruptly abandoned their Bible-thumping employer when he did not pay them as promised. And, despite Ervin's kind words about Lidel, uttered tactfully from a half-century's distance, there are indications that he viewed the revivalist as nothing more than a common huckster.

In *The Man Who Invented Florida*, the quasi-fictional Ervin tells Tuck and Joseph that their scheme to sell a youth-restoring elixir evokes unhappy memories of his childhood brush with evangelism: "I never pictured you in the water-sellin' business. That flimflam preacher that used to take me around, he did a little of that. Called it medicine. I just figured never to go back to it. What he did to us boys…"

While the Lidel interlude may have done little to advance the brothers' spiritual lives, it did further sharpen their performing skills. By the early 1930s, a Rouse quintet consisting of Ervin, Gordon, Jimmy, Earl, and Herbert had developed a crowd-pleasing, relatively polished hillbilly musical-comedy act, and were traveling together via automobile to appearances at theaters throughout the Northeast, Midwest, and Southeast, billing themselves as "The White Ducks," "The Red Hot Smoking Tar-Heels," or "The Corn-Fed Hill Billies."

Because motion pictures had brought extinction to vaudeville, many of these bookings would have been "independent vaudeville," a term coined by *Billboard* magazine to describe venues at which live acts were sometimes presented between films. "I was on the road when I should have been back home picking cotton," Ervin said in 1977, although he certainly did not mean it.

Sometimes, the entire Rouse clan would rendezvous at Jimmy's home in the Edgewood section of Danville, Virginia. "About three times a year, they'd all end up at our house," says Elizabeth Rouse Walters. "Uncle Ervin was so handsome back then, and all the girls were just crazy about him. Of course, our neighbors loved it when my uncles were in town because they could stand in their yards and hear this wonderful music. I looked forward to their visits, and cried my eyes out when they left."

While in Danville, which was a hotbed of hillbilly music, various combinations of brothers would perform to raise traveling money. It was such an impromptu apperance that musician Claude Casey, then in his late teens, first saw Ervin play. Casey, who died of complications from Alzheimer's disease in 1999, lived near Jimmy, and the pair frequently joined forces for guitar and fiddle jam sessions. They would later form a band, The Pine State Playboys, and make records for RCA Victor.

"I believe I first saw Ervin when he was ten or twelve years old," Casey recalled in a 1982 interview with Country Music Foundation historian John Rumble. "[Earl] and Ervin were going from tobacco barn to tobacco barn, and their mother and father were carrying them in a car. There was always a crowd at a tobacco barn, you see. Most of the farmers would be bringing the tobacco in, waiting for the sale the next morning." Later, Casey would perform as an honorary Rouse Brother, playing guitar or harmonica and sharing in the proceeds.

Yet, perhaps in part because of their frustration over Ervin's unpredictability, Jimmy and Herbert eventually stopped performing with their younger brother; Jimmy pursued his own musical career with Casey, while Herbert appears to have worked at various non-show business jobs in North Carolina before settling in Arcadia, Florida. It then fell to level-headed Gordon to act as defacto manager for the remaining trio—now known as the Rouse Brothers—affixing his signature to contracts, distributing earnings, and making certain that enough cash was set aside to cover expenses. He also acted as his temperamental brother's proverbial keeper. "Gordon would have to start on Ervin an hour before a show," recalls Carrie. "He'd say, 'Ervin, it's time to go to work.' Ervin would just sit there. One time, Gordon said, 'Ervin, if you don't get ready now, then I'll just go on home and we'll forget about it.' Then, at the last minute, he'd get ready."

Certainly, the group worked steadily; when Gordon did not have a paid engagement already booked, the brothers simply wheedled owners of clubs and restaurants into allowing them to perform for tips—a practice known as "busking."

In the spring of 1932, however, the boys had gone their separate ways when Earl encountered James H. Smith, a respected building contractor and patriarch of a hospitable, music-loving central Florida family. "Daddy never met a stranger," recalls Elon Smith Schieber, now living in the Conway section of Orlando.

She says her father was driving through the small town of Pine Castle in southern Orange County when he spotted a young man with a guitar strapped to his back trudging alongside U.S. 441, then a desolate, two-lane road. "Daddy loved to play the fiddle and he loved music, so I'm sure that's why he stopped," Elon continues. The hitchhiker introduced himself as Earl Rouse, and said that he was headed to Miami—some three hundred miles south—to perform in a nightclub. "Daddy asked Earl where he intended to spend the night, and Earl said he didn't know—so Daddy brought him home to spend the night with us."

Home was a large, four-bedroom house in the Boggy Creek area of Osceola County—then rural and isolated, now the gateway to Disney World—where Smith lived with his wife, Lillian Jane Cox, along with four daughters; Lillian, then six; Mildred, then eight; Elon, then twelve; and a son, Lloyd, then eighteen. "I was quite fascinated by someone who had been so many places and was such a great showman," recalls Elon. "After supper, Daddy played the fiddle and Earl played the guitar, and they had a really good time."

Obviously, Earl found the Smiths' hospitality to his liking—his one-night stay stretched into six weeks—and the Smiths came to regard Earl as part of the family. "All of us and our neighbors loved Earl and his singing and music," says Elon. "He was about the same age as my brother, Lloyd, and they practiced guitar together. They also went out together, hunted and fished together, and really enjoyed each other."

When Earl finally set out for North Carolina, he promised to return soon, and to bring his brothers, Gordon and Ervin. "He said to me, 'My brother, Ervin, is about your age (actually he was three years older), and you ought to meet him,'" Elon recalls. "Sure enough, six months later, the three of them drove up."

Elon says she thought fifteen-year-old Ervin was "cute," with his mop of wavy black hair, crooked grin, and surprisingly shy demeanor. He was thin and rangy, and spoke in a thick, eastern North Carolina brogue that would become difficult to understand when he was old and ill, but was probably endearing when he was a youth. "Ervin was very serious," she recalls. "I think he just grew up too fast, and was thrown in with a crowd that he shouldn't have been with."

For his part, Ervin was enchanted by his young hostess, a pretty girl with a lively personality and a multitude of beaux. The following day, Ervin and Gordon volunteered to pick Elon up from school and, when the unsuspecting teenager slid into the front seat of the brothers' well-traveled Chevrolet, Ervin, displaying atypical boldness, leaned over and kissed her on the cheek. Elon still chuckles at Gordon's deadpan reaction to his brother's spontaneous show of affection: "Ervin, sometimes you make me feel downright unnecessary."

During that first visit, the Rouses stayed with the Smiths for a week, establishing a routine that would continue for years, and forming friendships that would last a lifetime. "We didn't have a phone, and usually we wouldn't have any notice that they were coming," Elon says. "But they'd come around every spring, and maybe also in the fall, on the way down to Miami to play clubs. They'd just drive up in the yard, open the car windows and start playing music. We'd hear them, wake up and put on the coffee."

For Ervin, Gordon, and Earl, Orlando was essentially a rest stop between wherever they had come from and southern Florida; consequently, they typically did not have performances booked in the area. Still, recalls Elon, the brothers would often pile into their car after eating supper and head into town to go busking.

The Smiths occasionally accompanied the Rouses when they played Orlando dates—scheduled or spontaneous—and Elon, along with others who saw them perform, say that their live act was a wacky tour d' force of amazing musicality and infectious silliness. Dressed in hillbilly garb—Ervin would often wear a long-tailed tuxedo coat with his overalls—the boys would open the show with a rouser such as *Put That Pistol Down, She'll Be Comin' Round the Mountain,* or *Alabama Jubilee.* Then, Ervin would cut loose, playing *Indian Love Call, Turkey in the Straw,* or the trick fiddler's anthem, *Pop Goes the Weasel,* while holding his fiddle atop his head, behind his back, or underneath his upraised leg.

During the chaos, Gordon and Earl would keep time on guitars—sometimes Gordon would "second" on the fiddle—while feigning exasperation and swapping down-home quips. The crowds loved both the music and the cornpone interplay. "They put on as good a show as you'd see anywhere," Elon says. "Ervin was happy to play music, once you could get him to play when he was supposed to."

After returning to Kissimmee, the brothers would tally the evening's proceeds, then continue playing music until the wee hours. Once their coffers were sufficiently filled, Elon recalls, they would bid their farewells and head south. "We were always sad to see them go," she says. "They were such fun, and seemed to enjoy their lives so much. As for Ervin, I never saw his bad side. To me, he was a very likable person."

Little is known of the Rouse Brothers' other activities during the mid-1930s; presumably they were traveling, stopping to perform wherever they might draw a crowd. Elizabeth Walters believes that some combination of siblings appeared on *Major Bowes and His Original Amateur Hour*, a hugely popular radio program broadcast live from the Capitol Theater in New York.

The Bowes phenomenon drew thousands of hopefuls—many of them destitute—from small towns and rural areas across the country. Indeed, the influx of starry-eyed paupers became so overwhelming that CBS was compelled to change its policy and limit entrants to New York area residents only. However, this restriction could be easily circumvented by claiming a flophouse or even a city-run shelter as a permanent address.

The Rouse Brothers, of course, were not amateurs. But Bowes, who contended that most legitimate amateurs were void of talent and would drive listeners away, frequently booked lesser-known vaudevillians as ringers. He also enjoyed tossing an occasional hillbilly band into the mix of would-be crooners and comedians.

Claude Casey, for one, had hitchhiked to New York in 1934 and appeared on the program as a solo act, billing himself as "The Carolina Hobo." Casey, who won twenty dollars and a measure of hometown fame for his trouble, would certainly have told the Rouses about the experience, and encouraged them to give it a shot. So, although it is impossible to confirm, the brothers may well have showcased their talents on *Major Bowes* while barnstorming the Big Apple in 1935 or 1936. "I understand that they won the competition," says Elizabeth. "After that, they were able to get jobs all over New York."

In fact, there exists evidence that the Rouses may have recorded for New York City-based American Recording Corporation (ARC), a predecessor of Columbia Records. ARC, which had been acquired by Consolidated Film Industries in October 1930, had, in turn, purchased the Brunswick Record Corporation (BRC) from Warner Brothers Pictures in December 1931. The combined ARC-BRC operation would eventually boast a stellar artist roster, including Roy Acuff, Gene Autry, Bill and Cliff Carlisle, the Chuck Wagon Gang, Al Dexter, Red Foley, the Light Crust Doughboys, and Bob Wills, among others.

But, in addition to these luminaries, a group called the Three Floridians recorded four songs for the label in May 1934: *Duval County Blues, My Family Circle, The Death of Young Stribling,* and *The Jacksonville Stomp,* none of which were ever released. Information on the session sheet is sketchy, and nowhere are members of the mysterious trio listed by name.

Are the Three Floridians actually the Rouse Brothers? It would appear so, although, in truth, none of the brothers were yet Floridians; their permanent home, such as it was, remained in North Carolina. They did, however, spend winters in Florida, and worked frequently in Jacksonville, which is located in Duval County. Further, *My Family Circle* is the same title that the brothers would use five years later when recording the gospel standard *Will the Circle Be Unbroken* for RCA Victor's Bluebird label. *The Death of Young Stribling* has no apparent Rouse connection; it is a tribute to a popular heavyweight boxer, William L. "Young" Stribling, who had been killed in a motorcycle accident near Macon, Georgia, the prior year.

Finally, an intriguing notation at the bottom of the session sheet reads: "This group is associated with Luther Higginbotham." Higginbotham, apparently, was a performer who had cut *Duval County Blues* for ARC the previous year in Chicago. His version of the tune was likewise never released and, as far as can be determined, he made no other recordings. Therefore, the nature of Higginbotham's connection to the Three Floridians, or to the Rouse Brothers, remains unknown, and the masters in question have been lost or destroyed. Luther Higginbotham, it seems, is a mystery for another day.

ARC definitely recorded the Rouses—this time under the name Earl Rouse and Brothers—in June 1936. According to company files, Ervin, Gordon, and Earl cut eight songs at ARC's New York studios. However, only two sides were ultimately released: *I'm So Tired,* backed by *Pedal Your Blues Away,* both composed by respected music publisher Bob Miller, a Tin Pan Alley stalwart who, for the remainder of his life, would be a friend and advisor to the siblings. (Miller's catalogue—including *Orange Blossom Special*—was eventually acquired by a competitor, Leeds Music Corporation, which ultimately became MCA Music Publishing Inc., now a division of Universal Music Publishing Group.)

The Memphis-born Miller had been a pianist, a band leader, and a radio personality before moving to New York in 1928, where he joined Irving Berlin Music as an arranger. That same year, he wrote and recorded the immortal Depression-era farmers' lament, *Eleven Cent Cotton and Forty Cent Meat*. The song, which stretches over twelve verses, was covered by Vernon Dalhart, among others, and became a hillbilly classic.

Miller, who received formal training at the Southern Conservatory of Music in Memphis and the Chicago Conservatory of Music, was no hillbilly. But he had a knack for writing and recording topical songs with populist themes that spoke directly to rural audiences. *The Farmer's Letter to the President, Farm Relief Blues, Bank Failures,* and *The Rich Man and The Poor Man* were indictments of a system seemingly gone awry. Miller also cut anti-Prohibition songs, such as *The Dry Votin', Wet Drinkin', Better-Than-Thou Hypocritical Blues*, and songs based on current events, notorious crimes, and high-profile gangsters.

After leaving the Irving Berlin Company, Miller worked as an A&R man for the Columbia and Okeh labels, managing the hillbilly and race (blues) divisions, before opening his New York-based publishing company, Bob Miller Inc., in 1933. He stopped recording in 1935, but continued writing, eventually penning some seven thousand songs under his own name and under a variety of pseudonyms.

Miller's best-known composition: the 1942 Elton Britt paean to patriotism called *There's A Star Spangled Banner Waving Somewhere*, which became one of the biggest-selling country records ever to that time. This weeper about a crippled boy who longs to assist in the war effort sold more than two-and-a-half million records and, at President Roosevelt's insistence, was sung by Britt at the White House.

"Bob Miller is a figure from country music's early history who fascinates me for several reasons, chief of which is his unmerited obscurity," writes former Country Music Foundation Researcher Ronnie Pugh in the *Journal of Country Music*. "Yet he strikes me as Tin Pan Alley's closest parallel to Nashville's Fred Rose. Both were pianists, both made vocal records (pop and country), and both wrote numbers of great songs. Each produced records for other artists, managed careers much better known than their own, and launched lucrative publishing firms." Rose is in the Country Music Hall of Fame and Miller is not, Pugh contends, mainly because Rose had the good fortune of signing and producing Hank Williams and landing Roy Acuff as his business partner.

How, then, did the unheralded Rouse Brothers become acquainted with such an industry luminary? Ervin told Randy Wayne White a story indicating that Miller, or a Miller associate, first heard the trio purely by chance, as the brothers were busking in Kissimmee. In *The Man Who Invented Florida*, Ervin claims that he and Earl—Gordon, for whatever reason, is not mentioned—were playing outside a barber shop, passing the hat, when an unnamed "Atlanta musical agent" overheard the commotion, and immediately arranged for the brothers to travel to New York for a recording session.

However, this account appears fanciful. Most likely, the brothers sought Miller out and auditioned for him. In interviews years later, Ervin refers to trudging along the streets of New York, trying in vain to gain audiences with publishers and bookers. Perhaps Miller, who knew good hillbilly music when he heard it, was willing to listen.

Indeed, the prolific publisher "always championed the dignity, purity, and separate identity of rural music," according to Pugh. In a 1946 interview, Miller himself described what he listened for when evaluating a song: "Nowadays, people like their emotions straight. They want to either cry or laugh. That's the essence of real hillbilly. It's elemental, simple, and without subtlety."

Elemental, simple, and without subtlety are certainly adjectives that describe both the Rouse Brothers and their music. Consequently, it is perhaps not surprising that Miller took an interest. Still, the only memorable song recorded by the Rouses during this first collaboration, *Some Old Day*, was not released. It became popular decades later, but by then it had inexplicably slipped from their grasp. The released sides, *Pedal Your Blues Away* and *I'm So Tired*, can best be described as bizarre and mediocre, respectively.

Pedal Your Blues Away, for example, was not a hillbilly song; it was a silly pop trifle peppered with hipster slang: "You'll find lots of happiness as you spin along/Things are hunky-dory as you fly/In the middle of your heart you'll find a new song/With your palsy-walsy riding by your side." Earl, whose raspy but powerful tenor is sometimes compelling on hillbilly material, sounds comical when carefully enunciating these vapid lyrics. (An amusing relic of its era, *Pedal Your Blues Away* was revived in the 1970s by "Keep On Truckin'" cartoonist and erstwhile recording artist Robert Crumb and his Cheap Suit Serenaders.)

Earl also solos on *I'm So Tired*, struggling unsuccessfully to tame his North Carolina accent while lamenting: "I went out to milk/But I didn't know how/I milked the goat/Instead of the cow/I'm so tired/So awfully tired/I'm so tired I don't know what to do."

Released on the Melotone label, *Pedal Your Blues Away* and *I'm So Tired* were described by the record company as "Vocal with Old Time Playing." Unfortunately, Ervin's atypically subdued fiddle is overshadowed by Earl's awkward wailing. Not surprisingly, the tunes failed to make an impact. Unreleased cuts from the 1936 session include another Miller composition, *Please Let Me Walk With My Son*, along with *Are You Angry Little Darling, Toll, Dixieland Echoes, Under the Double Eagle,* and *Some Old Day*.

Herein lurks yet another mystery: although it is generally believed that Ervin composed *Some Old Day*, the session sheet credits Jack (Earl's nickname) Rouse with authorship. Yet, the tune remained uncopyrighted until November 14, 1955, when it was registered by Flatt & Scruggs using their wives' names—Louise Certain and Gladys Stacey—as pseudonyms. Shortly thereafter, Flatt & Scruggs recorded the hard-charging, chain-gang lament and made it a bluegrass standard.

"Earl wrote *Some Old Day*," says Gene Christian. "Not Ervin, and not Flatt & Scruggs. That's what I always understood from both Ervin and Earl. As to why he didn't copyright it at the time, I don't know. Hell, he probably didn't know how." Of course, Bob Miller knew how. Therefore, his failure to protect *Some Old Day* is a puzzling—and costly—oversight for such a savvy operator.

How Flatt & Scruggs ultimately obtained the song is also unclear. Most likely, it was brought to them by an industry jack-of-all-trades named Troy Martin, who co-produced the Flatt & Scruggs version of *Some Old Day*. Martin, a contemporary of the Rouses who hailed from Danville, was known to appropriate unprotected works and copyright them on behalf of his clients. Even more telling, *Some Old Day* was published by Golden West Melodies, a company with which Martin was then affiliated.

Still, ownership aside, it would appear that Ervin was not the only Rouse Brother to have composed a popular tune saddled with an authorship controversy. The lyrics to *Some Old Day* read as follows:

> *I've been walkin' out in the rain,*
> *tied to the dirty old ball and chain.*
> *Oh dear mother I'll come home some old day.*
> *Some sweet day they'll turn me loose,*
> *from this dirty old callaboose.*
> *Oh dear mother I'll come home some day.*
>
> *(Chorus)*
> *Some old day,*
> *you'll wait for me and pray.*
> *Oh dear sweet mother I'll come home some old day.*
> *Some sweet day they'll turn me loose,*
> *from this dirty old callaboose.*
> *Oh dear mother I'll come home some old day.*
>
> *Oh dear mother I've hurt you so.*
> *I've been cruel to you I know.*
> *Oh dear mother I'll come home some old day.*
> *Tell my brother, my sister and dad,*
> *they're the best friends that I've had.*
> *Oh dear mother I'll come home some old day.*

In addition to recording, during the mid- to late 1930s the rambling siblings passed through Maces Springs in mountainous southwest Virginia, where they made the acquaintance of Mother Maybelle Carter—a meeting that would prove quite fortuitous thirty years later, when Maybelle's future son-in-law, Johnny Cash, began asking questions about *Orange Blossom Special.*

The original Carter Family, widely acknowledged as the first family of country music, consisted of Alvin Pleasant Delaney (A.P.) Carter, his wife, Sara Dougherty, and Sara's younger cousin, Maybelle Addington, who was married to A.P.'s brother, Ezra. The pioneering trio had made its first recordings in August, 1927, for Ralph Peer and Victor Records and, by 1930, had released such instant classics as *The Storms Are On the Ocean, Keep On the Sunny Side, Wildwood Flower, John Hardy Was a Desperate Little Man, I'm Thinking Tonight of My Blue Eyes, Wabash Cannonball, Anchored in Love*, and *Worried Man Blues*.

Carrie says that the Rouses and the Carters initially met in the late 1930s via a Virginia-based fiddler whose name she cannot recall. However, a likely candidate is Ervin's friend Tommy Magness, who had performed primarily in North Carolina—on radio stations WWNC in Asheville and WBT in Charlotte—before joining Roy Hall and Blue Ridge Entertainers on WDJB in Roanoke.

"They [Ervin, Gordon, and Earl] used to stay with Maybelle and her girls [Helen, Anita, and June] whenever they came through that part of the country," says Carrie. "Maybelle loved to cook, and she enjoyed fussing over them. If the Rouse Brothers liked you, and if you'd have them, then you could count on them staying with you for a while."

THROUGHOUT HIS TRAVELS, ERVIN had continued to correspond with teenaged Elon, and the pair eventually fell prey to the kind of moony, long-distance romance that is inevitably doomed from the outset.

In his letters, which are unfortunately lost, Elon says that Ervin recounted his travels, stated his desire to start a family, and mused about "cutting out this nonsense" and getting an education. "He told me in a letter that he was going to ask me to marry him," recalls Elon. "But he would often write about things that he never did, so I didn't really think he'd follow through."

However, in early 1939, Ervin appeared at the Smith home—uncharacteristically without his brothers—and offered Elon, then a high-school senior, a diamond engagement ring. "I had to tell him no," she says. "I wanted to finish school, and I realized that all the traveling he did would make marriage difficult. Plus, I realized that, although I was very fond of him, I wasn't in love. Well, he was heartbroken, and went to see my mother, who tried to soothe him."

Surely Ervin was, in his way, in love with Elon, and probably found her solid, Norman Rockwellian family life to be intriguing. Nonetheless, the young fiddler had been a nomad since the age of eight and, despite statements to the contrary, he was not prepared to give it up.

James and Lillian Smith must have harbored mixed feelings about the potential union; fond as they were of the Rouse boys, and of Ervin in particular, they also recognized that his irregular lifestyle would surely lead to marital disaster. As an amiable houseguest, Ervin was fine; as a son-in-law, he could not have been what the Smiths had in mind. Therefore, it is safe to speculate that all parties were, to a greater or lesser degree, relieved when it became apparent that Elon was not interested in becoming Mrs. Ervin T. Rouse.

Fortunately, after the initial awkwardness had passed, relations between the Smiths and the Rouses remained warm. And, although Elon and Ervin gradually drifted apart, they would renew their friendship forty years later, when Ervin realized that his days were numbered, through several lengthy telephone conversations.

"We talked about our past together," Elon says. "I felt sorry for him. It seemed as though he had given up on life. He was drinking and not taking care of himself. He asked me to come down and visit him, but I never made it. The next thing I heard, he was gone."

By JANUARY 1938, ERVIN and Gordon had relocated permanently to Miami, where they shared an apartment until Gordon met and married Carrie White, a pretty waitress who had caught his eye at Gene's Barbecue, a popular eatery where the brothers often performed. The newlyweds then moved to a trailer park ("And I do mean trailers—not mobile homes," adds Carrie) at Northwest 2nd Avenue and 79th Street.

Earl, who had been married since 1934 to a woman named Evelyn Umholtz, returned to North Carolina and formed a husband-and-wife singing team billed as "Jack and Jackie," while Lloyd Smith, who would die a hero's death at Iwo Jima, joined Ervin and Gordon as their manager and booking agent. "That only lasted about a year and a half," says Elon. "They [Ervin and Gordon] were used to going where they wanted, when they wanted."

During the years just prior to World War II, the Rouse Brothers, now a duo, seemed to be gaining some momentum. The decision settle in Miami may, at first blush, seem curious for dyed-in-the-wool hillbilly musicians; yet, given the nature of their act and its dual audiences, it is clear that there was a method in their apparent madness.

First, Miami proper was not the cosmopolitan racial and ethnic melting pot that it would later become; indeed, by 1940, fully forty percent of the city's male residents had been born in Georgia. The city also attracted displaced farmers from the Florida Panhandle and other Deep South states, creating a large, built-in audience for down-home music in scores of working-class taverns. And many of these rural refugees had money to spend; Florida's economic recovery, bolstered by New Deal initiatives and the nation's military buildup, was well under way. "The people of Florida now are eating high on the hog, "boasted Governor Fred P. Cone, a Lake City banker known as "Old Suwannee."

Second, Miami Beach already boasted dozens of luxurious, oceanfront resort hotels that attracted an affluent, out-of-state clientele by offering opulent amenities and extravagant floorshows. "It is impossible to challenge the claim of Miami Beach that it is the greatest leisure destination in the nation," crowed a pre-war tourism publication. "It is everything that the ordinary American wants when in search of winter relaxation." Northeasterners arrived on luxury trains such as the Orange Blossom Special, while Midwesterners drove along some four thousand miles of connecting roads known as the Dixie Highway. One way or another, more than two million tourists made their way to the Sunshine State in 1940.

Ervin and Gordon, who had always considered themselves to be essentially comedic nightclub entertainers and not mainstream musicians, knew from their vaudeville experience that good rube acts were always amusing to affluent urbanites. Therefore, the duo found regular employment at Miami's Olympia Theater, Coral Gables' Biltmore Hotel and, in the summer of 1938, at Miami Beach's Royal Palm Club, then one of the largest supper clubs in the Southeast, where they appeared with orchestra leaders Paul Whiteman and Glenn Miller. ("Paul Whiteman said that if Ervin could have read music, he'd have hired him," says Louallie.)

In a letter of reference, club manager M.L. Daye noted that "they [the Rouse Brothers] were originally engaged for two weeks, but they became so popular that we held them over almost indefinitely." Bookings at other posh resort hotels followed—the Sea Isle, the Versailles, the Ritz Plaza, the Cadillac, and the Lord Tarleton—as did dates at nightclubs throughout Florida, and along the eastern seaboard.

For eight weeks, Ervin and Gordon also hosted their own radio program, inevitably named *Barn Dance*, which was broadcast live on Saturday nights over WKAT in Miami Beach. "They drew the largest studio audience ever seen in this district," wrote station owner Frank Katzentine in another letter of reference, "and they had a large listening audience. They are as good a hill-billy (sic) outfit as I have ever heard."

And, as always, the boys spent every available evening busking, sometimes accumulating more in tips than they earned as a supporting act at the Royal Palm Club. "They played anywhere and everywhere," says Carrie. "It didn't matter, as long as there were people to listen."

Claude Casey joined the brothers in Florida for several months in late 1939 or early 1940. In addition to performing with Jimmy Rouse as a member of The Pine State Playboys, Casey had also been a rambling, Rouse-style busker and a featured performer in various hillbilly bands, including a stint with Fat Sanders and His Country Cousins. "[With Fat Sanders] we dressed with little tight-skin britches, you know, and little derby hats," Casey recalled. "I mean, we looked like we were from the hills, to some people. Fat was a showman. I think he'd been in vaudeville. His wife was named Louella. The Hillbilly Striptease Dancer is what they called her. She had on about six or seven pairs of red underwear, you know, so she wasn't really stripping, but it brought a lot of people to the shows."

When Sanders injured his eye and the show disbanded, Casey hitchhiked to Washington, D.C., where he pawned his guitar, and then back to Danville, where he moved in with his brother and made plans to apply for a job in the cotton mill where he had worked as a teenager. But one Sunday afternoon, Ervin and Gordon unexpectedly dropped by with a proposal. "They said, 'Let's go to Miami,'" Casey recalls. "I said, 'No, I'm going up to the mill to get me a job there.' They said, 'Aw, don't do that. Come on, let's go to Miami. Boy, things are good in Miami.'"

It did not take much persuading for Casey to abandon the idea of swapping music for mill work; he climbed in the brothers' Chevrolet and the trio headed south. The trip, Casey says, was vintage Ervin and Gordon: "About thirty or forty miles down the road, [Ervin] says, 'You got any money?' I said I didn't. He said, 'You see that gas tank? That's all we got left. Not too much!' I said, 'Well how in the world are we getting to Miami?' He said, 'Don't worry; we're getting to Miami.' Then I said, 'What are you going to do, rob a bank?'"

Gordon pulled the car into a service station and had the attendant fill up the tank as Casey nervously wondered what kind of larceny the brothers had planned. After the gas was pumped, Ervin asked the attendant if he'd like to hear some music. "The guy said, 'No, I don't care for music,'" Casey recalled. "Ervin said, 'Let us play a little music. Got a guy back there who can really sing and yodel.' The guy said, 'I don't care.' So Ervin just reached over in the car and got the fiddle and started playing, and the rest of those guys sitting there said, 'Golly!'"

As a crowd began to gather, Ervin, Gordon, and Casey played several tunes and passed the hat. They did not collect enough to pay for the tank of gas, but the attendant figured that the free concert more than made up for the shortfall.

This risky scheme—filling up first and then offering to perform after pleading poverty—was audacious, even to a veteran busker like Casey. But it worked. "The guy said, 'Forget about that, you can have the gasoline,'" Casey recalled. "So, that's the way we got down to Miami."

Fringe musicians often lived a precarious existence, but Casey and the Rouses were kindred spirits in that regard. Discussing his career forty years later, Casey undoubtedly spoke for Ervin, Gordon and countless others like them who had chosen a traveling minstrel's life:

"If anybody has ever worked with picks and shovels…for fifty cents a day and loved music, it gets in your blood. It's just hard to explain, but I've gone hungry, and I know there are a lot of other fellows…who have gone hungry that loved music. Like one fellow told me, 'I would rather starve to death doing something I love than go the other way. You follow?'"

FLORIDA FOLKLORIST AND CIVIL-RIGHTS ACTIVIST Stetson Kennedy wrote in his classic 1942 book *Palmetto Country* (re-issued by University Presses of Florida) that "the northernmost part of Florida is farther south than the southernmost part of

California [and] with the exception of a few spots in Florida, the region is also psychologically the Deepest South."

Robert Russell Dees, who would become known worldwide as Chubby Wise, was born on October 2, 1915, in this singular land of rolling sand hills, scrub oaks, pines, Spanish moss, and cabbage palms. Music reference books list his birthplace as the north-central Florida town of Lake City, and further report that his mother died in childbirth, occasioning his adoption by a paternal aunt and her husband, whose surname was Wise.

In fact, Chubby was born in St. Augustine, Florida, to a woman of Spanish descent named Maggie Rake Lewis, a distant relative and mistress of a railroad electrician named John Henry Dees. Although information regarding Maggie is scarce, St. Johns County marriage records indicate that she was fifteen years old when she wed a man named W.J. Lewis in 1905.

Whether or not she was still married when she became pregnant with Chubby is unclear; neither Maggie nor her husband reappear in St. Augustine city directories until 1918, when "Maggie Lewis" is listed as a widow living with three men surnamed Rake, presumably her brothers, on Cuna Street.

Yet, marriage was apparently out of the question under any circumstance, and neither partner in this fateful affair wished to rear an illegitimate son. Therefore, John Henry pleaded with his sister, Barbara, and her husband, Alfred Robert "Bob" Wise, to act as surrogate parents.

The Wises were a farm family, and grew flue-cured burley tobacco—the kind used in the manufacture of cigarettes—and Sea Island cotton. Both were important crops in Columbia County, although tobacco rose to prominence when a boll weevil infestation just prior to World War I devastated the region's cotton industry. Like the Rouses, they were poor but self-sufficient.

Still, with five daughters, ranging in age from ten to seventeen, Bob Wise was not anxious to assume responsibility for yet another mouth to feed. Barbara, however, persuaded her skeptical husband that they had no choice but to accept the infant into their home, and to raise him as their own. So, at two weeks of age, Chubby was loaded aboard a horse-drawn buggy and transported by his biological mother to the Wise farm, located five miles south of Lake City.

Initially, at least, Chubby was ignored by his ill-tempered uncle and doted upon by his aunt and his cousins, who enjoyed the novelty of having a baby boy in the household. However, as the years passed, Bob grew increasingly resentful of the young interloper's annoying presence. "When I was little, he wasn't quite so rough on me," said Chubby in 1994. "I don't know why he had a change of heart, but when I got bigger, it got to where he couldn't hardly tolerate me."

In fact, according to Rossi Wise and others, Chubby was subjected to intensifying levels of brutality, and on several occasions might have been seriously injured— or worse—had Barbara not intervened. "Chubby didn't dwell much on his childhood," says Rossi. "I figured if he wanted me to know about it, he'd tell me. But he did talk about a time when he was plowing, and I guess he was doing it wrong. That old man [Bob Wise] said that he was going to kill him, and throw his body into the spring. Barbara was out there, and she told Bob that if he touched that boy, he was the one that was going to get killed."

Chubby also claimed that his uncle once threatened to flail him with a bullwhip, and backed off only after Barbara pointed a shotgun squarely at her husband's forehead and vowed, "If you hit him with that whip, you're dead."

Confirming the generally derogatory impression of Bob is Carl Dees, one of three sons sired by John Henry after he married a woman named Stella Mae Downing and moved, without Chubby, from Lake City to Miami. "He was a brutal human being," says Carl, now retired from the U.S. Navy and living in Dothan, Alabama. "He just didn't want Russell there."

Bob's cruelty was heightened by his excessive drinking, according to Audrey Nelson, a childhood friend of Chubby's. "My uncle lived next door to us, and he and Bob Wise would go out and get drunk together," she says. "My mama would hear them coming, and she'd hand me a loaf of bread and a jug of milk and send me out back to stay until she thought it was safe to come in. I spent many a night out in the hog pen waiting for her to come and get me."

But Bob was hardly Lake City's only volatile drunkard; bootleg liquor was a scourge in Columbia and Baker counties, and had been for decades. Initially, most moonshiners—so named because they plied their trade by moonlight—were farmers, who supplemented their meager incomes by surreptitiously brewing homemade whiskey using river water and cane syrup. These illicit entrepreneurs sold their wares locally, at turpentine camps and at hangouts such as Big Sally's, a notorious house of ill repute.

Ultimately, however, the manufacture and distribution of moonshine became big business in north-central Florida, with professional bootleggers extending their reach throughout Florida and the Southeast. Baker County, with just 5,300 residents spread across 375,000 acres of swamps and forests, was dubbed by "The Shine Capitol of the State" by the *Times-Union*, thanks in large part to a succession of compliant local sheriffs who allowed the industry to flourish unchallenged.

Yet, despite its seamy side, Lake City was, in many ways, an idyllic place for a youngster to grow up. Dubbed "the Gateway to Florida," this picturesque, flourishing community of about three thousand souls was described in a 1925 edition of *The Saturday Evening Post* as "surrounded by pecan groves, towering live oaks, and rolling hill slopes whose contours suggest Southern Maine or Vermont rather than tropical Florida."

Roughly half the out-of-state tourists driving to southern resort destinations—more than seventeen hundred vehicles daily at the height of the season—passed through town, and civic leaders worked hard to leave a favorable impression.

The community's social life centered around church events, political rallies, square dances, and high-school sports, while the downtown Opera House hosted minstrel shows and other traveling musical and theatrical troupes. During the summer, band concerts were held in the town square, and every youngster eagerly anticipated the annual arrival of the circus. "Of course, the circus was the greatest event of the year," wrote Gerald Witt, a former mayor. "The parade of the elephants, camels, caged beasts, clowns, and show people to the music of the calliope will never be forgotten." Outdoor recreation was also popular, with families flocking to White Springs, Suwanee Shoals, Ichetucknee Springs, and Ocean Pond to picnic, swim, and bask in the greater Suwannee River Valley's considerable natural beauty.

At least for the benefit of interviewers, Chubby depicted his gothic childhood as happy and tranquil. During the week, he walked the obligatory mile or more to a one-room elementary school, Shady Grove, where a formidable spinster, Miss Fannie Taylor, used a well-worn paddle to enforce decorum. "Uncle Chubby would sometimes just lie on the ground looking up at the sky," says Pamela Wendell, a great-granddaughter of Bob and Barbara. "When his teacher would ask him what he was doing, he'd just say he was dreaming." The youngster also enjoyed fishing, exploring, and teaching himself to play the guitar, an activity at which he displayed substantial natural aptitude.

Chores were many and varied, depending upon the season, but Chubby particularly favored cane-grinding time, when he could gnaw on the sweet, reedy stalks as he worked. "Instead of using a tractor to pull that mill, we had an old mule hooked to the sweep," Chubby recalled in 1996. "It would go around and around, and I'd stand there and feed that sugar cane between those rollers. That was my job—that, and fightin' them yellow jackets."

Then, on weekends, he clattered into Lake City driving a mule-drawn wagon laden with watermelons, which he sold for six cents each. "Sometimes, when I'd get back home, my uncle [apparently meaning Bob] would say, 'Well, you done a good job, boy,' and he'd give me a nickel," Chubby continued. "Now, that was a big deal. You could get an ice cream cone for a nickel."

He even conjured up a handful of sanguine holiday memories, highlighted by the year he received a cap gun and a red wagon instead of the anticipated assortment of oranges, apples, peppermint sticks, and Brazil nuts. "That was the biggest Christmas I ever had," he said. "Man, I wore that wagon plumb out."

As a youngster, Chubby began playing guitar and banjo at community "frolics," meaning parties or dances, often held in private homes. Sometimes he backed Bob Wise, who played the fiddle. "I've loved music as long as I can remember," Chubby said in 1987. "When I was a little boy—I'll say six or seven years old—I learned to play three chords on an old five-string banjo—dropthumb style, we called it. I also fooled around with an old flattop guitar. I never will forget, the first money I made was playing at one of those dances. Back then they'd pass the hat and say, 'These boys got to have money for their strings.' Me and my dad [again, apparently meaning Bob] made thirty-seven cents apiece. And I'll tell you, I was the richest boy in Columbia County with that thirty-seven cents."

Chubby used the terms "uncle" and "dad" interchangeably, creating some confusion for biographers. Until he was about twelve years old, he assumed that Bob and Barbara were his natural parents, and that John Henry Dees was an uncle. Finally, however, the whispers and the snickers became so worrisome that he went to Barbara and demanded a full accounting.

"I'm told that Uncle Chubby was devastated when he found out," says Pamela. "Other kids in the community had been teasing him about [being illegitimate]. Then, when the truth finally came out, Barbara made it clear to Uncle Chubby that she loved him like one of her own, and that he was even more special because he had been chosen. Well, he accepted that, and he never held any hard feelings toward Barbara. She was the only mother he ever knew, and he loved her regardless."

Unfortunately, however, Barbara's love would not be enough to forestall the tragedy and hardship to come. In 1926, after yet another confrontation with Bob, Chubby was sent—probably for his own safety—to spend several days with another aunt, Essie Dees Prescott, and her husband, Buddy. (John Henry had moved south the previous year.)

Chubby, who was walking back to the Prescott home after buying ice cream at the downtown drug store, passed a construction site where steel girders were stacked near the sidewalk. He climbed atop the obstruction, and was balancing himself when the load collapsed, pinning his leg between two beams and nearly severing his foot just above the ankle. "It was hanging on by the tendon," Chubby said. "You could have cut it off with a pair of scissors."

The injury was severe, and at first doctors at Lake Shore Hospital were certain that amputation was inevitable. Fortunately, a difficult bone graft was successfully performed, saving the leg but mandating a long and arduous recuperation.

Chubby's problems, however, were far from over. Several days following surgery, Barbara visited the youngster's hospital room to announce that she was leaving Bob, and was taking up residence with her daughter and son-in-law, Tennie and Maynard Sweet. Unfortunately for Chubby, she added, there would be no room for him at Tennie's home, nor would he be able to return to the farm, which had been sold.

In essence, this emotionally and physically wounded twelve-year-old, who would be unable to walk without the aid of crutches for three years, was informed that he would now be expected to fend for himself.

Given the circumstances, it is tempting to judge Barbara harshly for seeming to abandon her extraordinarily luckless nephew in his hour of need; however, it is likely that she simply could not impose an injured child upon her daughter, who was already caring for three youngsters of her own.

So, following his release, Chubby spent a brief period of time at Daddy Flagg's Home for Boys in Jacksonville before returning to Lake City and a dreary, hand-to-mouth existence as a ward of the community. "Chubby didn't have a permanent home after that," says Rossi. "He sold oranges and pencils on the street; he stayed wherever he could and with whoever would have him." Agreed Carl: "Russell was kicked around so much it's a wonder he didn't grow up to be a criminal. He didn't know where his next meal was coming from."

Often, Chubby called upon various cousins—whom he had previously regarded as sisters—generally waiting until nightfall before hobbling to their doorsteps and asking for accommodations. "Oh, no, I never got turned away," he said. "They could see that I was a young'un who needed help. But when I felt the atmosphere start to get cold, then I knew it was time to move on."

Without question, Chubby's plight reflects poorly on the adults in his life. Yet, he consistently refused to speak harshly of those who had abandoned him, abused him, and ignored him. "Chubby would not utter a bad word about nobody," Rossi recalls. "In fact, years later, when Bob Wise was dying, Chubby was at his bedside, holding that old man's hand. He was such a forgiving person, and he didn't hold grudges."

At least one positive development resulted from the accident and its shameful aftermath: During the months he was bedridden and confined to a wheelchair, Chubby somehow obtained a fiddle and taught himself the basics.

Then, while being shunted among an assortment of relatives and family friends, he attended a square dance at the Lake City home of Bryan Purcell, a one-time Florida State Fiddling Champion, and was instantly captivated by what he heard and saw. Chubby especially enjoyed a novelty tune called *The Cackling Hen*, during which Purcell's fiddle emanated barnyard clucking sounds. "I still remember sitting in the corner, listening," Chubby said. "I loved that fiddle so well that I said to myself, 'That's what I'm going to do—learn to play like that man.'"

So, a determined Chubby resolved to master the devil's box, practicing constantly and accompanying faraway string bands featured on WSM's *Grand Ole Opry* broadcast. "By the time I was fourteen or fifteen, I had gotten pretty good," Chubby said. "The Lord was good to me. I don't mean to brag, but I really am grateful. I wouldn't know a note from a mule's foot, but I could hear a fiddle tune and it wasn't long before I was playin' it."

In fact, fifteen-year-old Chubby was confident enough in his abilities that he entered—and won—his first fiddling contest, which was held north of Lake City at the Deep Creek School. He did not recall what he had played—possibly *The Cackling Hen*—but he did recall the prize money: three dollars. Emboldened, Chubby was soon in demand for square dances and parties throughout Columbia County, and scheduled these engagements around a mind-numbing job "pushing hot dogs" in an all-night diner.

In 1931, sixteen-year-old Chubby finally did leave Lake City behind—physically if not emotionally—when he moved briefly to the St. Augustine home of yet another aunt, Jane Dees Cappallia, and her husband, Gonzales, an ill-tempered St. Augustine street-sweeper who was apparently no more anxious to welcome a bastard nephew into the fold than Bob Wise had been.

The Cappallias, their three daughters, and a company of assorted relatives—including, ironically, some members of the Rake clan—lived in a large, three-story home at 36 Harding Street. "There was always trouble there," Carl says. "I can't explain why Russell went." Could he have been seeking his biological mother? Perhaps, but city directories in the early 1930s no longer list Maggie Lewis, and there is no indication that the two ever met or spoke. Perhaps St. Augustine was appealing simply because it was not Lake City. Nonetheless, Chubby's experience in this atmospheric town of ruined fortresses, creaky Victorian homes, and narrow, cobblestone streets was not a happy one.

The breaking point apparently came after the Cappallia clan decided to visit John Henry in Miami, and began the long southward trek with perhaps a half-dozen family members packed into a Model T Ford. Chubby was driving when the vehicle ran off the road and overturned, seriously injuring several passengers and further convincing Gonzales that his unwanted nephew ought to seek permanent shelter elsewhere.

Shortly thereafter—and probably at Gonzales Cappallia's insistence—Chubby moved to Miami and was finally reunited with his biological father, who by then had four sons; Leo, Harold, Lloyd, and Carl. John Henry had been an electrician at a Florida Power and Light Company steam generating plant in Miami Beach, but like many others had lost his job as the Great Depression tightened its grip. The ever-resourceful Chubby, however, managed to find employment as a bicycle delivery person with Western Union and as a dishwasher at a local restaurant, while John Henry was eventually hired by the federal government's Works Progress Administration (WPA) for a dollar and a quarter per day.

"We weren't just poor, we were plain pitiful," says Carl, who was eight years old when his stepbrother moved in. "Russell already drank, smoked, and chewed tobacco, and I remember pulling him along Northwest Second Avenue in a wagon, looking for cigarette butts people had flipped out of their cars. He'd pick them up and put them in a sack, and we'd go home and take out the tobacco so he could use it to put together a smoke. I'll, tell you, that's living high on the hog, ain't it?"

Despite hard times, the year he spent at 153 Northwest 68th Street was probably as close as Chubby ever came to experiencing a relatively normal home life. He attended the seventh grade at Miami Edison High School, worked at his part-time jobs, and earned extra money by offering twenty-five-cent guitar lessons to the children of his schoolteachers.

"We all got along good, and my family treated Russell very well and made him feel like he had a home," recalls Carl. "Now, my mother, she had to get on him sometimes. Russell was lazy, partly because he was so big, and he didn't want to do anything to help around the house. Plus, he could eat a half-dozen eggs and a pot of grits for breakfast."

It was during his Miami interlude that the teenaged fiddler first met the Rouses, who were wintering in Florida. Carl recalls that Ervin, Gordon, and Earl visited the Dees home on several occasions, and that the brothers and Chubby would frequently go busking together before returning to enjoy late-night, kitchen-table jam sessions. "Ervin was a damn genius; the best who ever lived," Carl recalls. "Chubby could play the fiddle, but he couldn't touch Ervin. Nobody could. Plus, Ervin wasn't just a great fiddler; he played mandolin, banjo, guitar—anything that had strings on it."

Yet, if the Rouse Brothers believed that they had wheedled complimentary accommodations a'la the Smith family, then Jane Dees quickly dashed their hopes. "My mama would finally run their ass off," says Carl. "She didn't put up with much." Still, Ervin and Chubby—who were roughly the same age and shared much in common—developed a close friendship, and Chubby was anxious to learn all he could from this well-traveled young man who was actually earning a living with his music.

Then, in 1932, Chubby abruptly left Miami and returned to Columbia County. "I think he just got tired of going to school," says Carl. "Plus, he was a rambler by nature. He couldn't stay in one place for long, even if he was in a good situation."

Upon his arrival, Cubby apparently moved back in with his Uncle Buddy and Aunt Essie and resumed playing guitar, banjo, and fiddle at local gatherings. It was at a square dance that he first set eyes on Geneva Kirby, a pretty teenager who was the daughter of prominent farmer Edgar Kirby and his wife, Maude. "Russell was playing the guitar with a little group," recalls Geneva, who still lives near Lake City. "I was dancing, and he saw me. Well, when they took a break, he asked me to show him where the water bucket was, and I did. Then he asked if he could take me home, and I said, 'No, my brothers are here, and they can take me.'"

Undaunted, Chubby quickly realized that way to Geneva was through her family. Several of her five brothers frequented a Lake City pool hall, so Chubby made it a point to drop by and befriend them—not a difficult task for such an eager-to-please extravert. After shooting a few games, he found himself with an invitation to visit the Kirby home for dinner. With both a literal and a figurative foot in the door, Chubby began his courtship of Geneva in typical fashion, escorting her to church functions, taking her on picnics to Ichetucknee Springs, and sitting with her on the front porch swing as evening drew near.

Chubby and Geneva married in December 1933, and Geneva left the comfort of her childhood home to set up housekeeping in a one-room, three-dollar-per-week apartment. Sadly, it would not be a happy union. "Geneva was a nice, quiet country girl," says Audrey Nelson. "She wanted Chubby to settle down and be a farmer, and her parents even offered them a tract of land to get started." But Chubby, who had come to harbor a loathing for manual labor, declined, declaring to his dubious in-laws that "a mule's ass ain't gonna be my compass."

However, the job that Chubby ultimately secured, clearing tree-stumps for the WPA in preparation for construction of a small airport, was surely no less odious. "I was standin' out there holdin' a shovel, and I said, 'This just ain't gonna get it for me,'" he recalled. "I wasn't fit to kill doing that kind of work. I said to Geneva, 'Honey, this dog ain't gonna hunt. We've got to go to Jacksonville, where I can play music, and where there are people to hear me.' Man, I loved that music. I couldn't do without it."

But Geneva, who was by then pregnant, wisely opted to move back home with her parents while Chubby scouted new territory.

THE YOUNG FIDDLER WAS certainly not alone in looking toward Jacksonville, a deep-water port straddling the northern St. Johns River, for a new start. Pockets of the city, such as the Springfield neighborhood north of downtown, were populated in significant numbers by country people who had left their depleted farms in rural north Florida, Georgia, and Alabama for jobs in the city's factories.

Indeed, this gritty, blue-collar bastion was condescendingly regarded by many Floridians as being more akin to Georgia—the border of which lay just a half-hour's drive from the heart of downtown—than to the state's more glitzy resort destinations. That image was reinforced by a Federal Writers Project (FWP) guidebook, published in 1939, which described what was then the state's largest city (population 129,459), as "a working son in a family of playboys."

"I knew absolutely, without knowing how I knew it, that something called the Springfield Section of Jacksonville was where all of us from Bacon County [Georgia] went, when we had to go, when our people and our place could no longer sustain us," wrote Harry Crews. "I had spent a lifetime hearing about the city. Jacksonville came up in conversations like the weather. Farmers' laconic voices always spoke of Jacksonville in the same helpless and fatalistic way. It was a fact of their lives. They had to do it. Everybody had to do it. Sooner or later, everybody ended up in the Springfield Section, and once they were there, they loved it because it was hope, and hated it because it was not home."

By late 1933, the Wise family—which now included an infant daughter, Marvelene—occupied a small apartment at 324 West Union Street, located in a seedy Jacksonville neighborhood consisting of pawn shops, bars, upstairs hotels, and boarding houses at Springfield's northeastern edge. The apartment's stove was coin operated, and Geneva recalls having to serve half-cooked biscuits when she ran out of quarters.

Chubby drove a jitney cab by day—the fare was ten cents to any destination within the city limits—and entertained in beer joints by night.

Eventually, he assembled a rag-tag combo that included, in addition to his fiddle, a banjo, a guitar, and a washboard for rhythm. "Our salary was free lunch the next day," Chubby said. "We'd play in a bar until it closed, and we had a kitty for people who wanted a special request to throw a nickel or dime in."

Because many Jacksonvillians played as hard as they worked, there were plenty of venues at which enterprising musicians could ply their trade. A 1938 Jacksonville city directory lists no fewer than one hundred businesses under the heading "Liquors Retail," including everything from relatively respectable meeting places at the upscale George Washington, Roosevelt, Seminole, and Mayflower hotels to neighborhood hangouts with names such as Barney's Place, the Blue Horse Shoe Bar, the Paradise Tavern, and the Stag Bar.

Saloons offered bone-tired laborers from the shipyards and the paper mills a chance to unwind with a cold brew, to wax nostalgic with some down-home picking and, on occasion, to unleash their frustrations on offending outlanders. "These [bars] are tough joints," a U.S. Army private told Stetson Kennedy. "They'll murder you, caress you, and bless you. I was in one, and just because I'm a Yankee, a cracker pulled a knife on me. He reached around my ribs and I was in the hospital three weeks."

One evening Geneva, who had never before been inside a bar, decided to walk a block or two and make an unannounced visit where Chubby was performing. The band was on a break, and her garrulous husband was sitting alongside a small stage with a woman giggling and squirming in his lap. "Grandma just walked up behind Granddaddy and tapped him on the shoulder," says Rebecca Mangrum, one of Marvelene's three offspring. "When he looked around and saw her, he was so star-tled that jumped up and dumped the woman on the floor. Grandma never said a word. She just walked out and started home. Granddaddy was right behind her, telling her that it wasn't what it looked like, and that he was just being nice to the customers. Naturally, Grandma didn't buy that—but it was the last time she went into a bar."

Drinking, of course, was not the only vice thriving in the River City. Main Street, which marked downtown's eastern boundary and terminated amid riverfront warves and warehouses, was described in the FWP guide as "a boisterous street, its side-walks thronged well into the night." The guide did not mention, however, that pros-titution was rampant, although generally ignored by bribable city officials. When law enforcement did feel compelled to take some sort of action against houses of ill repute, it typically involved little more than cursory health inspections, unenforced quarantines, and temporary closings.

For example, in the February 15, 1938 edition of *The Times-Union*, it was reported that Jacksonville Sheriff Rex Sweat and representatives of the state Board of Health, "in a drive to protect citizens who patronize such places," had examined an assortment of red-light houses, and had closed several because of unsanitary conditions. Nonetheless, as one madam confidently told Kennedy, "We were told to close up before, and it didn't mean a thing."

Cab drivers—Chubby among them—were exposed to the city's burgeoning sex industry on a daily basis. Some savvy cabbies, in fact, received fees in exchange for delivering customers to preferred houses or hotels. In 1940, a Jacksonville attorney named Harry Silver was disbarred after it was revealed that he had paid the fines of jailed prostitutes who were willing to "work off" the debt. One woman, who testified that she had been recruited by Silver, claimed that "dates were priced at three dollars; we got a dollar, Silver got a dollar, and the cab drivers got a dollar."

Whether or not Chubby participated in Silver's enterprise is unknown, but, with a family to support, it is unlikely that he would have declined an opportunity to pocket easy money. "Russell told me about some things that happened while he was driving a cab that you wouldn't believe," says Carl. "He said he really got a rearview mirror full."

Such an environment was, perhaps, not entirely healthy for a person with Chubby's predilections. "By his own admission, Chubby was a hellraiser," recalls Colonel Tom Riggs (the title is of the honorary Kentucky variety), president of Orlando-based Pinecastle Records, for which Chubby would make his final recordings. "He settled down later, but his drinking probably started at some of those places he played [early in his career]." That Chubby would abuse alcohol is not surprising, considering his painful personal history. But clearly, nightly proximity to hard liquor exacerbated the problem, as it did for countless other entertainers who began their careers in honky-tonks. "Playing those places was when Chubby started drinking," says Geneva, apparently unaware that her husband had been a drinker since high school. "I hated it. Playing the fiddle is what he wanted to do. I knew that. But I also knew that I didn't want him drinking."

Geneva hastens to add that Chubby was not an abusive drunk, as his uncle had been. In fact, she says, he was usually mellow and jovial when he came stumbling home in the wee hours. Still, she feared for her family and longed for a stable home life.

Ervin and Gordon had also been known to take a drink, although the brothers at that time enforced strict rules against imbibing on the job, both for themselves and for the musicians whom they occasionally employed. For Ervin, however, alcoholism—along with something even more sinister—would eventually accelerate his shocking physical and emotional decline.

IV

Same Train, Different Track:
Variations on a Theme

You know, that's going to be a famous train like the Old '97; that is, if somebody does something about it.
Lloyd Smith, manager,
to Ervin and Gordon Rouse

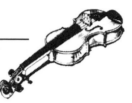

There are basically two stories purporting to explain how—and where— *Orange Blossom Special* was composed. Both hold that the song was written in a burst of creative energy and inspiration after Seaboard Air Line's diesel exhibition tour visited one of two cities: Jacksonville (Chubby's version) or Miami (Ervin's version). Ervin's story, for the most part, is true; Chubby's story, for the most part, is not.

After he gained a measure of fame, Chubby discussed the song more frequently— and commanded a wider audience—than did the reclusive, little-known Ervin, who was collecting royalty checks regardless, and was apparently uninterested in having a debate over authorship claims. Therefore, it is Chubby's account that has been cited in several authoritative source books as the quasi-official, final word on the matter.

Yet, the writing of the *Special*—the melody, if not the lyrics—appears to have been an evolutionary process, which began in the early 1930s with a now-lost Rouse tune called *South Florida Blues*, and ended on October 20, 1938—three days *before* the exhibition tour got under way—when Gordon, traveling with Carrie and Ervin on a busking excursion up the east coast, delivered the lead sheet for a "fiddle tune" called *Orange Blossom Special* to the Library of Congress copyright offices in Washington, D.C.

Does Chubby's story contain any factual elements? Was Ervin even in Jacksonville during the train's high-profile stop at Union Station?

No advertisements specifically touting a Rouse Brothers nightclub appearance could be found in a search of *The Times-Union* archives. In fact, several of their favorite haunts, most notably the Temple Theater and the Mayflower Tavern, were specifically promoting other entertainers. However, the Roosevelt Patio ("Where Novelties Are Originated!") was heralding a new "all-star revue," which was to feature seven unnamed attractions. Since the brothers had played the downtown hotel's showroom before—once accepting second billing to a trained-dog act—they could well have been included in the Roosevelt's package.

In fact, the Rouses never specifically denied Chubby's claim that they were in Jacksonville—although they usually ignored it, perhaps viewing it as irrelevant—and Geneva, the only living person in a position to know, specifically recalls the visit. "Yes, I remember when Chubby brought that boy [Ervin] home," she says. "It was way early in the morning. They woke me up when they came in. So I made them some coffee, and that boy just kept pouring sugar into the cup. We had sugar-rationing back then, you know, and I thought, 'I won't have a bit left when he leaves.'"

According to Chubby—who told essentially the same *Orange Blossom Special* story for five decades—on the night the song was written, Ervin and Gordon had strolled into a bar where he and his trio were performing. "At intermission, Ervin wanted to know if he could play the fiddle and pass the hat," Chubby said. "So, he played for about fifteen minutes, he and his brother, just a fiddle and guitar. He was a great fiddle player—a trick fiddler—one of the finest. He'd just tear an audience all to pieces. If there was three dollars [in the audience], he'd come out with a dollar fifty of it."

This statement, too, is credible; the brothers—especially Ervin—enjoyed nothing more than busking, even after completing a paid engagement, and regardless of the hour. "He [Ervin] called everybody 'Doc,'" Chubby said. "He'd look at me and say, 'Hey, Doc, I tell you what. I'll rub my bow and you flog your box and we'll pick 'em a tune.' He was a real country boy, Ervin was. He had facial ticks. He'd brink his eyes when he talked."

Following the barroom revelry, the most commonly accepted *Special* story places Ervin and Chubby—both well lubricated from a busy evening of fiddling and imbibing—wandering in the wee hours around Union Station, where the Orange Blossom Special was still parked, although no longer open for tours. Gordon had, apparently, declined further bar-hopping, retiring instead to whatever modest accommodations the brothers had secured.

"We were at Union Station, and we were down there drinking beer," said Chubby, who, like Ervin, knew how to spice up a yarn. "We had done closed up all the beer joints, and we were sittin' there drinkin' and got to talkin' about that cotton-pickin' Orange Blossom Special train. On the way home, I said, 'Ervin, go home and eat breakfast with me.' So, we went home at about three in the mornin', and he said, 'Chubby, let's write a fiddle tune and call it *Orange Blossom Special*.' I said,

'Alright, we'll do it.' We got our fiddles out, and wrote that melody in about forty-five minutes while my wife was cookin' breakfast.'"

As Chubby told it, Ervin suggested that the pair have their musical creation copyrighted as soon as possible. Chubby, however, demurred: "I said, 'Ervin, I haven't got time to fool with a fiddle tune. I've got to check on my cab in a few minutes, and try to go make some beans to feed my young'un. If you can do anything with that fiddle tune, buddy, then it's all yours.' I remember them exact words as if it was yesterday."

If Ervin was in Jacksonville at the time—and, again, there is no reason to believe otherwise—it is then safe to assume that the pair did, at some point, go to Union Station and view the train. How could they have resisted? It also follows that eventually they would have returned to Chubby's apartment to swap fiddle tunes while enjoying a hearty breakfast and gradually sobering up.

Geneva, who had been rousted out of bed and given kitchen duty, does recall some mention of the train, and the playing of a fiddle tune that sounded very much like the melody now known worldwide as *Orange Blossom Special*. However, when gently pressed for more detail, she essentially repeats Chubby's well-worn account of the conversation. In fairness, however, she is being asked to reach back seven decades, and to recall what must have seemed, at the time at least, to be unimportant banter between her night-owl husband and his sugar-guzzling buddy.

Indeed, it is the widely accepted contention that the *Special* was written during this visit that is demonstrably untrue. The tune had been copyrighted the previous month—the date is clearly stamped on the original submission—and could not, therefore, have been conceived and completed while the long-suffering Geneva prepared a hot meal.

Was the *Special* discussed and played? Naturally, it would have been. But playing a song together is not the same as writing a song together. The indisputable fact is, by the time Ervin and Chubby were conducting their impromptu jam session on West Union Street, the history making tune was a fait accompli.

Nonetheless, this scenario quickly became accepted as gospel—much to the annoyance of Ervin's family, if not Ervin himself. Louallie recalls an incident in the late 1940s, when she and Ervin attended one of Chubby's performances near Washington, D.C. She says that an announcer, having been told that Ervin was in the audience, introduced him from the stage as "the man who helped Chubby Wise write *Orange Blossom Special*." Says Louallie: "That just made me so angry. I think Chubby was embarrassed, because he just hung his head. But Ervin didn't say much about it. He just said, 'What difference does it make?'"

Typical of subsequent published accounts is this passage from a meticulously researched book, *Bluegrass: A History* (University of Illinois Press), by Neil V. Rosenberg: "*Orange Blossom Special* was composed in Jacksonville, Florida by two young fiddlers, Robert "Chubby" Wise and Ervin Rouse…in a practice typical of the time, Wise gave his interest in the song to the Rouses [Ervin and Gordon], who copyrighted it."

Or, this passage from the scholarly liner notes of a Rounder Records Corporation train song compilation, which features a Johnson Mountain Boys rendition of the *Special*: "Wise, to his enduring regret, relinquished all claims to the tune, and it generally appeared over Rouse's name alone."

The erroneous assumption, of course, is that any rights to *Orange Blossom Special* were ever Chubby's to give.

ERVIN AND GORDON TOLD an entirely different story on the relatively rare occasions when they were asked by interviewers to expound upon the tune's origin. Conveniently ignoring their Jacksonville excursion, which they probably viewed as unnecessarily cluttering the narrative, the brothers insisted that they had first viewed the dazzling diesel in Miami, and had added lyrics to their previously copyrighted tune during a subsequent automobile trip between southern Florida and Kissimmee.

In fact, the Orange Blossom Special did arrive in the Magic City on Wednesday, November 16, for the southernmost stop on its exhibition tour. That same day, the brothers said, manager Lloyd Smith had planned to drive them to Kissimmee, where they would visit the Smith family—including Ervin's soon-to-be-ex-sweetheart, Elon—and perhaps arrange some bookings. "Our manager took us downtown to watch the christening of the Orange Blossom Special," Gordon said in 1992. "We saw the ceremony, and our manager said to Ervin, 'You know, that's going to be another famous train like the Old '97; that is, if somebody does something about it.' That very afternoon, we decided to give it a try."

Certainly, the ceremonies would not have been out of the way; the Seaboard Air Line passenger station, then located at Northwest 7th Avenue near 20th Street, was perhaps a five-minute drive from Little Trailers, where Gordon and Carrie had set up housekeeping. (The train station has long since been demolished, although a massive, Mediterranean-style stucco archway was spared the wrecking ball, and has been preserved at the entrance to what is now a modern office park.)

On the previous evening, hundreds of people had assembled to watch as the Special stopped just north of Miami, in Hialeah, where a gated canopy of palms had been constructed across the tracks, marking a symbolic entrance into the metro area.

Colonel Henry Anderson, co-receiver of the railroad, had then accepted several bouquets of flowers from civic organizations—one, from the president of the Hialeah Parent-Teacher Association, had been purchased with contributions from local schoolchildren—before receiving the keys to the city from Hialeah Mayor Carl Ault.

Following the presentations, Mary Tigertail, a Seminole Indian, had solemnly swung open the gates, ushering the Special along its way to Miami proper. The train, hauling its customary gaggle of junketeering elected officials, and local dignitaries, had finally arrived downtown around 10:40 p.m., much to the delight of several hundred additional spectators assembled to catch a glimpse.

Official welcoming ceremonies the following day were comparable to those held in Jacksonville—large crowds, soaring speeches, considerable pomp—and the festivities clearly dazzled the Rouses. Enroute to Kissimmee, Gordon recalled, Lloyd stopped at a drug store, where he bought a pencil and a legal pad. Then, he offered to sit in the back seat and transcribe lyrics if Gordon would take the wheel. "My brother and I, we were up in the front of the car just driving along," Gordon said in 1985. "Lloyd would keep tearing the sheets of paper off and throwing them out the window. No telling how many sheets of paper we threw out." However, Gordon claimed, by the time the exhausted trio arrived at the Smith home, *Orange Blossom Special* was essentially complete.

Claude Casey, in his 1982 oral history interview with John Rumble, confirmed the fact that the Rouses had for several years been playing a tune similar to the *Special* called *South Florida Blues*. "I know there's a lot of people who say they helped Ervin do this and they helped Ervin do that, you know," Casey said. "But I know that Ervin—we were playing a song that we called *South Florida Blues*. Finally, they had a dedication of the [train] in Miami, and that's where Ervin got the idea to call the *South Florida Blues* tune *Orange Blossom Special*."

Of course, there is a slight inconsistency in Casey's recollection as well. *Orange Blossom Special* had been copyrighted, using that name, before the Miami dedication ceremonies took place. But the point is, the tune, or something close to it, had been in the Rouse Brothers' repertoire for some time. The dedication ceremony, apparently, inspired them to add words and perhaps pick up the tempo a bit. "*South Florida Blues* was basically the same as *Orange Blossom Special*," recalls Carrie. "It was a little bit slower, and had more of a blues-type sound to it. But it was really the same song."

So what was Chubby thinking when he tried to take credit for helping to write the tune? It is possible that he did contribute something, but not in the way or at the time he claimed. "Ervin told me he taught Chubby *South Florida Blues* in the early thirties," contends Louallie. "Ervin was always teaching Chubby things on the fiddle." Therefore, it is possible—although not provable—that Chubby suggested some up-tempo variations to *South Florida Blues* and, over the years, concocted a simplified, semi-factual story that linked him more directly to its musical successor, *Orange Blossom Special*.

Gene Christian is one of the few people—perhaps the only person—who ever specifically quizzed both Chubby and Ervin about the *Special* while the two fiddlers stood literally face to face. Chubby, having temporarily left Hank Snow's Rainbow Ranch Boys in the early 1960s, was a guest at Gene's Miami home when Ervin also came to call. "I asked them, point blank, who wrote the song," says Gene. "Hell, I'd been hearing these different stories for years, and I wanted to know what they'd say."

In Ervin's presence, Gene recalls, Chubby claimed only that "I was there" when the tune was composed. Laconic Ervin, apparently finding nothing worth tussling about in Chubby's non-answer, passively nodded, and diplomatically volunteered nothing about *South Florida Blues*, or about the Miami to Kissimmee automobile trip with Gordon and Lloyd Smith.

However, Gene and others say that Chubby was not always so willing to downplay his involvement. "Another time [when Ervin was not present] Chubby told me he gave Ervin *Orange Blossom Special* in exchange for a quart of whiskey," Gene adds, chuckling. "You can take that for what it's worth. I know I did."

And in a 1986 interview with the Associated Press, Chubby did not back down even when asked about a "controversy" involving his claim to authorship. "That was just the melody I helped write, not the lyrics," he said. "I gave Ervin my half of the song. But it didn't hurt my stature any. I've made a lot of money, not directly but indirectly, on the *Orange Blossom Special*. It has got me a lot of jobs and, in sense, a lot of dollars."

In 1993, Gordon addressed the contentious subject more directly than usual during a poignant, videotaped interview conducted by his cousin, Preston Rouse, at Preston's home near Kinston. At age seventy-seven, Gordon appears frail; his face marked by tumors and his breathing labored. But his raspy voice rises and he accentuates his words with hand gestures when asked by Preston to address Chubby's claims.

"Chubby Wise had never heard *Orange Blossom Special* until we played it for him," says Gordon, who forcefully reiterates the standard Rouse version of events, varying from published accounts only by adding that their father, Ernest, was also a passenger in Lloyd's vehicle when the lyrics were written. Although he doesn't specifically mention *South Florida Blues*, he seems to allude to it when he says, "We decided to write a tune—well, we had a tune already."

As for Chubby, Gordon says, "It's very easy to say that you done somethin' when you didn't do it. You keep on sayin' it, and folks don't know whether it's true or not. Chubby made out like just because he met us in Jacksonville, that he had somethin' to do with the tune. That's all wrong; all untrue."

Seemingly without basis is a tale related in the book *The Stories Behind Country Music's 100 All-Time Greatest Songs* (Boulevard Books) by Ace Collins. Without citing sources, Collins repeats the Rouse account, adding that Lloyd had previously persuaded Seaboard Air Line executives to allow the brothers to debut *Orange Blossom Special* at the train's Miami christening. While the idea might have had considerable promotional merit, there is no evidence that Lloyd arranged anything of the sort; neither Ervin nor Gordon ever mentioned having performed at the ceremony, and there is no mention of the Rouse Brothers on a schedule of events published in the *Miami Herald*.

Collins also writes that Lloyd clandestinely copyrighted the tune under his own name, sparking a year-long legal struggle with Ervin and Gordon. This is untrue; the registration form clearly states that *Orange Blossom Special*, Copyright Number E 179156, is owned by "Ervin Thomas Rouse, c/o J.H. Smith [James Smith, Lloyd's father], Kissimmee, Florida." The Smith name indicates only that the brothers' business matters were being handled by their Kissimmee-based manager, and does not by any stretch of the imagination indicate duplicity on Lloyd's part.

Equally spurious is a contention by Texas fiddler Leon "Pappy" Selph that he, not Ervin or Chubby, was the author of *Orange Blossom Special*, and that he debuted it onstage at the *Grand Ole Opry* in 1931. Selph is best-known for leading the Blue Ridge Playboys, a 1940s western swing combo consisting of pianist Moon Mullican (with whom we shall become better acquainted), singer Floyd Tillman (*Slippin' Around*), and songwriter Ted Daffan (*Born to Lose*).

In February 1997, the ailing but still feisty old codger related this story, versions of which he had told for decades, to a reporter from Houston radio station KTRU: "I was with the [*Opry*] backup band. Well, things rocked on and one night they said, 'Leon, could you play about three or four minutes onstage? One of the entertainers has come up sick; won't show or ain't gonna show.' I said, 'Okay, I'll do my *Orange Blossom Special*.' When I got through playin' it, I had a standing ovation, and Bill Monroe said, 'Man, I've gotta have that song.' So, I learned it to him, and he made it for Columbia in 1934."

Selph further claimed that Chubby magnanimously offered to record the *Special* in 1952, saying, "Pappy, you're a good friend and I enjoy playing with you, so I'm gonna make your song. My records are sellin' like hotcakes, and I'll make you some money."

There are several glaring inconsistencies in this story, not the least which is the fact that there was no *Opry* backup band in 1931. (Possibly, Selph was referring to the WSM staff orchestra, which provided pop-oriented musical programming for a network of stations but had no direct affiliation with the *Opry*.) Further, an unknown Bill Monroe was toiling in an oil refinery that year, made no recordings at all until 1936, and did not appear on the *Opry* until 1939. Finally, Selph did not explain— nor was he asked to explain—how a man named Ervin T. Rouse came to own the tune's copyright.

Yet, the widely respected Western Swing Hall of Famer repeated this implausible yarn so often that, when he died in 1998, several published obituaries propagated the myth that he had "introduced" *Orange Blossom Special*.

How, then, does the often-overlooked Gordon fit into this jumbled mosaic of claims and counter-claims? Carrie insists that her well-meaning husband should have registered the *Special* as a collaboration between himself and his brother, but failed to do so "only because he didn't have any education; he thought you had to copyright a song under just one name."

Of course, the *Special* is first and foremost a fiddle tune, and it is doubtful that Gordon contributed much—if anything—to the melody. Still, because Gordon apparently did help to write the lyrics, Ervin might well have acknowledged at least a moral obligation to share the royalties.

Yet, according to Carrie, her brother-in-law felt no such responsibility; other family members and fair-weather cronies apparently benefited far more from the fiddler's largess than did his life-long protector and steadfast performing partner. "Ervin was very free-hearted with his money," says Carrie. "But with Gordon, it might be fifty dollars here and twenty dollars there. Never much."

Therefore, based upon the available evidence, it is safe to state that the *Special's* melody is, in fact, the same or nearly the same as an earlier Ervin T. Rouse tune called *South Florida Blues*—to which Chubby may or may not have contributed— and that the lyrics are the result of a collaboration between Ervin and Gordon, with a possible assist from Lloyd Smith. Precisely when—and why—Ervin changed the name of *South Florida Blues* to *Orange Blossom Special* is unknown; but as the copyright date conclusively demonstrates, it occurred sometime prior to the much-discussed exhibition tour.

So, while it is impossible to conclude that the *Special* is totally devoid of Chubby's influence—indeed, few popular songs could be described as being entirely original— there is no reason to believe that his role was significant enough to earn the designation "uncredited co-author."

In fact, Chubby's official International Bluegrass Music Association (IBMA) performer profile, written when he was posthumously inducted into the organization's Hall of Honor in 1998, appropriately contains carefully worded hedges and caveats when discussing the *Special*.

The brief tribute, written by bluegrass historian Lance LeRoy, mistakenly states that both Chubby and Ervin were Jacksonville cab drivers—an error that has found its way into print before. But LeRoy then carefully avoids presenting anecdote as fact when he writes: "Chubby Wise often asserted that he 'had a hand' in creating the classic *Orange Blossom Special*…He also said he refused a co-writer share, which he alleges was offered by Rouse." The remainder of the profile, as it should, focuses on the many other accomplishments that have ensured Chubby Wise's place in musical history as perhaps the greatest and most influential bluegrass fiddler of all time.

Dubious authorship claims aside, there is no disputing the fact that Chubby was, at the very least, a great popularizer of *Orange Blossom Special*. With Bill Monroe, then with Hank Snow, and finally as a solo star on the bluegrass festival circuit, "Fiddlin' Chubby" took the *Special* around the world.

For Ervin, as well, the tune should have been a career-maker. Instead, despite several priceless opportunities to capitalize on its success, his life and career began a slow, downhill spiral that has remained one of country music's most heart-breaking untold stories.

V

Would Have, Could Have, Should Have:
Orange Blossom Special on the Record

Native-born hillbillies from the sticks usually provide entertaining music, but in most cases they're short on comedy and showmanship.
Meyer Horowitz

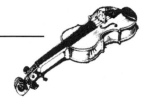

W e walked all over New York, and were turned down by all the music publishers," Ervin once recalled. "We were told that, 'Your music will never amount to anything.' We were discouraged and encouraged to stay out of the music business. There were several times when I got so discouraged from being told that my songs would never sell that I nearly quit."

Bob Miller, however, believed in the Rouse Brothers. Despite the commercial failure of their 1936 collaboration, he was willing to work with them again. After all, like the Rouses, Miller had come to New York as a young man, determined to make a living with his music. But he had lasted just a few weeks before running out of money and returning to Memphis. Miller, therefore, was a believer in second chances—particularly for artists in whom he had faith.

Although the music business has changed substantially over the years, the role of the music publisher has remained essentially the same. In addition to handling administrative functions, such as the registration of copyrights and the collection of monies owned, the publisher "plugs" the song, securing recording commitments and making certain that appropriate revenue-generating opportunities are exploited.

Unfortunately for hillbillies, large publishers that dominated popular music prior to World War II paid scant attention to the country genre, at least in part because much of early country music consisted of folk tunes already in the public domain. If a new song was published at all, it was typically steered through companies owned by savvy record producers such as Eli Oberstein, Dave Kapp, W.R. Calaway,

Art Satherley, and Ralph Peer. (Peer, in fact, had been among the first to recognize that country publishing could be lucrative; in 1926, he offered to help Victor Records expand its hillbilly business at no salary in exchange for control of the copyrights he obtained.)

Miller, whose name is today less well-known than those of his publishing peers, was equally shrewd. Plus, he was genuinely fond of old-time music, regarding it as a legitimate art form worthy of preservation and promotion. Therefore, in early 1939, Bob Miller Inc. published *Orange Blossom Special* along with three additional Ervin originals: *(I've Got Those) Craven County Blues, Bum Bum Blues*, and *We'll Start Love All Over Again*.

Miller also arranged studio time for his proteges with Bluebird, an RCA Victor budget-line subsidiary specializing in hillbilly and race records. Although he may or may not have believed that the Rouse Brothers could establish themselves as recording artists, Miller obviously viewed Ervin's songs as potential hits for others.

(I've Got Those) Craven County Blues is a catchy tribute to Ervin's old stomping grounds, and to the North Carolina moonshine industry:

> *In the hills of Craven County,*
> *we make our licker so sweet,*
> *Oh, my pappy's got a still,*
> *way down by Brice's Creek.*
>
> *Oh Lord, I've got the Craven County Blues.*
> *Oh Lord, I'm cravin' my Craven County corn.*
> *My pappy drank a gallon,*
> *the day that I was born.*

Bum Bum Blues is a standard, woe-is-me hillbilly ditty about being down on one's luck:

> *Now I've come to let you know from the start,*
> *I've done my bumming in every part.*
> *I've been made fun of and called names,*
> *I've been turned down by all the dames.*
> *I've got de bum, de bum, de bum bum blues."*

Finally, *We'll Start Love All Over Again* is a maudlin plea for forgiveness and renewal proffered by a cheating spouse:

> *Oh darling I'm sorry I went to stray,*
> *oh sweetheart I'll no more pretend.*

I'm sorry, so sorry, that's why I say,
we'll start love all over again.

As for the *Special*, it was published with two verses and two "extra" verses. Interestingly, the tune has never been recorded—even by the Rouse Brothers—using the complete lyrics, which read as follows:

Look-a yonder comin',
comin' down the railroad track!
Look-a-yonder comin,'
comin' down the railroad track!
It's the Orange Blossom Special,
a-bringin' my baby back.

Talk about a-trav'lin,'
it's the fastest on the rail.
Talk about a-trav'lin,
it's the fastest on the rail.
It's the Orange Blossom Special,
a-comin' down the Seaboard trail.

(Extra verses)
Goin' down to Florida,
and get some sand in my shoes.
Goin' down to Florida,
and get some sand in my shoes.
I'll ride the Orange Blossom Special,
and lose these T.B. blues.

If you want to write me,
I'll tell you how to 'dress my mail.
If you want to write me,
I'll tell you how to 'dress my mail.
In care of the Special,
at the end of the Seaboard trail.

Then, with their songs safely protected—or so they thought—the brothers inexplicably waited six months before recording them. In late January, 1939, Ervin and Gordon—joined by Jacksonville musician Loren "Sleepy" Gibbs— packed up their overalls to join a traveling musical revue headlined by Paula Stone, the platinum-blonde daughter of stage and screen star Fred Stone (perhaps best known as the original "Scarecrow" in the theatrical production of *Wizard of Oz*).

Paula, a singer and a dancer with a handful of B western films to her credit, had just completed a Broadway run with her father; her sister, Dorothy; and her mother, Allene Crater, in the musical comedy *Ripples*. She and her husband, bandleader Duke Dingley, had organized a musical variety show, the *Paula Stone Revue*, which was slated to tour Midwestern theaters when *Ripples* closed.

It is unknown how the brothers became attached to this troupe, which on occasion also featured African-American comedian Stepin Fetchit (real name: Lincoln Perry). But they were apparently hired by Dingley following an audition in Miami, and traveled by car, along with Carrie and Sleepy's wife, Lucille, to dates in Evansville, Indiana; Chicago, Illinois; and Madison, Wisconsin.

In Chicago, the ensemble lingered for two weeks at the Berkshire Hotel while Paula traveled to California to appear in a film, *Idiot's Delight*, which is best remembered today for screen idol Clark Gable's awkward song-and-dance routine to *Puttin' On the Ritz*. "We didn't have a telephone or even a radio in our room," says Carrie. "So, we spent a lot of time going to the movies and playing Chinese checkers, because five people at a time could play. In fact, we played Chinese checkers so much that I thought I was going to turn Chinese by the time we left town."

In Madison, the rag-tag company—with the exception of Duke and Paula, who had wisely made advance reservations—was unable to locate a hotel with any vacancies. So, Gordon canvassed residential neighborhoods, knocking on doors and seeking lodging in private homes. "He finally found us a place to stay." Carrie says. "We slept on Army cots in someone's den. And it's a good thing, too, because it was freezing cold and snowing outside."

The March 25, 1939 edition of the *Wisconsin State Journal* reports that "Fred Stone's dancing daughter" and the Duke Dingley Orchestra—the Rouses are not mentioned—played a two-day stand at the Capitol Theater, performing four shows daily between screenings of the film *Nancy Drew, Detective.*

The brothers and Sleepy—a guitarist who, like Claude Casey, was introduced onstage as a Rouse Brother—presented their usual act. Paula, who had spent her life in the company of vaudevillians, was favorably impressed, telling Ervin that she could help the trio break into the movies. (Stepin Fetchit, whom Carrie describes as being entirely unlike the shuffling, bug-eyed dullard he portrayed in films, also lauded the brothers' showmanship. Since the Rouses also exploited stereotypes for laughs, the pioneering comedian may have considered them to be kindred spirits).

Perhaps Paula was sincere, but financial troubles plagued the tour, which was ponderous and expensive to mount, and the brothers found it increasingly difficult to wring their weekly pay from Dingley. "They got just enough for expenses—gas and hotel rooms—and that was it," Carrie says. "Duke was always saying, 'We'll get you caught up next week.' But he never did. So, when the show came back to Raleigh, they decided to leave." Sleepy returned to Florida, but Ervin, Gordon, and Carrie stayed several months in North Carolina, performing as a trio in rural schoolhouses and small-town theaters, and sometimes sharing the stage with Earl and his wife.

From there, the Rouse Brothers—this time including Earl as well as Sleepy— were booked at the well-known Village Barn in New York City's Greenwich Village; a venue described in *Billboard* magazine as "New York's most successful nightclub using the homespun motif." The two-hundred-seat facility, first opened in 1929 and located at 52 West Eighth Street, offered New Yorkers lowbrow floorshows consisting of hillbilly singers, comedians, and assorted vaudeville novelty acts along with ballroom dance bands. Between sets, audience members joined in square dances, musical chairs, and sack races.

Although it all appeared quite authentic, owner Meyer Horowitz had lamented to *Billboard* that "native-born hillbillies from the sticks usually provide entertaining music, but in most cases they're short on comedy and showmanship." Therefore, he had concluded, "synthetic hillbillies [primarily Jews and Italians] are, as a rule, more desirable in a night club than real ones."

Horowitz's analysis is correct in the same way that a white comedian in black-face could normally be counted upon to present a more broad—and certainly more offensive—caricature of stereotypical African-American behavior than would an actual African-American. Likewise, some "genuine" hillbillies did not believe that their music and their culture were particularly funny and, as a result, were not especially adept at playing for laughs.

Imagine, then, Horowitz's delight at encountering the Rouse Brothers, who may have come to his attention through Bob Miller, or who may have simply shown up for an audition. Could it be? Authentic rustics from North Carolina (by way of Florida) who possessed both musical virtuosity and show-business savvy?

Enchanted, Horowitz booked the three brothers and Sleepy for two weeks, and then held them over for two months. The quartet played three shows a day, seven days a week, working from 7:30 p.m. to 2:30 a.m. Pay was a hundred sixty dollars weekly—divided four ways—and meals at the club.

The boys—plus Carrie and Lucille—shared a small apartment in Greenwich Village, enjoying New York's sights by day while playing to enthusiastic crowds by night. "Meyer Horowitz sure got his money's worth," says Carrie. "He'd watch the act every evening, and he'd always sit at a table with me. And he left strict instructions with his staff: He was not to be interrupted as long as he was watching the Rouse Brothers."

At some point during the engagement, Earl returned to North Carolina. But Horowitz wanted to keep Ervin, Gordon, and Sleepy for as long as possible, offering them a one-year contract and suggesting that they might parlay the resulting exposure into Broadway engagements and perhaps a movie deal. "But it was cold, and we wanted to get back [to Miami]," says Carrie. "Besides, Ervin just wasn't in the mood. He said, 'There ain't enough damn money in the world to make me want to stay in New York.'"

A decade later, reflecting on his lifelong love-hate relationship with the Big Apple, Ervin wrote a song called *A New York Boy Gone Hillbilly*, in which he casts himself against type as a city slicker who, after being forced into a shotgun wedding with a mountain girl, happily abandons the Great White Way for Appalachia.

The cornball ditty, which was never recorded, further demonstrates that, as a lyricist, Ervin Rouse would never be confused with Irving Berlin. Yet, it also exemplifies his adeptness at exploiting hillbilly archetypes:

> *My wife she's tall and rangy,*
> *and just about six-foot-three,*
> *she looks just a little bit mangy,*
> *but she means just as much to me.*

> *In a hog's hollow we've got Broadway,*
> *we get our water and lights free,*
> *so you take New York and let us be,*
> *we're happy gone hillbilly.*

Would the fortunes of the Rouse Brothers have been advanced had they agreed to accept a quasi-permanent position with Horowitz? Possibly. At least one well-known hillbilly performer's successful career was launched in this manner: Judy Canova, the Jacksonville-born comedienne, came to Horowitz's attention as a teenager, and was anointed a Village Barn regular in the early 1930s.

Canova—along with brother Leon and sister Diane—had cobbled together an act called "Anne, Judy, and Zeke, the Three Georgia Crackers," which included comedy routines, country dancing, yodeling, novelty tunes, and even hog calls. From the Village Barn, the trio had graduated to Broadway in a 1934 revue called *Calling All Stars*, which in turn led to a successful film and recording career and a nationally syndicated radio program for Judy, who was, for a time, Republic Pictures' top moneymaking female star.

Horowitz, who seems to have detected similar potential in Ervin and Gordon, no doubt repeatedly invoked Canova's example when trying to convince the brothers to remain in New York—but to no avail.

Ultimately, however, the brothers established a routine of remaining in the Deep South during the winter and traveling to the Northeast during the summer; therefore, they were able to return to the Village Barn most every season until 1953, when Horowitz replaced hillbilly entertainment with a Gay '90s revue.

And, although stage and screen stardom never resulted from the Rouses' long but sporadic affiliation with the New York nightspot, Ervin and Gordon apparently did appear on a Horowitz-produced television program, which originated from the night-club and was fed by NBC to its East Coast and Midwest affiliates throughout 1948 and 1949. A clipped newspaper advertisement, undated and unidentified, indicates that "those famous trick fiddlers from North Carolina," along with Howard Woods and his Orchestra, performed on the broadcast at least four separate times during one month-long summer engagement. (For reasons unknown, the brothers did not appear in *Village Barn*, a low-budget, 1949 feature film inspired by the television venture.)

As it happened, while the brothers worked for Paula Stone and Meyer Horowitz, *Orange Blossom Special* almost got away from them. In January 1939, Rouse buddy Tommy Magness, along with Roy Hall and His Blue Ridge Entertainers, waxed the *Special* and seventeen other selections in Columbia, South Carolina, for the Vocalion Division of ARC, the same label that had recorded the Three Floridians and the Rouse Brothers four years earlier.

How Magness learned the tune is unclear, but since the Blue Ridge Entertainers had previously been based in Winston-Salem, North Carolina—where they played on radio station WAIR—it is probable that someone from the group saw it per-formed by Ervin and Gordon during one of the brothers' frequent forays through the Tar Heel State.

Regardless, the first recorded version of *Orange Blossom Special* was not released; in Columbia's archives, a note scrawled upon the session sheet reads: "Hold. Don't release. Rouse Brothers refuse to sign a [licensing] contract." Another note states: "Don't release—publisher [Miller] promises trouble."

For decades, it was thought that this rare gem was lost. However, the Magness-Hall recording surfaced in late 1999 on *Soundtrack for a Century*, an extraordinary twenty-six-CD boxed set compiled by Sony. This previously unheard rendition, which employs no lyrics and features only a fiddle and a guitar, is tightly played and follows Ervin's composition virtually note for note.

Although it is assumed that Magness is the fiddler, a brief dialogue near the tune's end involves an exchange between Hall and someone named "Bob," possibly guitarist Bob Hopson. Note the reference to Jacksonville, further suggesting that that the Blue Ridge Entertainers associated the *Special* with the Rouses:

> Hall: *Hey, Bob, where you goin'?*
> Hopson: *Goin' down to Jacksonville. Where you goin', Roy?*
> Hall: *Gonna ride this Orange Blossom Special on down to Columbia, South Carolina.*

Then, in February 1939 yet another unauthorized version of the tune—rather transparently dubbed *Train Special*—was recorded for Bluebird by harmonic player cum fiddler Walter Hurdt and His Singing Cowboys, and was released as the B side of a traditional fiddle showpiece called *Lost Dog*.

To be charitable, Hurdt could have been unaware that he was stealing a previously published work—but Bluebird A & R man Eli Oberstein, who frequently changed the titles of songs he recorded to hide their legitimate copyrights, surely was not. In any case, Hurdt's clandestine effort, which is plodding and ineptly played, deservedly sank into oblivion.

PRIOR TO WORLD WAR II, New York, Chicago, and Los Angeles—not Nashville, where the powers-that-be still used the moniker "Athens of the South" instead of "Music City, USA"—were the municipalities in which the nascent country music recording and publishing industries flourished.

So, it was to Manhattan and Victor's Studio No. 1 that Ervin and Gordon finally returned on June 14, 1939, for what was likely their third recording session. All that is known of this seminal event must be discerned from the session sheet, which affirms that, in addition to *Orange Blossom Special*, the brothers also cut *Bum Bum Blues* and *(I've Got Those) Craven County Blues*, along with new versions of their earlier ARC efforts, *Please Let Me Walk With My Son, My Family Circle (Will the Circle Be Unbroken),* and *Some Old Day.*

Unfortunately, of the six completed sides, the *Special* is the only cut that is currently in print: on *Classic Country Music*, a Smithsonian Institute boxed set available via mail order. The tune also appears on *The Railroad in Folksong,* an out-of-print 1966 RCA Victor Vintage Series compilation now much prized by collectors.

Bum Bum Blues, (I've Got Those) Craven County Blues, and *My Family Circle (Will the Circle Be Unbroken)* have escaped extinction, although only a handful of 78 rpm disks are known to exist. Neither *Please Let Me Walk With My Son* nor *Some Old Day* could be located. (A curious footnote: Earl, not Ervin, is listed on the session sheet as Gordon's vocal partner on *Please Let Me Walk With My Son.* However, there is no indication that Earl was present in New York, and Ervin later referred to the session as consisting only of "me and my brother Gordy.")

For better or worse, the Bluebird cuts are hard-core hillbilly. Mostly, it is for worse. *Bum Bum Blues* and *(I've Got Those) Craven County Blues* are distinguished mainly by their showy fiddle runs, while *My Family Circle (Will the Circle Be Unbroken)* is undermined by Ervin's jarringly nasal lead vocals, tempered by Gordon's high harmony on the chorus.

Unquestionably, of the surviving 1939 Rouse Brothers recordings, the *Special* is far and away the most memorable. Indeed, it is worth the entire price of the Smithsonian's excellent compilation just to hear the ebullient duo, without pretension and with nothing to lose, gleefully unleashing their crowning achievement.

The *Special* opens with Ervin, who employs an exaggerated "black" dialect and shouts: "All a-booooooard! Popcorn! Peanuts! Goo-Goos! Yes sir, buy 'em on dis train; de first train gwine south!" Then, as the fiddle simulates a train whistle and the guitar lays down a steady beat, the brothers, raising their voices in tight, reedy harmony, render the first two verses as originally written.

Exquisite tension builds until the first instrumental break, when, in a burst of maniacal energy, Ervin and his frantic fiddle take command. He plays with lightening speed, then, using the so-called jiggly-bow technique (a repeated, rhythmic bowing pattern that mimics a train's chug-a-lug), he eases off before attacking the melody with renewed vigor.

Finally, the brothers improvise a dialogue of the sort that would appear on virtually every future recording of the *Special* employing lyrics:

> Ervin: *Lord, have mercy!*
> Gordon: *Meeee, too.*
> Ervin: *Hey, Gordon!*
> Gordon: *Uh, huh?*
> Ervin: *What's the name of this train?*
> *Gordon: It's the Orange Blossom Special.*
> Ervin: *That right?*
> Gordon: *Uh, huh.*
> Ervin: *Where you gwine 't get off, boy?*
> Gordon: *I think I gwine 't get off down about Jacksonville,*
> *Florida. Where you gwine?*
> Ervin: *Miami, Florida, Miami, Florida. I'll get off at Miami*
> *on the Seaboard Line, right at the end!*

Forty years later, Ervin talked about the session with Randy Wayne White, and told the writer a hilarious yarn about staying in a fancy New York hotel featuring an oddly configured "drinking fountain" in the bathroom. The story, which White adapted for *The Man Who Invented Florida,* is probably utter nonsense—but it is indicative of Ervin's determination to reinforce his backwoods persona at every opportunity. Once again inexplicably substituting Earl for Gordon, the fiddler recalls that he, unlike his brother, refused to sip from the strange appliance, which was, in fact, a bidet. "I might get down'n my knees to drink whiskey, but not water," Ervin tells Earl. "Lord knows, somethin' ain't natural about that."

Following their Bluebird session, the boys returned to Miami brimming with optimism. But, strangely enough, *Orange Blossom Special* was not the first song to be released, nor was it on the A side when it finally did emerge, indicating that neither Miller nor Bluebird executives regarded the tune as unusually noteworthy.

Instead, in August 1939 the label pressed and distributed *Please Let Me Walk With My Son,* backed by (at long last) *Some Old Day.* In October came *My Family Circle (Will the Circle Be Unbroken),* backed by *Orange Blossom Special;* followed in November by *Bum Bum Blues*, backed by *(I've Got Those) Craven County Blues.*

Advertising flyers distributed by the record company to its dealers feature a photograph of the Rouse Brothers—in full hillbilly regalia—and tout their music under the category "Old Familiar Tunes," alongside those of Carl Boling and His Four Aces, Montana Slim, Bill Boyd and His Cowboy Ramblers, and Daddy John Love. Still, despite what appears to be at least some promotional support, none of these releases sold well.

Ervin and Gordon later claimed that they had unintentionally violated an American Federation of Musicans (AFM) regulation, which had compelled the union to threaten litigation against Bluebird. Consequently, the brothers said, the label had abruptly withdrawn their records from the market.

This improbable story is perpetuated in Ervin's obituary, published in the South Florida Bluegrass Association's newsletter, a portion of which reads: "The Rouse Brothers' version [of *Orange Blossom Special*] ran into problems with the musicians' union in New York. They [Ervin and Gordon] inadvertently, through a lack of understanding more than intention, ran afoul of union regulations, and had apparently dealt with a non-union label or publisher—which is not clear—and they were blacklisted as far as their recordings were concerned at that time."

Yet, Bluebird's catalogue indicates that the first and third releases stayed on the market for nearly a year, and that *My Family Circle (Will the Circle Be Unbroken)* and *Orange Blossom Special* remained in print well into 1942.

It is factual that, unlike most hillbilly performers of the era, Ervin and Gordon were union members: AFM Local 655 in Miami. They joined primarily because the resort hotels at which they often appeared were union operations. But the card-carrying duo had not, in fact, dealt with a non-union label, a non-union publisher, or non-union musicians. (A typewritten notation on the session sheet plainly reads, "Union Musicians Used.")

So, is there any conceivable way that a union dispute could have derailed the Rouse Brothers' version of *Orange Blossom Special*? Harold Bradley, highly respected president of the Nashville local and a pillar of the music industry establishment for more than a half-century, says that he can discern no apparent violation based upon the information provided. "All I can say is, that story certainly doesn't seem right," he states.

Why, then, did the brothers believe, or appear to believe, that their records had been "withdrawn," or "blacklisted?" Most likely, they were referring to a 1941 standoff between the American Society of Composers, Authors and Publishers (ASCAP), the performing rights licensing organization with which Miller and the Rouses were associated, and the National Association of Broadcasters (NAB).

ASCAP, founded in 1914, assessed fees against music users—hotels, nightclubs, motion picture producers and broadcasters—then passed along performance royalties to its writer and publisher members. (Mechanical royalties, based only upon record sales, were paid by record companies.) At the root of the problem was money.

For the privilege of playing ASCAP-licensed selections—which encompassed most American music published after 1884—radio stations remitted a percentage of their annual gross advertising sales.

However, a five-year contract between ASCAP and NAB was due to expire on December 31, 1940, and the licensing organization, assuming that broadcasters had no choice but to acquiesce, planned to impose a one hundred percent rate hike. So, in protest—just three months after the Rouse Brothers' session—NAB announced formation of an ASCAP competitor called Broadcast Music Inc. (BMI).

Then, when no accommodation with ASCAP could be reached, broadcasters instituted a ban on the older organization's songs that lasted through the first ten months of 1941. In the meantime, radio stations mined public domain material while building BMI's catalogue with new work from composers whom ASCAP had previously shunned—particularly writers of hillbilly, gospel, race, jazz, and most ethnic music.

Where did these machinations leave Ervin and Gordon? Although some publishing companies with large country catalogues—most notably Ralph Peer's Southern Music and M.M. Cole of Chicago—changed their affiliation from ASCAP to BMI, New York-based Bob Miller did not. Consequently, the Rouse Brothers' recordings could not have been played or sung over the airwaves for most of 1941.

Still, although the radio ban was undoubtedly an impediment, it is an overstatement to contend that it alone wrecked the *Special*. At that time, record sales and airplay were not inexorably linked; indeed, until a 1940 U.S. Supreme Court ruling clarified the situation, many broadcasters assumed that recorded music could not legally be used, prompting their continued dependence upon live talent.

Also, the *Special* was on the market for more than a year before the ban went into effect, which means that it had time to be heard before being shelved.

In fact, the Rouse Brothers' recordings were unsuccessful not because of nebulous union rules or publishing company disputes, but because of changing times and tastes. For example, by 1940 most country records were sold not to individuals for home use, but to jukebox operators, who serviced hundreds of thousands of the coin-operated devises. Unfortunately for the Rouses, jukeboxes were not effective outlets for acoustic music, which was difficult to hear in clamorous environments such as taverns and restaurants.

Ernest Tubb, who began his career as a Jimmie Rodgers imitator, learned this valuable lesson in 1941, when he was told by a Fort Worth vendor that "as soon as the crowd gets in and gets noisy, they can't hear your records; they start playing Bob Wills." From that time forward, the Texas Troubadour was electrified and amplified.

Jukeboxes aside, recording was problematic for the Rouses because their act was built around flashy trick fiddling, a highly visual art form. "You just had to see 'em play," says Gene Christian. "The showmanship, that was what made 'em special."

Even so, under normal circumstances the brothers might have tried again. But beginning on August 1, 1942, an AFM strike against record labels all but halted commercial recording activity. Union President James C. Petrillo contended that jukeboxes and increasingly common all-disk radio programs were throttling demand for live music, and sought the establishment of a trust fund to aid unemployed musicians.

By the time the strike was settled two years later, a war-related shortage of domestic shellac mandated that record companies severely curtail their output for the duration. Understandably, none were willing to expend their precious allocations on unproven acts.

The Rouse Brothers, then, were both out of luck and out of style. Crooners Eddy Arnold and Red Foley, western swingmeisters Bob Wills and Al Dexter, singing cowboy Gene Autry, honky-tonker Ernest Tubb, and Appalachian warbler Roy Acuff dominated country music in the 1940s, while Bill Monroe's supercharged sound—the generic term "bluegrass" would not come into popular usage until the mid-1950s—had supplanted traditional string bands and old-time fiddlers.

A few hillbilly duos, such as Henry D. "Homer" Haynes and Kenneth C. "Jethro" Burns, successfully combined comedy with music. But Homer & Jethro were best known for catchy novelty songs and clever parodies; most notably *Baby It's Cold Outside* (with June Carter) and *The Battle of Kookamonga*. Ervin and Gordon, whose humor could charitably be described as broad, simply lacked the sophistication to emulate Homer & Jethro's formula.

In hindsight, perhaps Ervin should have gone it alone. Gordon was, by all accounts, a delightful person but only a passable musician. Although Ervin's unwillingness to learn new material would have prohibited a career as a session sideman, he might have adopted a comedic persona and caught on as a featured performer in a country ensemble, as Speck Rhodes did with Porter Wagoner and Pete "Brother Oswald" Kirby did with Roy Acuff. After all, nobody knew how to parlay hillbilly clichés into laughs better than Ervin.

As a solo act, Ervin might also have followed the lead of Louis Marshall "Grandpa" Jones and Dave "Stringbean" Akeman. Both men, perhaps best known for their television stints on *Hee-Haw*, also enjoyed long careers as *Opry* stalwarts, and were celebrated by city-slickers for their musical authenticity during the folk revival of the early 1960s. Within his comfort zone, Ervin was as good or better a musician than either Jones or Akeman—and no one could say that he wasn't authentic.

Sadly, however, the befuddled fiddler was simply too erratic to be dependable, and too inept to have pursued a career as anything other than a vaudeville-style busker. "Ervin just never wanted to work for anybody else," says Gene. "You know, sometimes when you take a man out of his element, he just gets lost. Ervin was the best at what he done, but he got too comfortable with it. Times changed, but you couldn't move Ervin."

Nonetheless, *Orange Blossom Special* chugged along, albeit with others at the controls. Tommy Magness, for one, performed the tune on radio and at personal appearances, and eventually fronted a band called "The Orange Blossom Boys" in honor of the show-stopper that he, not the Rouse Brothers, had recorded first. More importantly, however, he brought the *Special* to the attention of Bill Monroe after joining the Blue Grass Boys.

During a 1982 interview with *Bluegrass Unlimited*, former Blue Grass Boy Cleo Davis recalled how the *Special* came to be part of Monroe's repertoire:

"We [the Blue Grass Boys] were in Stauton, Virginia, with a great fiddler friend of mine, Tommy Magness, who was fiddling with us at that time. He came up with a fiddle tune called the *Orange Blossom Special*. We were doing a two-day stand at the Vigilight Theater, and Tommy and me were rooming together. I had my guitar in the room, and he had his fiddle, and he played me the *Orange Blossom Special*, and man, I thought I'd never heard such a train tune. *Train 45* wasn't that good, and neither was *Lee Highway Blues*. The *Orange Blossom Special* took it all, and Tommy knew the words. We went over the words and learned the song. And we went downstairs and got a portable recorder at a music shop, and tried to record it in the lobby. We couldn't get a true sound in the lobby, so the man took us in the public rest room and locked the door. We set the recorder on the john, and me and Tommy Magness recorded the *Orange Blossom Special*. I sang tenor in the duet. While in the bathroom, we also recorded *Peach Pickin' Time in Georgia* and *The Hills of Roane County*. When we got back to Nashville, we called Bill over to listen to it. He liked it. Tommy had picked up an old record by the Rouse Brothers, who were good friends of Chubby Wise, an old Florida boy. Chubby and the Rouse Brothers wrote it, and Chubby gave it to the Rouse Brothers. They copyrighted it and recorded it, but Tommy Magness and me took it to Nashville. Bill, he let Tommy and me do it on the *Grand Ole Opry* the next Saturday night. The following Saturday night, me and Bill did it, and from then on, me and Bill did it."

Ironically, however, neither Davis nor Magness appear on Monroe's recording of the *Special*. Davis left the Blue Grass Boys in late 1940, moving to Lakeland, Florida, and landing a country music program on radio station WLAK. Magness rejoined Roy Hall in 1941, and was replaced by a former band member, Art Wooten.

It was Wooten, bassist Bill "Cousin Wilbur" Wesbrooks, and guitarist Pete Pyle who traveled with Monroe to Atlanta in October 1941 to cut the *Special* and seven other songs for RCA. Not surprisingly, the Kentuckian and his troupe nail the train tune. Monroe and Pyle sing the *Special's* opening verse, then let Wooten's scorching fiddle take center stage.

The dialogue is expanded to encompass the entire ensemble, which allows the musicians a chance to banter while being introduced to the listening audience:

Wooten: *Comin' right on down the line, now, pulling up a heavy grade. Hey, Bill, where you gonna get off this train at?*

Monroe: *Down about Atlanta, Georgia, boy. Where's you gwine?*
Wooten: *I'm going up about Nashville, Tennessee. Where are you going, Cousin Wilbur?*
Wilbur: *I'm going down to Birmingham, Alabama.*
Wooten: *What for?*
Wilbur: *Ain't no ham like Birmingham!*
Wooten: *Pete, where you gonna get off?*
Pyle: *Well, I'm Memphis bound, I believe.*

The *Special* quickly became Monroe's concert showpiece as well. And, as various Blue Grass Boys—including such notables as Lester Flatt and Earl Scruggs—struck out on their own, they carried the tune with them. Gradually, then, Ervin's "little ole fiddlin' piece" became a standard for virtually every acoustic combo playing Monroe-style music.

Concurrently, Tennessee native Fiddlin' Arthur Smith, who, according to Charles Wolfe, "elevated fiddling from simply a folk music to a folk art," also adopted the *Special*, and performed it "with the usual histrionics that have come to characterize that song" on radio and at personal appearances throughout the 1940s. Smith, himself an excellent trick fiddler who played for a time with cowboy singer Jimmy Wakely, found that high-rollers at Las Vegas casinos reacted to the *Special* just as enthusiastically as did rural crowds at county fairs.

Still, it is doubtful that Ervin derived much financial benefit from the growing popularity of his tune. It had not yet appeared on a best-selling record, and the fan base for early bluegrass, while enthusiastic, remained outside the musical mainstream. He may have earned nominal sums from Monroe's recording and others, but it is doubtful that ASCAP, which only half-heartedly monitored the independent radio stations on which most country records were played, was very effective at tracking and collecting performance royalties.

Meanwhile, in Florida, Chubby Wise was also playing the *Special,* and was soon to evolve from locally popular old-time fiddler to bluegrass pioneer.

VI

Chubby Wise and
the Birth of Bluegrass

*I'll visit with anybody, have a picture made with anybody and auto-
graph for anybody. When I get to where I'm too good to do that I'll
stay at the house, brother, and get out of show business.*
Chubby Wise in 1988

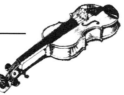

S hortly after the Rouse Bothers departed Jacksonville, Chubby Wise moved his
small family sixty miles southwest to Gainesville (population 10,465).

Although it was home to the University of Florida, Gainesville in the mid- to
late-1930s remained primarily an agricultural center; Alachua County farmers produced corn, peanuts, pecans, tobacco, watermelons, vegetables, citrus, potatoes,
tung oil, forest products, dairy, poultry, and beef cattle. Indeed, so common were
wayward cows grazing along the shoulder of old U.S. 41 (now U.S. 441) that
motorists sometimes collided with the animals—and were held liable for damages,
since bovines were presupposed to have the right of way.

Also, the community was very much a part of Stetson Kennedy's *Palmetto
Country*: Deep South in ambiance and attitude, and with considerable vice thriving
behind a virtuous facade of blue laws.

According to *Alachua County: A Sesquicentennial Tribute* (Alachua County
Historical Commission), jook joints "were generally out of the city limits, with
something like a filling station in front of a two-story building, often with cabins
out back [to facilitate prostitution]. Some were known as places of danger, because
there were often reports of fights, a number of them being fatal. Tales were told
of other attractions being available, including alcoholic beverages—although the
county had been legally dry for years."

The Ku Klux Klan, in an effort to preserve the morals of male university students, had torched several houses of ill fame in the mid-1930s, and had later managed to rally a vocal faction of concerned citizens behind an effort to ban from campus a Roman Catholic priest who was "preparing the innocent students for seduction by Rome by organizing a Dramatic Club."

Yet, Alachua County also exemplified old Florida at its most breathtaking; just fifteen minutes southwest of Gainesville, Marjorie Kinnan Rawlings was living and writing at Cross Creek, rhapsodizing about the "half-wild backwoods country" surrounding her now-famous Cracker cottage. And the fishing was fine. Chubby, an avid angler, surely joined fellow fishermen on the Santa Fe River, where red bellies, blue bream, stumpknockers, and catfish were abundant.

Chubby landed a day job driving a city bus—"If there was a bus or a cab to be driven, Russell was gonna drive it," states Carl Dees—but soon found full-time musical employment with a popular, Gainesville-based dance band called the Jubilee Hillbillies. (It was as a member of this group that the increasingly rotund Robert Russell Wise appears to have been saddled with the nickname "Chubby").

The Hillbillies, despite their backwoods moniker, performed western swing and pop standards in addition to country music and, from 1941 through 1942, showcased their versatility via a daily broadcast on radio station WRUF, which was owned by the university.

Following Pearl Harbor, able-bodied band members were routinely drafted or joined the armed forces. Because of his childhood injury, Chubby was exempt from military service and, for a time, attempted to keep the Hillbillies viable. But an opportunity arose in March 1943 that was simply too exciting to pass up.

"I was listening to Bill Monroe on the *Grand Ole Opry* on Saturday night," Chubby said in 1982. "I heard Bill announce that Howdy Forrester [Howard Wilson "Howdy" Forrester, Monroe's fiddler] had to go into the Navy, and that this would be his last night with them. That told me something. I said, 'Bill's going to need a fiddle player.' The next Monday, I took a train [Chubby, like Ervin, was always terrified of flying and, in any case, could probably not have afforded an airline ticket] to Nashville. I just sat around until the weekend. On Saturday night, I threw the fiddle under my arm, went backstage [at the Ryman Auditorium, then home of the *Grand Ole Opry*] and told the man at the door, 'My name's Wise, I'm from Florida, and I've come to see Bill Monroe. I want to have a job. Now, he's got to have a fiddle player, and I'm a fiddler.' So, the man said, 'Alright, he's in his dressing room.'"

Backstage at the *Opry* was—and still is, to a lesser degree—an accessible and informal place, bustling with performers, their families, their friends, and their fans. On any given Saturday night it was Hillbilly Central, packed with up-and-comers and down-and-outers, song-pluggers and pickers, who wandered in an out at will. Yet, even in this happily chaotic environment, Bill Monroe could not have been an easy man to approach.

A musical genius and a visionary, Monroe was also an aloof and imperious man, described in the 1960s by folklorist and bluegrass music promoter Ralph Rinzler as "a legendary figure in the world of country music; his regal bearing, pride almost to the point of arrogance, terse expression and profound musical dynamism have given rise to countless tales among the few who know him, and the many who admire him."

However, the garrulous Chubby, unintimidated by the *Opry's* icy demeanor, undoubtedly established his credibility by reminding Monroe of his reputed connection to the *Special*, and then auditioned by playing *Katy Hill* and *Footprints in the Snow*. "He didn't grin much," Chubby said of Monroe, whose musical standards were notoriously exacting and intractable. "But he just shook his head as if to say, 'Yeah, man, that's what I want.' I never will forget it. That's the only two tunes the man heard me play, and he hired me on the spot."

Monroe then instructed the newest Blue Grass Boy—who had spent three restless nights at the seedy Clarkson Hotel—to retrieve his clothes, and to be at the bus prepared to leave for a North Carolina engagement in two hours.

Could it really have been that easy? In fact, Monroe's musicians frequently were hired in this manner. In 1949, a young factory worker from Sneedsville, Tennessee, appeared backstage at the Ryman after hearing that guitarist/vocalist Mac Wiseman was leaving the Blue Grass Boys. Jimmy Martin, who would later achieve stardom fronting the legendary Sunny Mountain Boys, recalled in a 1999 interview how Chubby offered encouragement and praise during his impromptu audition:

"He [Monroe] took me in there and asked Mac Wiseman to let me have the guitar, which was the one that Lester Flatt had played with Bill. It was Bill's Martin D-28 herringbone. So, I sang one with Bill, then I played a solo, *Poor Ellen Smith*. Then I played *Orange Blossom Special* with Chubby Wise. Bill asked Chubby what he thought, and Chubby said, 'Lordy! I thought Lester Flatt had it, but this boy's flat got it!'" Martin got the job, and would shortly thereafter appear on classic Monroe recordings such as *Uncle Pen*, *Walking in Jerusalem*, and *On and On*.

Before departing Nashville with Monroe's entourage, Chubby telephoned Geneva, who had moved to back Lake City with eight-year-old Marvelene and was living with her parents. "I was glad for him," Geneva says. "I was always proud of his music. But I didn't want him to be gone from home so much."

Nonetheless, with Marvelene in tow and a precious few belongings stowed in a suitcase, she caught a train the next day for Tennessee and a new life.

WILLIAM SMITH MONROE, WHO would be honored by President Ronald Reagan as "the only living American who created a style of music," was born on September 13, 1911, in the Jerusalem Ridge community near Rosine, Kentucky, the youngest of eight children. His farmer father, James Buchanan "Buck" Monroe, was a stepdancer; his mother, Melissa, played fiddle, accordion, and harmonica.

Young Bill, who was introverted and painfully self-conscious due to crossed eyes (later corrected), took up the mandolin somewhat grudgingly, since older brothers Birch and Charlie already played the fiddle and the guitar. He was generally ignored by his siblings and teased by his peers, and later recalled his childhood as "a sad life, a lonesome life."

Bill's mother died when he was eight; his father when he was fifteen. So the youngster was cared for by his uncle, Pendelton Vandiver, an old-time fiddler whom Bill would later immortalize in the bluegrass classic *Uncle Pen* ("Uncle Pen played the fiddle, Lord how it'd ring/You could hear it talk, you could hear it sing."). Pen was much in demand for square dances, and would use Bill as a backup musician on either guitar or mandolin. In addition, and perhaps equally important, Pen bolstered Bill's self-esteem by treating him as an equal.

On the liner notes of Bill Monroe's *Uncle Pen*, a 1969 album released by Decca, Monroe praised the old man as much for his kindness as for his musicianship: "A man that old, and crippled [Pen had suffered a broken hip that failed to heal properly], that would cook for you and see that you had a bed and a place to stay and something for breakfast and dinner and supper, and you know it come hard for him to get…"

Concurrently, Bill and an African-American fiddler and guitarist named Arnold Shultz teamed to play dances and parties around west-central Kentucky, with Schultz fiddling and Bill seconding him on guitar. But it was Schultz's country-blues guitar picking—by all accounts he was extraordinarily skilled—that left the biggest impression.

"There's things in my music, you know, that come from Arnold Schultz," Monroe said in 1980. "I use a lot of his runs in my music. I don't say I make them the same way he did, because he was powerful with it." Later, when asked to list the three greatest old-time musicians, Monroe stated: "It all leads back to this old colored man from Kentucky." Schultz, who died in 1931 at the age of forty-five, was never recorded—but his sound can be heard in the music of Monroe and many mainstream country artists.

When Uncle Pen died in 1930, eighteen-year-old Bill was reunited with Birch and Charlie in East Chicago, Indiana, where they had migrated to find work as the Great Depression worsened. Bill and his brothers labored in an oil refinery, and played music radio station WJKS in nearby Gary.

Also, the trio and their girlfriends joined a touring dance team affiliated with Chicago's *WLS Barn Dance* program (Bill was still proudly showcasing his old-time hoofing skills as an octogenarian). Birch, however, soon left the group, leaving Bill and Charlie to seek full-time musical careers as the Monroe Brothers.

In 1934 the duo landed a sponsor—Texas Crystals, makers of a laxative—and in 1935, after appearing on company-sponsored programs on radio stations KFNF in Shenandoah, Iowa, and WAAW in Omaha, Nebraska, they moved to the Carolinas, to WIS in Columbia, South Carolina, and finally to WBT in Charlotte, North Carolina. There, they performed mostly traditional songs, albeit with a blues predilection, and earned considerable regional popularity with their sweet vocal harmonies and vigorous instrumental breaks.

In 1936, Bill and Charlie were dropped by the financially troubled Texas Crystals, then quickly picked up by a larger competitor, the Crazy Water Crystals Company of Mineral, Wells, Texas. Their WBT program was called *The Crazy Crystals Barn Dance*.

In February of that year, at the behest of Eli Oberstein, the brothers traveled to Charlotte to record the first of some sixty sides for Bluebird, which over the next two years released distinctive Monroe Brothers renditions of traditional gospel songs, such as *What Would You Give in Exchange for Your Soul?*, and seminal bluegrass hybrids, such *as Nine Pound Hammer*.

However, the brothers split acrimoniously to form separate bands in 1938, and by the following year Bill Monroe and the Blue Grass Boys—consisting of Monroe, guitarist Cleo Davis, bassist Amos Garen, and fiddler Art Wooten—had been hired by the *Opry* on the strength of *Muleskinner Blues*, a Jimmie Rodgers hit that Monroe's rafter-reaching tenor seemed tailor-made to sing. (Monroe's astonishing vocal range would spawn a popular one-liner: "That was so high it would take Bill Monroe to sing bass to it.") He would then complete two more sessions for RCA— including the Atlanta session at which the *Special* was recorded—before beginning a legendary association with Columbia Records in 1945.

When Chubby first approached Monroe in 1943—"like a big rooster from Florida with my fiddle under my arm"—the Kentuckian was among the *Opry's* biggest attractions, traveling with a circus tent because most small towns did not have venues capable of accommodating the throngs that his show attracted. He and his troupe toured almost constantly, sometimes working six or seven days a week performing three or four shows a day in addition to their Saturday night *Opry* segment.

Ricky Skaggs, a bluegrass musician who achieved mainstream popularity in the 1980s, describes the excitement surrounding a Monroe personal appearance in the 1940s: "When they were on stage, it sounded like the Beatles were on stage," Skaggs says. "You'd hear these country people screaming at the top of their voices, hearing this new music no one had heard before. It was a new sound; it was a new day for this music." And it was a bargain: admission was sixty cents for adults, thirty cents for children.

Chubby was clearly in tall cotton. But oddly enough, he briefly left hillbilly music's hottest road show in April 1945 to join Curley Williams and the Georgia Peach Pickers, a combo whose style veered more toward western swing.

Curley, who would later write the Hank Williams hit *Half as Much*, was also an *Opry* cast member from 1942 through mid-1945, and may have persuaded Chubby that a stint with the Peach Pickers would be more lucrative and less pressure-packed than remaining with Monroe, a notorious tightwad who was unyielding in his view of how bluegrass music ought to be played.

Whatever the case, when Williams and his troupe left Nashville for the West Coast, where western music was booming and a film career was beckoning, Chubby stayed behind and rejoined his formidable mentor in March 1946. It proved to be a fortuitous decision, as celluloid stardom eluded Williams; he and the Peach Pickers appeared in only one movie, *Riders of the Lone Star*, with Charles Starrett.

It was this definitive combination of Blue Grass Boys—Chubby, bassist Howard Watts (a Gainesville friend of Chubby's known professionally as Cedric Rainwater), guitarist Lester Flatt, and banjoist Earl Scruggs—that most musicologists agree provided the genesis of bluegrass music as it would be defined from that time forward.

Wrote Doug Green in *Country Roots* (Hawthorn Books): "Monroe's bands have included brilliant musicians ever since, but that particular group was a very special one, full of excitement, confidence, and the exhilaration of creation. Since they were together for nearly three years (rare with Monroe, as with many hard-traveling bands), they developed a smooth cohesiveness and a highly polished sound that have set them still further apart from later versions of the Blue Grass Boys."

That sound was preserved on a series of twenty-eight immortal sides, many of which were recorded in Chicago for Columbia Records during September 1946 and October 1947. The output from those sessions—*Why Did You Wander?, Toy Heart, Will You Be Loving Another Man? Footprints in the Snow, Blue Moon of Kentucky, I'm Going Back to Old Kentucky, Little Cabin Home on the Hill, It's Mighty Dark to Travel, Molly and Tenbrooks, Remember the Cross*, and *Little Community Church*—represents "classic bluegrass at its zenith," according to Bill C. Malone, author of the scholarly *Country Music U.S.A.* (University of Texas Press).

Agrees Lance LeRoy: "It is inconceivable that any serious student of music would dispute the assertion that [the Columbia recordings] were the first to define for the world the music now called bluegrass. These releases made a far more profound and widespread impact on the genre than any single event before or since."

It was the inclusion of Scruggs, with his three-finger banjo picking style, which has been most widely credited with rounding out Monroe's sound and broadening its appeal—but the impact of Chubby's rich, bluesy fiddle passages cannot be overstated. (It should be pointed out that the multi-talented fiddler also contributed some fine guitar work to several of Monroe's gospel cuts.)

Wrote Richard Smith in *Can't You Hear Me Callin': The Life of Bill Monroe* (Little, Brown): "Chubby Wise was firmly establishing the bluegrass style of fiddling. Chubby took his cues from the vocals, producing music that was incisive yet not harsh, powerful yet tender."

In a 1974 interview with Charles Wolfe on WMOT-FM, the campus radio station at Middle Tennessee State University, no less an authority than Monroe himself rated

Chubby among the best of his many renowned former fiddlers—although his praise was as parsimonious as his paychecks.

Comparing Chubby with Howdy Forrester, Monroe said, "Chubby's a little bit more a lonesome-type fiddler, and he plays some blues in it. And Howdy—now, he's the first man who played with me that played double-stop [two notes played together in harmony], and Howdy knows that neck all the way, and he knows how to get that tone out, give the fiddle a chance. Chubby might could have beat Howdy on a song, but Howdy would have beat Chubby on a fiddle piece like *Cotton-Eyed Joe* or stuff like that. So it balances out."

Aspiring musicians everywhere listened closely to Monroe's recordings, and sought to imitate the sound of each instrument. Consequently, the erstwhile outcast from Lake City influenced a new generation of fiddlers, some of whom would go on to make musical history of their own.

Among the youngsters that Chubby inspired was Kissimmee-bred virtuoso Vassar Clements, who would join the Blue Grass Boys in 1949. Clements recalls first meeting Chubby in 1944, when Monroe's show played Osceola High School.

"My family shared a house with a man named Bun Bass," says Clements, then sixteen years old. "Somehow, he knew Chubby. So, one night after a show, Chubby came over, along with Monroe and Zeke Clements [a cowboy singer unrelated to Vassar]. Of course, they brought their instruments, and let me sit in and pick with them. I was trying to learn the guitar and the fiddle then, but I just played guitar that night. I had been listening to those people for years on our old battery-powered radio, and I idolized them. Let me tell you, that was quite an experience for a young man."

However, it was Chubby's music that most excited Clements, inspiring him to drop the guitar in favor of the fiddle. Five years later, when Clements auditioned for Monroe, he got the job in large part because he had learned to copy Chubby note for note.

"I went to Nashville and met Bill backstage at the *Opry*," says Clements. "It cost me twenty-five cents to get in. Well, Bill remembered me from Florida, and let me play for him. At that time, I didn't know any fiddle tunes except the ones I'd copied from Chubby, but luckily those are the ones he asked me to play—*Footprints in the Snow, Blue Moon* of Kentucky and, of course, the *Special*. Well, he liked what he heard and hired me."

Ultimately, Clements would develop his own distinctive and decidedly progressive sound, earning five Grammy nominations and establishing himself among the industry's foremost fiddle stylists. He later worked with bluegrass pioneers Jim and Jesse McReynolds and Jimmy Martin, and was featured on the Nitty Gritty Dirt Band's landmark album *Will the Circle Be Unbroken*.

In the late 1970s, Clements performed with the Earl Scruggs Revue and the Grateful Dead, appeared as himself in the Robert Altman film *Nashville,* and became one of Music City's most sought-after session musicians. Still, he considers Chubby to be the best bluegrass fiddler who ever rosined up a bow. "He just had the prettiest notes," says Clements. "He could get more out of one string than most people could get out of five. Nobody else had that tone; nobody else could get that feeling out of the instrument."

Another Wise admirer is Richard Greene, a classically trained violinist who played with Monroe from October 1966 to January 1967, and later recorded the *Special* with a bluegrass-rock fusion group called Seatrain.

In 1996, when questioned about his role in bringing "the symphonic sound of the violin" to bluegrass music, Greene replied: "Symphonic is a very general term. I think a classical sound is a better way to put it. And, to be really accurate, I would say that Chubby Wise, who was Bill's fiddler on the recordings when the music tipped from old-time to bluegrass, was the first one to do that. I don't know if he was a classically trained musician, but it doesn't matter. He brought those values to bluegrass music, and that created a serious challenge for all the fiddlers that followed him. They could never have his tone; and no fiddler between him and me had that sound. They had fiddle sound, which is a different thing. You can't fault it; it's a beautiful, pure sound, but it doesn't have the fullness of tone that is involved in classical violin."

George Custer agrees with Greene's assessment of Chubby's impact: "You can learn the mechanics of playing the fiddle, or the violin, just as a visual artist can learn the mechanics of using a paint and a brush. But the great fiddlers, just like the great painters, learn to personalize their work. Chubby painted his sounds in multicolored variations. And his music had a beautiful, bluesy sound. Perhaps not quite as guttural as Negro blues, but there is an element of blues that makes his work so distinctive."

While working with Monroe, Chubby pursued other musical opportunities. In 1946, for example, he wrote the melody for former Blue Grass Boy Clyde Moody's hit record *Shenandoah Waltz*, basing his composition upon a tune called *The Sidewalk Waltz* by Cajun fiddler Harry Choates. "I heard that song while we were on tour in Texas," Chubby said. "Somebody put a nickel in a jukebox, and man, I cocked my ears up. That was the prettiest sound I'd ever heard in my life. As long as I was there, I was shoving nickels in—I wanted to hear that song over and over. Then I went back to hotel, got my fiddle out, and in about thirty or forty minutes I had *Shenandoah Waltz* wrote."

Of course, the sharing—or the swiping—of melodies was a hallowed country music tradition, perhaps best exemplified by two widely known standards that employ precisely the same tune: *Great Speckled Bird* and *I'm Thinking Tonight of My Blue Eyes*. Often—but not always—such appropriated works were ancient folk melodies long in the public domain. "Bill Monroe said he would hear a tune he liked, and would write it just as close to that tune as he could without [copying it exactly]," said Chubby, perhaps a bit too defensively. "There's no law against that.

That's how most [popular country and bluegrass songs] were born—don't you ever forget it."

Additionally, Chubby earned renown as a studio musician in genres outside bluegrass, backing crooner Red Foley—Chubby's fiddle highlights Foley's tearful canine classic *Old Shep*—gospel singer Wally Fowler and, most notably, Hank Williams. The Williams sessions, for MGM Records, took place in Nashville on November 6 and 7, 1947, and also included Zeke Turner, one of Red Foley's Pleasant Valley Boys, on electric guitar; and Jerry Byrd, who had backed both Foley and Ernest Tubb, on steel guitar.

With the AFM strike looming, producer Fred Rose was attempting to stockpile as much Williams material as possible, and had personally assembled this no-nonsense trio after forbidding Hank to use his own band. "You just do your part, and they'll do theirs," Rose told his temperamental protégé, adding that each tune had to be nailed in one take.

Although Williams' style was far removed from bluegrass, Chubby demonstrated his adaptability on a trifle called *Rootie Tootie*, along with two songs that would become Williams standards: *Honky Tonkin'* and *Mansion on the Hill*.

Mostly, however, Chubby's years as a Blue Grass Boy were spent traversing the nation's highways. Naturally, the veteran cabby did most of the driving for Monroe and, like every touring musician, he had his share of road stories. He particularly enjoyed relating an incident regarding the sudden but short-lived religious conversion of Uncle Dave Macon, who happened to be aboard Monroe's vintage Chevrolet bus as Chubby navigated an icy mountain road in West Virginia.

As Chubby told it, the hard-drinking Macon, who always kept a bottle of Jack Daniels in what appeared to be a physician's medicine satchel, awoke from his slumber to find the bus fishtailing and sliding as Chubby fought to retain control. The colorful old showman, who referred to his companions as "Goodboy," quickly assessed the situation, and fearing that the end was near, began "preaching" to a distracted Chubby, concluding his sermon with a vow that, if he survived, he would change his ways: "You know Goodboy, I'm thinking. I'm gettin' old. Ain't gonna be around much longer. I'm gonna have to slow down on my nippin.' I nips a little too much sometimes." When the bus safely reached the bottom of the treacherous slope and came to a halt, Macon cleared his throat, turned to the musician seated behind him, and said, "Hey, Goodboy, hand that black bag up here."

Chubby always laughed uproariously—as did his listeners—when he repeated this yarn. However, the Uncle Dave anecdote may have been apocryphal; old-time guitarist Walter Bailes, for one, claimed that the incident happened near Newport, Tennessee, in a bus carrying the Bailes Brothers, the McGee Brothers, and Curly Fox along with the backsliding Uncle Dave.

Still, musicians—particularly married ones—had safety concerns quite apart from highway mishaps. Gene Christian joined the Blue Grass Boys in 1950, first replacing legendary hellraiser Benny "The Big Tiger" Martin on fiddle, then moving to the bass after Chubby was hired.

Once, when preparing to leave for a weekend tour, Gene was seated in the back seat of a new Hudson alongside Monroe and Bessie Lee Mauldin, the *Opry* star's longtime girlfriend and frequent traveling companion. Chubby was at the wheel, and had just cranked up the engine when shots rang out. Monroe's estranged wife, Carolyn, was running across the parking lot, firing a revolver at the vehicle. It could not be assumed that she was merely being melodramatic; two years earlier she had savaged her philandering husband's leg with an ice pick.

"That was a brand new car, and Bill had just told Chubby to take it easy for the first five hundred miles so it could get broke in just right," recalls Gene. "But it got broke in a lot faster than he figured. We hauled out of there, and I was scared half to death. Bill didn't have much to say about it; just somethin' like, 'Aw, she's crazy as hell.'"

Elaborate practical jokes also relieved the tedium of constant travel, and many were at Chubby's expense. Vassar Clements says that Monroe, not known for his sense of humor, once arranged with local police to have Chubby "arrested" following a show.

"The police came backstage and told Chubby that he had to come with them, that he was under arrest," Clements says. "Chubby didn't suspect that anything was going on. He said, 'Under arrest? What for?' The police said something like, 'You know what you did.' Well, they started to take Chubby out, and he was yelling back at Monroe, 'Bill! Bill! Tell 'em who I am!' Bill just shook his head and kept walking. He let 'em take Chubby into town and lock him up before he finally cut the joke off."

VII

Sweeter Than the Flowers:
Triumph and Tragedy

Carrying Sweeter Than the Flowers *was just like a woman carrying a baby. Now, a song is in your heart and soul just like a child. It's a load to write about your own mother, and our mother was a very sweet woman. She loved all of her children—she had 15 head of children—and we all loved her. And when she passed away, our main remembrance of Mama was that she was more sweeter than any flower.*
Ervin T. Rouse in 1977

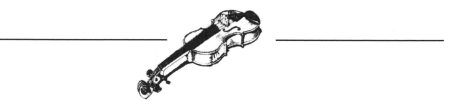

By 1940, discouraged by the indifference greeting their Bluebird releases, Ervin and Gordon had returned to Florida, and had resumed their bread-and-butter Miami Beach resort hotel appearances along with busking.

But Ervin, now twenty-three and still smarting over Elon Smith's rejection, was more anxious than ever to inject a degree of stability into his life by getting married and starting a family of his own. In fact, he already had a likely partner in mind: a North Carolina teenager named Hattie "Louallie" Whitehurst.

The star-crossed pair had met three years earlier, when Ervin, Gordon, and Earl performed in the town square at Winterville, North Carolina, just south of Greenville. Louallie, then sixteen, was pretty, sweet-natured and, as an added bonus, played the guitar and sang. "A next-door neighbor told me that the Rouse Brothers were going to be downtown," says Louallie. "Ervin's sister [Bettie McGowan] had a friend who was a friend of my brother's, so I knew who they were. Well, I went to their show, and Ervin was the best entertainer I'd ever seen."

Subsequently, the two music-lovers developed an intense but sporadic romance, hindered—or perhaps helped—by Ervin's long absences. "He was a handsome man then," recalls Louallie. "About five-foot-ten, with a head of curly black hair. But he traveled most of the time, and we only saw one another a couple of times a year, usually when the brothers were coming through [eastern North Carolina] on their way to New York."

Then, in the summer of 1940 Louallie's life changed in dramatic fashion. Bettie's husband died suddenly, leaving his thirty-five-year-old widow with several income-generating commercial buildings in downtown Greenville. Alone but financially secure, Bettie decided to leave North Carolina and its bittersweet associations for Miami and a new life. Seeking companionship for the drive, and perhaps playing matchmaker, she asked Louallie to come along. "I was anxious to make the trip," Louallie says. "Bettie said she was going to rent an apartment, and that I could stay with her as long as I wanted. But I never had any intention of getting married. I intended to have a nice vacation and then go back home."

Louallie, however, was dazzled by the Magic City—and by Ervin. She enjoyed the lively nightspots that Ervin and Gordon frequented, and was particularly thrilled when the brothers asked her to join them onstage for a series of performances at a Hollywood lounge called the Banyon Club. "I could yodel in those days," says Louallie. "They'd play and I'd sing whatever was popular. We had so much fun."

But, when she cut her finger and developed blood poisoning, Louallie was sur-prised at Ervin's abrupt callousness. "The blood poisoning had made me very, very sick," she recalls. "The owner of the club took one look at me and told me that I ought to be home. Ervin, though, became angry. He said that he had to work regard-less of how he felt—which was certainly true—and that I ought to do the same thing. The way he reacted really hurt me."

Yet, galvanized by Ervin's talent, Louallie attributed this outburst—and others like it—to an artistic temperament. In fact, she says, Ervin was typically gentle, polite, and solicitous. Ultimately, he apologized for his rough edges, professed his love, and asked Louallie, as he had Elon, if she could find happiness married to a traveling musician.

Enchanted, Louallie said that she did not wish to remake the young fiddler into something that he was not, and could never be. "I didn't expect that Ervin would do anything other than play music," Louallie says. "I didn't want him to do anything else. Music was his life, and I understood that from the beginning."

On January 21, 1941, Ervin T. Rouse and Hattie Whitehurst were quietly wed by a notary public; the ceremony was held in a private home, and no family members were present. (Bettie was married two months later, to a blind trumpet player named Howard "Hal" Lane, leader of a locally popular three-piece combo.) The newlyweds purchased a small frame home at 3729 Northwest 20th Court in the Alapatta section of Miami, a well-kept, working-class neighborhood populated largely by young families. Gordon and Carrie, having escaped Little Trailers, lived nearby, at 1067 Northwest 101st Street.

"Obviously, I didn't go back to North Carolina," Louallie says. "But it didn't take me long to realize that Ervin had no idea what it took to make a happy marriage. He was smart about music, but he lacked any common sense." This indisputable fact could not have come as a complete surprise. Yet, Ervin was difficult to resist, combining as he did musical brilliance with equal measures of earthy charisma and childlike vulnerability.

Louallie, undoubtedly, was swayed by the total package: an intriguing, enigmatic man working in a glamorous profession; a man with whom life would be an adventure, far removed from the monotony of her sleepy hometown. She was not the first young woman to choose such a path, nor was she the first to regret it.

Certainly, it was clear from the outset that Mr. and Mrs. Ervin T. Rouse were not destined to lead a typical suburban lifestyle. In the summer of 1941, Ervin, Louallie (who was by then three months pregnant), Gordon, and Carrie—along with Ervin's small dog—set out on a sweltering cross-country odyssey in Ervin's 1939 Chevrolet.

The brothers, perhaps energized by praise from the likes of Meyer Horowitz and Paula Stone, were determined to reach Hollywood and break into western movies; not an altogether absurd notion, since celluloid singing cowboys always needed comical sidekicks.

The Rouses were surely aware that Leonard Slye, a singer with the Pioneer Trio (later the Sons of the Pioneers), had walked into Republic Pictures without an appointment and had walked out with a contract and a new name: Roy Rogers. And, of course, youngsters everywhere were enthralled by the wholesomely bloodless screen exploits of Gene Autry, Bob Baker, Johnny Bond, Smith Ballew, Dick Foran, Ken Maynard, Tex Ritter, Jimmy Wakely, and many others who wielded both guns and guitars with equal expertise.

Indeed, the late 1930s and early 1940s saw Hollywood emerge as a mecca for country musicians and cornpone comics. (Cowboy star Buck Jones lamented that children "would get the wrong idea that all you need to stop an Indian or a rustler is a loud voice accompanied by a hillbilly band.") So, although the brothers may have set a reasonable goal, they went about trying to achieve it in typical Rouse fashion: on a proverbial wing and a prayer, and with only the sketchiest itinerary in mind. The "plan," if it could be described as such, was to purchase a fourteen-foot trailer large enough to sleep four, and to start driving—stopping along the way just long enough to perform in favorably disposed bars and hotels, thereby earning enough money to continue the journey.

The brothers and their wives would follow the Gulf of Mexico through the Florida panhandle, skirt coastal Alabama, Mississippi, and Louisiana, then ramble through the heart of Texas enroute to New Mexico, Arizona, and finally, the Golden State. The route was Highway 90, which snaked through Tallahassee, Pensacola,

Mobile, Pascagula, Biloxi, Gulf Port, New Orleans, Lafayette, Lake Charles, Beaumont, Houston, and beyond.

What did Ervin and Gordon intend to do once they reached Hollywood? According to Louallie and Carrie, their freewheeling husbands did not give the matter much thought. It is conceivable, however, that Bob Miller may have provided some leads. The well-connected Miller, along with other music publishers in the late 1930s, had begun to produce western-themed songbooks, licensing the names and photographs of cowboy film stars to package and sell sheet music.

Also, the brothers were acquainted with another Miller protégé, cowboy yodeler Elton Britt, who had been based in Los Angeles since 1930 and would later record Miller's World War II anthem *There's A Star-Spangled Banner Waving Somewhere.* In Ervin's scrapbook is a Britt publicity photograph bearing the inscription, "To Gordon and Ervin: My best wishes to two swell boys."

The "swell boys" also knew Zeke Clements, an Alabama-born singer who had appeared in several B westerns as Charles Starrett's singing sidekick, and had provided the voice of "Bashful" in the Walt Disney animated film *Snow White and the Seven Dwarfs.* Although Clements had left Hollywood in 1939, returning to Nashville and the *Opry*, the "Alabama Cowboy" may have regaled the brothers with appealing tales of the glamour and potential stardom awaiting them on the west coast. (Clements, who died in 1994, opined in an unpublished interview with Charles Wolfe that Ervin and his siblings were "all of them crazy." Although he does not discuss how or where he and the brothers became acquainted, it is possible that they met at the Village Barn, where Clements also performed in the 1930s.)

In any case, the hopeful young gypsies racked up the miles by day, stopping to rest in tourist camps, parking lots, or anywhere else weary travelers might remain undisturbed for a few hours. "We had a very nice time," recalls Carrie. "I remember those as being wonderful times, even though we didn't have air-conditioning, and even though the trailer was small. On that trip, Louallie and I became like sisters."

Upon their arrival in a city sizable enough to support a nightclub or two, it was ever-dependable Gordon's responsibility to arrange for work. He undoubtedly explained to club managers—without having to exaggerate much—that the Rouse Brothers, popular Bluebird recording artists, had just completed a series of prestigious New York engagements, and happened to be passing through while enroute to Hollywood. Would there be any interest in booking these top-notch entertainers for a night or two? There nearly always was—especially considering that the duo would work for tips.

At times, they were treated like stars. In Mobile, Alabama, the Rouse Brothers headlined at the respectable Cawthon Hotel ("The Spot That Care Forgot"), and ultimately stayed two weeks at the behest of management. But they do not appear to have remained more than a night or two in any other city before arriving in wide-open Houston.

There, the venues were a far cry from the Royal Palm Club or even the Village Barn. At the Club Continental, for example, the "Hillbilly Comics" were billed behind Sue Webb, "Queen of the Hula;" and "Girls, Girls, Girls." At the Ranch Nite Club, the "Real Hillbillies From the Mountains of Tennessee (sic)" appeared in a "Giant Girl-Thrill Show" which also featured Mona Leslie, "The Girl With the Perfect Body;" and Jean Bayne, "Strip Artist."

The brothers also found work in Fort Worth, where at the Clover Club the "Aristocrats of Comedy" were billed behind Wilhelmina "The Queen of Strips;" Bobbie Corey, "The Girl You Must See;" Topsy Boyd, "The Girl Who Sits On Her Own Head;" Billie Martin, "The Girl in Cellophane;" and, again, the flawless Miss Leslie.

Yet, despite competition from scantily clad showgirls, Ervin and Gordon managed to more than hold their own, and audiences responded favorably to their preposterous shtick and their surprisingly proficient playing. "The Rouse Brothers have 'em rolling in the aisles at the Ranch Nite Club with their music ranging from hillbilly to classical," wrote an entertainment reporter with the *Houston Post*. "Believe it or not, these boys are marvelous musicians!"

Perhaps the strangest of the brothers' Texas engagements was at yet another Houston nightspot, the Reno Club, where the main attraction was the "Sensational Fat Girl Revue," in which young women weighing a minimum of three hundred pounds danced individually and as part of a corpulent chorus line. "Those girls could dance a lot better than the skinny ones could," recalls Carrie, who attended many of the brothers' shows—which sometimes ran until 2 a.m.—while Louallie, pregnant and uncomfortable, usually languished in the trailer. "We went into places that I wouldn't go into now," says Carrie, who became a born-again Christian in the 1950s. "But we were young, and back in those days it just didn't bother us much."

Still, the Rouse Brothers and their wives had tarried in the Lone Star State far too long—more than three months. In San Antonio, Louallie went into labor and was rushed to Nix Hospital, where on December 18, 1941, Ervin Thomas Rouse Jr. (called "Tommy") was born.

Among the well-wishers visiting the hospital was singer David McEnery, better known as Red River Dave, a San Antonio native who appeared on radio station WOAI and recorded for numerous independent labels. Dave and the Rouse Brothers, both of whom were affiliated with Bob Miller, had met during nightclub engagements, and had possibly even performed together during their extended Texas layover.

"Ervin was just thrilled," Carrie says. "He said he had to get back to North Carolina immediately and show off that baby to his family. To him, that was the only baby in the world." Because four adults, a newborn, and a dog sharing one car and one trailer would have made traveling arduous at best, Gordon and Carrie purchased a 1935 Chevrolet and another trailer for the trip back east, thereby aborting a six-month journey roughly halfway toward its original destination.

What had the brothers been thinking? Why had they lingered in Texas as Louallie's delivery date drew near? Most likely, Gordon had assumed that Ervin would agree to continue the trek regardless of when the baby was born, and therefore saw little urgency in accelerating an already pliant schedule. Also, the brothers had established a reputation in Houston, San Antonio, Fort Worth, and points in between as dependable crowd-pleasers, and as a result were much in demand at clubs, restaurants, and even rodeos. "It costs money to go to California, and we had just been living day to day," Carrie points out. "When you're making good money, you know, it's hard to walk away from that. Plus, I don't think any of us realized— and I don't even think I realized—the seriousness of having a newborn baby and being on the road."

Just as consequential in their decision to turn back was the December 7 Japanese attack on Pearl Harbor, which finally pushed America into World War II. The Rouse families, frightened and enraged by this shocking turn of events, concluded that the west coast had suddenly become a far less enticing destination than initially thought.

Therefore, anxious to return to comfortably familiar territory, Ervin, Louallie, and little Tommy headed for North Carolina, while Gordon and Carrie set out for Florida. At least for the time being, the film industry would have to manage without the Rouse Brothers.

IN THE SUMMER OF 1942, sixteen-year-old Gene Christian of Mt. Pleasant, Tennessee, was visiting his mother's home in a quiet southwest Miami neighborhood. The teenager, who played mandolin, guitar, and fiddle and would one day perform with Bill Monroe's Blue Grass Boys, had stepped outside for a breath of fresh air, and much to his surprise heard old-fashioned string music wafting through the sultry night air.

"I said to myself, 'Where the hell is that comin' from?'" he recalls. "Bein' from Tennessee, I was drawed to it like a fly to honey. Then, I realized it was comin' from a beer joint across the street. Well, I walked over there to see what was goin' on." The sweet sounds were being produced by two young men wearing hillbilly garb, one of whom strummed the guitar and cracked jokes, and one of whom said little but played the fiddle "like I hadn't ever seen or heard it played before."

The entertainers were Ervin and Gordon, engaged in an evening of busking. The brothers had generally stayed closer to home following Tommy's birth, although they had made return visits to Texas to play clubs in Houston, Edinburg, Bay City, and San Antonio; to Alabama to play the Cawthon Hotel; and to New York to play the Village Barn and other venues.

"Me and Gordy, we played every bar in Brooklyn for nickels and dimes," Ervin claimed in 1976. "Bars that had peanuts on the floor. Beer was a nickel a glass. Them drunks didn't have no money. We lived in a flop joint in New York City, and we played up and down Flatbush and back to Coney Island and the dives downtown.

Rough. Some rough places in my time." Back in Florida, Ervin continued, "we was working in dives and dumps, in the slums of Miami and other places. We got so we were playing in dives too much. We got a reputation for that, and the booking agents wouldn't let us play any of the good clubs."

Indeed, the south Florida entertainment milieu had changed since the outbreak of the war, compelling fringe entertainers to take work wherever they could find it. On Miami Beach, for example, travel had been restricted, while all but a handful of hotels had been leased by the federal government and converted into barracks and training facilities for military personnel.

The Biltmore, where the Rouses once headlined, had been retrofitted as a veterans' hospital, while the municipal golf courses, where duffers once cursed errant putts, had been trampled by soldiers in training. The war was uncomfortably close; from the shore, spectators could view blazing tankers and freighters that had been struck by missiles from prowling Nazi submarines.

Therefore, the Rouse Brothers came to depend upon the largess of patrons in hotel lounges, roadhouses, and restaurants in Dade and Broward counties, while occasionally traveling to Jacksonville and West Palm Beach, among other Florida cities, to appear in nightclub revues, as an added attraction at movie theaters, and on local radio stations.

Ervin occasionally struck out on his own, although he seemed particularly hapless without his brother's steadying influence. Vassar Clements, who then fiddled on Jacksonville radio station WJHP, recalls a time in the early 1940s when Ervin, traveling solo, arrived in the River City to appear on a broadcast hosted by a local singer named Tiny Greer and his band, the Bluefield Boys:

"Well, Ervin, he was loose as a goose. He was supposed to be at the station, but called to say he'd run out of gas. So, Tiny went out and helped him push his car off the road and bought him some gas. They got back just in time to go on the air and, once the program started, Ervin just started talking about this and that—you couldn't really follow what he was saying. Tiny was getting impatient because they didn't have much time. Finally, he said, 'Ervin, that's interesting, but don't you think we ought to play something?' Ervin finally played the *Special*. But that's the way he was. He'd just start driving until he ran out of gas, figuring somebody would come and get him. And when he was introduced, he'd talk until somebody told him to play."

So, it was a long-forgotten tavern at the corner of Southwest 8th Street and 7th Avenue, now squarely in the midst of Little Havana, at which under-aged Gene first encountered the Rouse Brothers, whose lively music was so reminiscent of the hillbilly string bands that thrived around south-central Tennessee. "I come right up to 'em and introduced myself, and told 'em I played a little, and asked 'em where they were goin' next," says Gene, now retired and dividing his time between Mt. Pleasant and a small ranch in Nebraska. "They were real nice to me, and told me they were headed to another beer joint or somewhere like that. I asked 'em if they'd please wait so I could get my car and follow 'em."

The brothers agreed, and Gene accompanied them to their second stop. There, he was the beneficiary of an unforgettable surprise: "Gordy said, 'Here, Gene, take my guitar and do a few numbers for the folks.' Then he got up and brought me on with a big buildup. Well, I'll tell you, I was thrilled to death. I did three or four tunes, and the people liked it. From then on, I hung right with Ervin and Gordy. I thought the sun rose and set with both of 'em. And the club owners were happy, because it didn't cost them a penny to have this great entertainment."

Exhilarated, young Gene shadowed the duo until the early morning hours, when all the bars had closed, then watched as they divided the fruits of their labor—more than a hundred dollars.

Now, looking back across six decades, Gene still vividly remembers studying these seasoned pros, then aged twenty-five and twenty-eight, as they deftly worked a room. "They didn't have no electric instruments," he recalls. "They didn't have no [public address system] so they'd be free to stroll. Ervin would always find a woman, walk over to her table and hand her the bow. Then, while Ervin held the fiddle and changed the chords, he'd let the woman play a song. I'll tell you what, the music still sounded just as pretty as could be. And everywhere they went, people knew 'em. They'd walk in the door and folks would say, 'Hey, there's them hillbillies! Come on in, boys!' They could flat get it. If you had them two, you didn't need nobody else."

Gene's powerful bond with the Rouses—and especially with Ervin—would endure for as long as the brothers lived. But, temporarily at least, world events were taking precedence. After spending several months as an apprentice busker, Gene left Florida for Tennessee, where he married fifteen-year-old Helen Norman, lied about his age, and joined the Army Air Corps. However, he would not see action, spending his hitch safely ensconced at Fort Bragg in Fayetteville, North Carolina. Upon his discharge in September 1944, he returned to his young wife in Mt. Pleasant and sought to establish a career in music.

"But hell, everybody was playin' hillbilly music in Tennessee," Gene says. "So I come back down to Miami, which was a big country music town in those days, and picked up right where I left off with Ervin and Gordy."

GREETINGS: HAVING SUBMITTED yourself to a local board composed of your neighbors for the purpose of determining your availability for training and service in the land or naval forces of the United States, you are hearby notified that you have been selected...

The Selective Training and Service Act of 1940, which authorized the nation's first peacetime draft, had been reluctantly extended by a divided U.S. Congress in August 1941. However, as events unfolded, it was fortunate that General George

Marshall's fledgling army had not been prematurely disbanded; following Pearl Harbor, America needed all the military might it could muster—and quickly.

During those anxious months, young men who had not enlisted would likely have received a much-dreaded form letter obliging their presence at a regional processing facility, at which time their physical, psychological, and moral fitness for military duty would be determined.

Gordon, flat-footed and blind in one eye, was exempt from service. (Ervin later claimed that he had jabbed Gordon's eye with an errant fiddle bow as the two performed. Carrie, however, says that her husband was injured as a child, when Ervin carelessly tossed a piece of firewood in his direction.) Evidencing no obvious physical disabilities, Ervin was ordered to Camp Blanding in Bradford County in March 1943. "He didn't want to go," says Louallie. "I suppose he was frightened."

Ervin would not have been the only young man fearful of being killed or maimed in battle. But this reluctant warrior was apparently prepared to do whatever was required to demonstrate, beyond a shadow of a doubt, that he did not belong in any uniform other than overalls, a tuxedo jacket, and a straw hat. "He told them he saw pink elephants on the walls," says Louallie. "Of course, he saw nothing of the kind."

Yet, despite this rather transparent invocation of a highly unoriginal barroom hallucination, military psychiatrists ruled that Ervin did indeed suffer from neuropsychosis (NP). As a result he was classified as 4-F—unsuitable for service due to physical, moral, or psychological reasons. "A Navy doctor told me he had a schizoid personality," recalls Louallie. "They were concerned that if he were in a combat situation, he might throw down his gun and run."

Was Ervin truly insane, or at least teetering on the brink? Four years later, he would be diagnosed as schizophrenic by a private physician; but at the time he was drafted, his manner seemed more self-centered than psychotic. "Ervin wasn't right," says Gene. "But I don't think he was *crazy* crazy, if you follow me—at least, not then."

From a distance of more than a half-century, it is not possible to say for certain. However, it may be instructive to review the criteria established in the 1940s for military service, and to compare those standards to what is known about Ervin's behavior and his state of mind.

The army's physical requirements were hardly stringent: the conscript must stand no less than five feet tall, and weigh no less than one hundred five pounds; he must possess no fewer than twelve serviceable teeth; he must be free of venereal disease and hernia; he must not be afflicted with flat feet or venereal disease; his vision must test at 20/40 or better. Still, more than forty percent of selectees were rejected for one or more of these reasons, with flat feet and dental defects being the primary culprits.

If the physical examination was acceptable, however, there followed a screening session with a psychiatrist, the purpose of which was to weed out "neuropsychiatric undesirables"—a blanket term that encompassed an array of perceived emotional shortcomings.

General Lewis B. Hershey, director of the draft, had stated that "an individual not feeble-minded enough or insane enough to require institutional care in civilian life may still be too feeble-minded or too disordered in mind to make a good soldier." Therefore, psychiatrists were fairly liberal in handing out NP evaluations; ultimately, of fifteen million men examined, more than twelve percent were rejected for neuropsychiatric reasons, with more than three hundred thousand others accepted and then discharged for previously undetected mental instability.

The examiner began by observing the selectee's coordination, while also watching for outward manifestations of a potential nervous disorder, such as nail-biting or excessive sweating. (A layperson might reasonably surmise that *not* sweating or biting one's nails under such circumstances would be far more curious.) Then, if a mental defect was suspected, the psychiatrist might ask questions such as, "Why does the sun rise in the morning and set at night?"

And, because homosexuality was then considered a mental illness, the examiner also sought to determine whether or not the selectee was physically attracted to men, often by simply asking, "Do you like girls?"

Yet, perhaps Ervin's ultimate ace-in-the-hole need not have been faked: his rustic upbringing and his laconic personality. General Hershey, who had insisted upon strict standards, later complained that many NP rejections were due to the fact that "Yankee" psychiatrists did not know what to make of unschooled young men, like Ervin, who had come from the rural South. "They were rejecting men no queerer than the rest of us," said General Hershey. Agreed one staff psychiatrist: "Boys from the southern hills...looked withdrawn, autistic, and were often diagnosed as schizophrenic, with no reference to their taciturn culture pattern."

Although Ervin was far better traveled than a typical country boy—or a typical city boy, for that matter—the terms "withdrawn," "autistic," and "taciturn" would still have aptly described the strangely disengaged fiddler as he must have appeared to others, particularly when observed outside his element. Consequently, Ervin's absurd pachyderm yarn may have been merely pink icing on the cake—particularly if a clueless, Northeastern-bred psychiatrist had conducted his screening.

In any case, either through diagnostic skill or educated guesswork, the army got this one right. Insane or merely eccentric, Ervin T. Rouse was no hero, and would undoubtedly have made a terrible soldier.

As for how he might have behaved in combat, Louallie recalls an incident in the early 1950s when a fight broke out in a bar where the brothers were performing. The combatants filed litigation against one another, and peace-loving Ervin was called as a witness when the case went to trial. The fiddler explained to the court that he had fled from the stage at the first sign of trouble, and had not seen a thing. "When they [the litigants] started their show," he said, "I stopped mine."

However, perhaps partially out of guilt, Ervin contributed to the war effort with a patriotic song called *I Am an American*, which was sung to the tune of the country hit *Are You From Dixie*? Its belligerent tone is ironic in light of Ervin's efforts to avoid military service:

> *Old Uncle wants you,*
> *and Uncle needs you,*
> *he'll be there in the lead.*
> *He's a shootin' desperado,*
> *you might get a smell.*
> *He'll be shootin' and leadin'*
> *old Stalin straight to—well...*

Another oddity about *I Am an American* is the reference to Josef Stalin. Though he was initially a Hitler ally, Stalin joined the allied effort after Germany invaded Russia in the summer of 1941. Why Ervin identified Stalin instead of Hitler as a bogeyman seems to be a case of confusion over which brutal dictator was which.

NOW RELOCATED TO MIAMI, Gene landed a day job driving a truck for a concrete block manufacturer—but he spent evenings busking with Ervin and Gordon "every damn time they'd let me."

In fact, Gene's presence was a decided plus for the act since he, unlike the Rouses, knew contemporary hits, and could answer requests for the latest releases from Acuff, Arnold, Tubb, Wills, and others whose tunes were appearing on *Billboard's* Most Played Juke Box Folk Records chart (the trade magazine would not adopt the term "country and western" until 1949.)

"Ervin and Gordy would get into it with each other quite a bit at that time," recalls Gene, who was sometimes called "Texas" because of his fondness for cowboy attire. "Hell, they were brothers. It was only natural. But Gordy was the businessman of the two, and there wasn't nothin' businesslike about Ervin."

Several times, Gordon found his brother's antics so maddening that he disbanded the act. During these periodic splits, Ervin sometimes aligned himself with other local musicians, who were invariably far less forgiving of his peculiarities, while Gordon teamed with Carrie and a succession of hired fiddlers in a trio he dubbed "The Everglades Ramblers."

Nonetheless, the Rouse Brothers were never apart for long. "They reminded me of Ira and Charlie Louvin," says Vassar Clements, referring to the Louvin Brothers, perhaps the most influential vocal duo in the history of country music. Ira, who died in an automobile crash in 1965, was erratic and difficult; Charlie was stable and amiable. "Gordon kind of picked up where Ervin left off. He wasn't the musician Ervin was, but he sort of kept things on an even keel."

Although their careers seemed to have peaked in the 1930s, there is no evidence that Ervin and Gordon were embittered by their failure to achieve national stardom. The duo gratefully entertained the VFW Ladies' Auxiliary, the American Legion, and other fraternal and civic organizations, usually receiving seventy-five dollars per show.

They also played between screenings at movie theaters throughout the state, appearing without embarrassment alongside undistinguished local talent and fading vaudevillians. At Jacksonville's Temple Theater, for example, the "Two Gentlemen from the Georgia (sic) Hills" appeared with Bob Dupree and Carlo, "Petite Swing Dancing Smoothies;" Jack Harvey, "Jacksonville's Favorite Tenor;" Billy and Ida, "WPDQ's Singing Cowgirls;" and The Amazing Martels, a pair of mentalists about whom it was modestly stated, "They Can Almost Read Your Mind!" At the Edison and the Paramount in Miami, the brothers were billed as "Those Funny Hill-Billy Hep Cats," and rather generously as "Famous Stage, Radio, and Screen Stars."

Nightclubs offered occasional bookings as well. Rube acts had fallen out of favor at Miami Beach's resurgent resort hotels, but the Rouse Brothers were still welcomed at less pretentious venues, particularly Miami's Club Grenada and Bali Club, and Palm Beach's Biltmore Hotel and Club 1001. At the latter venue, the "Kings of Comedy" were always headliners, and consequently earned their most generous paychecks: two hundred fifty dollars per week.

Concurrently, Ervin and Gordon participated in various benefits sponsored by AFM Local 665, and returned to radio with a thirty-minute program broadcast six days weekly on WKAT, where their modest, seventy-two-dollar-per-week salary was augmented by their ability to promote personal appearances.

If their slightly frayed routine was hardly mainstream, audiences seemed unbothered. For example, after a May 1944 appearance at a Miami Officer's Club dinner-dance, an Air Force captain wrote the brothers a rousing letter of reference, stating that their performance was "by far the best ever presented to us…and it might be added that we have had the privilege of having in our floorshows for the past eight months all of the leading entertainers who were working in the Miami area." The letter continued, "We wholeheartedly and sincerely recommend [the Rouse Brothers] as two very excellent entertainers who brought us more fun and enjoyment in forty-five minutes that we have had in a long time."

So, between busking and bookings, the brothers probably enjoyed adequate annual incomes through the early mid-1940s. Of course, their cash flow was sporadic, and from their earnings they paid travel expenses. Still, the Rouses and their wives had managed to purchase their own homes—Gordon and Carrie had paid cash for theirs—and to live as well or better than their more conventional blue-collar neighbors. "It was tight, but we never had any serious problems with money," says Louallie, who worked as a clerk in a hobby shop located within walking distance of their home. "Ervin made good money for the time."

Also reassuring—if sometimes exasperating—was the presence of other Rouse family members in Miami. Durwood (also known as "Stony") and Earl, along with their wives, had arrived in 1942, while Guy, a widower and perhaps the oddest of an odd bunch, had followed his siblings in 1945. Like Ervin and Gordon, Durwood and Earl were full-time musicians; Guy, who played several instruments, supported himself as a blocklayer. Most significantly, Bettie and Hal, despite having two small children, had taken in Ernest and Eloise, the brood's aging parents. Thus reunited, various combinations of brothers performed in nightspots throughout Dade and Broward counties, while the elder Rouses enjoyed familial proximity and warm weather.

"Oh, Lord yes, they [the brothers] would fight," recalls Earl's daughter, Elaine, who for years performed with her father and now lives in Danville, Virginia. "They were happiest when they were arguing, and they'd argue about anything: music, writing, money, you name it. But they all loved each other like little children. They were very close and were happy to be living close together."

However, the noisily familiar routine was shattered when Eloise, who had been seriously ill with heart problems, died on February 9, 1945, at the age of sixty-five. Ervin was devastated, as were his brothers and sisters. Grimly, the entire Rouse clan—with the exception of Jimmy—gathered in Greenville for a memorial service and burial in nearby Cherry Hill Cemetery. Jimmy and his band had been previously engaged to play a dance, and no one doubted what "Miss Ella" would have instructed her eldest to do. "My grandmother would have wanted my daddy to play the date," says Elizabeth Rouse Walters. "He was heartbroken, of course, but that's how important music was to the family."

A photograph taken outside the funeral home shows the remaining brothers flanking a dour-faced Ernest, who appears drawn and frail and is leaning on a cane. "They were all so upset," recalls Carrie. "Mrs. Rouse had always fussed over them so much. One thing I remember so well is how none of the brothers could stand to tell her goodbye. Before Mr. and Mrs. Rouse moved to Miami, the boys would visit them in North Carolina on the way to perform somewhere, and they'd get out of bed and sneak out of the house at the crack of dawn just so they'd be gone before she woke up. It was just too painful otherwise."

Ervin, however, was his mother's favorite—and she broached no criticism of her gifted son. "As far as Mrs. Rouse was concerned, if Ervin and I had problems, it was my fault," Louallie says. "It was so sad to me, because I had lost my mother when I was very young, and I was hoping that Mrs. Rouse could fill that role in my life. But she just seemed jealous that Ervin could love someone other than her." Agreed Carrie: "Mrs. Rouse cared deeply for all of her children, but she idolized Ervin, probably because of his tremendous talent. Anything Ervin did, that was okay." Not surprisingly, Louallie failed to find a confidant in her mother-in-law.

Depending upon the circumstances, everyone copes with the loss of a loved one differently. Still, mental health professionals agree that an emotionally stable person will typically pass through seven stages in the grieving process: shock, disbelief, numbness, fear, anger, depression and, finally, acceptance.

Many factors influence how long the process may last, and how severely its manifestations may be felt. "Absent grief reaction" is said to be present when a short-circuit occurs between the recognition of a loss and the acceptance of it. Indications of this disorder often include declining physical health, acerbated by major depression, erratic behavior, and substance abuse. Because Ervin had evidenced such symptoms prior to his mother's death, it is overly simplistic to blame his subsequent hardships entirely on this traumatic event. Clearly, however, his condition worsened in its aftermath.

Yet, from heartbreak a classic song emerged. Ervin, who was emotionally spent upon his return to Miami, vowed to write a memorial to the remarkable woman who had loved him deeply and unconditionally. Initially, he decided to call his musical eulogy *Sweeter Than Flowers*, only to find that a song bearing that title already existed. So, at Louallie's suggestion he added "the," and proceeded to compose one of the most morose "mother songs" in the history of country music.

"He wrote it sitting at our kitchen table," says Louallie. "It was difficult, because writing didn't come that easily to Ervin. He'd write a few lines and work out the tune on the fiddle—we usually didn't have a guitar at our house—until it was finally finished."

Decades later, Ervin explained the genesis of the composition to writer Dorothy Horstman: "Carrying *Sweeter Than the Flowers* was just like a woman carrying a baby. Now, a song is in your heart and soul just like a child. It's a load to write about your own mother, and our mother was a very sweet woman. She loved all of her children—she had fifteen head of children—and we all loved her. And when she passed away, our main remembrance of Mama was that she was more sweeter than any flower. We sang her song to hundreds of millions of people throughout our times and career in show business and we're mighty, mighty proud and happy that we had life in our bodies to do that."

The lyrics to *Sweeter Than the Flowers* read as follows:

> *Yes, as far as I can remember,*
> *she'll remain the rose of my heart.*
> *Mom took sick along in December,*
> *February brought us broken hearts.*
>
> *The reason we've not called a family reunion,*
> *we knew she wouldn't be there.*
> *But since we thought it all over, Mama,*
> *we know that your spirit is here.*

Oh no, I can't forget the hours,
your the onliest one, Mom, sweeter than the flowers.
Oh, no, there's no need to bother,
to speak of you now would only hurt father.

Well it looked so good to see us together,
but I had to look after Dad.
Oh, no, Mama, when I passed your coffin,
I didn't want to remember you dead.

They all gathered 'round, I stared at their faces,
all heads were bowed mighty low.
But that was one time we all had to face it,
though it hurt us so bad, you know.

Oh, no, Mama we'll never forget you,
and someday we'll meet you up there.

However, Ervin appears to have been contemplating some sort of a tribute to Eloise several years before her death. In fact, Zeke Clements claimed that Ervin composed *Sweeter Than the Flowers* in Cincinnati, where he was entertaining in a small bar and boarding in an apartment on the second floor. Natchee the Indian was also in Cincinnati, and the two fiddlers apparently spent some time together, perhaps joining forces for what would have been some memorable busking excursions.

According to Clements, who heard the story from Natchee and then related it to Charles Wolfe decades later, Ervin asked the owner of the bar at which he was engaged if he could use the telephone to call his mother on her birthday. The owner gave his permission, and intrigued by the strange, rambling conversation he overheard, jotted down some of Ervin's more saccharine statements—including "You are sweeter than all the flowers."

After the call, so the story goes, Ervin and the bar owner sat down together and started drinking beer while composing what would become a timeless tear-jerker.

This story may have elements of truth; given his devotion to Eloise, it is reasonable to believe that Ervin would have previously attempted to write songs in her honor. Further, it is possible that portions of such an homage may have originated under the circumstances described by Natchee; in particular, his description of the telephone conversation between Ervin and Eloise sounds credible.

But *Sweeter Than the Flowers* as it ultimately emerged clearly could have been written only after Eloise died. The lyrics pinpont specific dates—"Mom took sick along in December/February brought us broken hearts"—and accurately describe the sorrowful family gathering that took place at her funeral. Eloise was still very much alive in Natchee's narrative, and it is highly unlikely that Ervin would have allowed himself—or anyone else, for that matter—to speculate about her passing and its aftermath as fodder for a song.

After *Sweeter Than the Flowers* was complete, Ervin became obsessed with persuading a famous Nashville star—any star whose stature ensured radio play—to record it. He did not want this composition, and by extension Eloise, to be ignored and forgotten.

But Ervin's mental state was fragile; at the time of Eloise's death, the Rouses had two children—Thomas, then four years old; and Hattie Eloise, then two years old— and a third due at any time. (Harold Claude was born on February 21, just one week following the funeral.) Family deaths and family births rank among life's most stressful events, and Ervin, already near collapse, seemed overwhelmed when confronted in rapid succession with both.

At the same time, his marriage was faltering. Louallie understood that Ervin's late-night busking was a financial necessity—indeed, she sometimes sang with the brothers when Bettie agreed to baby-sit—but she was nearing the end of her patience with his drunkenness. "Louallie was frustrated, and you couldn't blame her," says Gene. "She was the sweetest person in the world, and she had those three kids to raise without any help from Ervin. She was a very knowledgeable lady; an educated person from a good family. And it seemed like Ervin just wasn't usin' his talent to better himself and his family's welfare." Further complicating matters, by December 1945 Louallie was pregnant again.

Although barroom busking hardly encouraged sobriety, Ervin did briefly make an effort to curtail his alcohol intake. "One time Ervin and me made a deal that we wouldn't drink while we was workin'," says Gene. "If he caught me takin' a drink, I gave up a night's pay. If I caught him, he gave up a night's pay. But everywhere we'd go, somebody wanted to buy us a drink. One night I said, 'Ervin, let's forget about that deal; I'm gonna have a beer.' And that was okay with him. We were the kings of the beer joints, so it's mighty easy to get caught up in that kind of life."

Then, sometime in the early summer of 1947, Ervin finally set out—ominously, on his own—for Nashville, where he intended to champion *Sweeter Than the Flowers*.

He had visited country music's nerve center several times previously, although without such a specific mission. The unreconstructed old-time fiddler was not interested in obtaining work as a session musician, nor did he possess the bravado required to put himself forward as a solo recording artist. Most likely, he enjoyed Nashville simply because the city was teeming with kindred spirits; struggling pickers, writers, and singers—a fair share of them talented misfits—who knew no other life than playing music.

What happened in during Ervin's visit is unknown. Carrie recalls only that the fiddler telephoned Gordon several times, asking his much put-upon brother to send money so that the trip could be extended. John Hartford, among others, believed that

Ervin may have guested on Roy Acuff's *Opry* segment, during which he performed brilliantly before sabotaging an opportunity for permanent membership.

Unfortunately, this story has not been confirmed and *Opry* rosters from the summer of 1947 do not list Ervin's name. Still, such an appearance could have been the result of an informal, last-minute invitation from Acuff, who wielded enough clout to spotlight whomever he wished. In any case, this possibly fanciful tale bears repeating if only because it seems so plausible, given Ervin's temperament.

Said Hartford: "The way I heard it, Acuff and some of those guys said, 'Hey, he [Ervin] is a natural; let's put him on the *Opry*.' So, Ervin performed, maybe as one of the Smoky Mountain Boys (Acuff's band), and was given a solo number. Well, he was such a great showman that he brought the house down. He did all his tricks, and even went out in the audience and let a woman take the bow and play while he held the fiddle. Afterward, Acuff and [*Opry* managers] decided to invite him to join. But they looked around, and Ervin was nowhere to be found. Finally, they saw him standing in front of the Ryman on the sidewalk, fiddling for tips. Apparently, he said that he liked being a street musician, and that he wasn't about to change for anybody. Of course, the powers-that-be decided that they couldn't have an *Opry* member playing on street corners, so the matter was dropped."

This much is known: Whatever else Ervin may or may not have accomplished in Nashville, he did not generate any interest in *Sweeter Than the Flowers*. He returned to Miami in July, physically exhausted and barely able to utter a coherent sentence. "I was shocked at Ervin's condition," recalls Louallie. "He seemed sober, but completely out of touch with reality. It was obvious that he was having some sort of breakdown."

Yet, immediately upon his arrival he insisted that his wife accompany him to a nearby bar, where he intended to perform. "I was a nervous wreck," continues Louallie. "I was terrified of what he might do or say when he got in front of an audience. But—this was the strangest thing—we went to this place where Ervin liked to play, and he got up and did *Sweeter Than the Flowers*. It was beautiful. In fact, I'd never heard him sing or play prettier than he did that night."

Still, over the next several days Ervin became increasingly delusional, baffling Gordon and Carrie when, after arriving unexpectedly at their home well after midnight, he ripped from the wall a seemingly innocuous calendar that pictured a young woman in a bathing suit. "He had suddenly become very religious, fanatical you might say," Carrie recalls. "He just tore that calendar down, fell to his knees, and started praying for us."

Adds Gene, who hastened to Louallie's side after being told that his friend was in trouble, "Ervin was talkin' about things that didn't make sense; I don't know how to describe it exactly, but it just seemed like he didn't know what the hell was goin' on."

Alarmed, Louallie and Carrie took Ervin to their family physician, who recommended that he immediately enter a "sanitarium," the bleak term then used to describe psychiatric hospitals. Ervin, however, refused to consider the prospect, voicing a ghastly premonition: "He said, 'If I go in there, something will happen to my baby,'" says Louallie, referring to the couple's ten-month-old daughter, Josephine.

Yet, recognizing that her husband was in desperate need of treatment and seeing no alternative, she signed the necessary forms to have Ervin committed to a private clinic called the Miami Retreat Foundation Sanitarium, located in northeast Miami. "I had been telling Ervin's family that he was physically and mentally sick," says Louallie, adding that his siblings—even Gordon—simply would not, or could not, accept that fact that their brother's behavior warranted serious concern. "Gordon would say, 'Ervin isn't acting right,'" agrees Carrie. "But until this incident, he would never come out and say, 'Ervin is mentally ill.'"

Psychiatrists at the Miami Retreat diagnosed Ervin as schizophrenic, and prescribed electroconvulsive therapy (ECT), more commonly known as shock treatment. ECT was discovered accidentally in 1938, when an Italian psychiatrist applied a pair of tongs used to stun hogs before slaughter to the temples of a seemingly intractable patient, thereby shocking him out of a delirious state in which he spoke only gibberish.

In subsequent years, psychiatrists worldwide adopted ECT, although it fell out of favor in the 1960s following the introduction of antipsychotic drugs, and in the wake of gruesome publicity regarding the use of ECT to punish and subdue troublesome patients.

Today, a highly refined version of ECT does appear useful in treating some mental disorders, including schizophrenia. In the 1940s, however, the procedure was primitive, traumatic, and of questionable efficacy. Patients did not receive general anesthesia or muscle-relaxing drugs to prevent spasms, and were held down by attendants as a brief electrical impulse coursed through their brains, triggering convulsions similar to epileptic seizures.

Typically, ECT would have been administered at least three times weekly, although it is unknown how many sessions Ervin underwent. Doctors told Louallie that he fought the treatments violently, possibly causing the series to have been cut short.

Were such drastic measures justified in Ervin's case, or had he simply suffered a situationally induced nervous breakdown, which might have been less painfully alleviated through rest and counseling? As evaluations of World War II draftees pointedly demonstrated, American psychiatrists were notorious for ascribing schizophrenia to a plethora of unrelated ailments and personality traits.

In one study, conducted immediately following the war, forty-six American psychiatrists and two hundred British psychiatrists watched a videotape of a patient who had hysterical paralysis of one arm and a history of mood fluctuations associated with alcoholism. Afterward, sixty-nine percent of the Americans diagnosed schizophrenia, while only two percent of the British reached the same conclusion. "Such international differences were unscientific and embarrassing," wrote Edward Shorter in *A History of Psychiatry: From the Era of the Asylum to the Age of Prozac* (John Wily & Sons). "They suggested that there was no science in psychiatry, but simply the weight of national tradition, making the discipline a branch of folklore rather than of medicine."

In the 1970s, with the advent of sophisticated medications targeting specific illnesses, more precise diagnosis of mental disorders became mandatory, leading to the adoption of universally recognized classifications. Now, although there is still no definitive medical test isolating schizophrenia, the simple or undifferentiated variety is thought to be present when a patient demonstrates a combination of behaviors: disorganized thoughts, preoccupation with specific rituals, inability to maintain personal relationships, decreased attention to personal hygiene, and general bewilderment at coping with the demands of everyday living.

Paranoid schizophrenia—a sub-type encompassing perhaps one-third of all schizophrenics—is also marked by delusions, hallucinations, anger, and volatile behavior. Likewise, many victims of mental disorders—particularly those afflicted with schizophrenia and depression—abuse alcohol and drugs. Therefore, it appears that Ervin's diagnosis was not without basis.

Why he was stricken is unknown; causes of schizophrenia may include brain structure abnormalities, neurochemical imbalances, in-utero viral infections, and heredity. (Ervin's father had been in a mental institution for what was described as a nervous breakdown, and several of his brothers, particularly Guy, displayed signs of mental illness during their lives.) In any case, the devastating malady is believed to have a biological basis, although stress may precipitate its onset in people who are predisposed.

"I have often said that there's a Nobel Prize waiting for the person who can pin down a cause," says Edward Zebooker, D.O., a psychiatrist and medical director at the Northeast Florida State Hospital in Macclenny. "But, because schizophrenia is a physiological disorder, we do know that treatments such as psychotherapy really don't help."

"Ervin later said that that if you weren't crazy when you got there [to the Miami Retreat], then you'd be crazy when you left," says Gene, who accompanied Louallie on several visits to see her husband. "He'd be beggin' me to get him out. There were people there who thought they were monkeys, and people who were walkin' around cluckin' like chickens. The damn place was kind of like a prison."

Louallie, who was only following the best medical advice she could obtain, must have nonetheless tormented herself, wondering whether or not having Ervin hospitalized was the correct decision. "Ervin's doctor told me, 'Once he gets out, you need to throw away that d-a-m-n fiddle," she recalls, carefully spelling out even this mild expletive. "I couldn't believe that. I said, 'Playing the fiddle is what he lives for.'"

Nonetheless, whether because of or in spite of his treatment regimen, Ervin seemed to gradually improve, and as his mental fog lifted, he came to enjoy entertaining fellow patients by playing the piano in a communal recreation room.

Then, fate dealt Ervin and Louallie yet another blow. Hospital policy was to keep newspapers out of the hands of patients, many of whom might be upset by the contents. But, on July 25, 1947, someone inadvertently left a copy of the *Miami Herald* sitting on a reception area coffee table. Ervin retrieved it and, casually turning the pages, stopped abruptly on page A-16, where divorce decrees, building permits, and deaths were listed in a column entitled "Vital Statistics." Under "Miami Deaths," one such vital statistic dryly read: "Rouse, Josephine. 11 months. 3729 Northwest 20th Ct., Friday."

Although Ervin had been unaware of any problems—Louallie, at the insistence of Ervin's doctors, had not yet told him—Josephine had developed a blistering fever several days earlier, and had died in Jackson Memorial Hospital of spinal meningitis. "That child [Josephine] was the sweetest baby I'd ever seen; just like a little angel," says Carrie. "And Ervin was never one to pick up newspapers. He couldn't care less about them. That's why it was so strange that he found out about it the way he did."

Surprisingly, the tragedy did not cause Ervin to slip further into an emotional abyss. Instead, although he reacted to the news with profound grief, he also became more focused on conquering his problems, and on demonstrating that he was well enough to rejoin his wife and family. Yet, when Josephine was interred at "Baby Corner" in Southern Memorial Park, only her mother, grandfather, aunts, and uncles stood by. Despite his apparent progress, doctors would not allow Ervin to attend his daughter's funeral.

Subdued and chastened, he was finally released about one week later, probably still feeling some disorientation and memory loss typically associated with ECT. Recalls Gene: "I seen Ervin and I said somethin' like, 'Well, are you ready to get back in the saddle?' Ervin just said, 'Yeah, let's get with it.'"

Almost immediately thereafter, the brothers and Gene were busking again and, by November, Ervin and Gordon had returned to nightclub work at two of their favorite venues: Club Granada in Miami Beach, on a show headlined by Irish balladeer Mike Peyton; and Club 1001 in Palm Beach, which touted the duo as "The Best Comedy Team to Play the Palm Beaches!" During a month-long engagement at Club 1001, the Rouse Brothers presided over a gala New Year's Eve floorshow, and must surely have been as glad as anyone who attended to see 1947 recede into memory.

In later years, Ervin would joke about his stint in a mental hospital and, in typical fashion, would toss in some flagrant misinformation while doing so. For example, he told Zeke Clements that it was imperturbable Gordon who had originally been institutionalized, adding, "I decided to stop in and see Gordy [in the hospital] on the way home to Florida, and they ended up keeping me there for two years."

BY THE SUMMER OF 1948, Gene was splitting his time between Miami and Mt. Pleasant, and was establishing friendships within Nashville's tight-knit musical community.

He fronted his own five-piece band—Gene Christian and the Country Pals—and appeared regularly on radio station WLAC with singer/promoter Big Jeff Bess, whose wife, Hattie Louise "Tootsie" Bess, would later eclipse her husband's fame as proprietress of Tootsie's Orchid Lounge, located around the corner from the Ryman Auditorium. In the 1960s, the shabby but welcoming Broadway landmark would become renowned as a home-away-from-home for aspiring singers, musicians, and songwriters, as well as for *Opry* stars wishing to guzzle a cold one before going onstage.

One Saturday morning in early May 1948, while at home in Tennessee, Gene awoke to spy an apparently abandoned automobile parked on the shoulder of the road, just beyond his gravel driveway. "It looked like maybe somebody had run out of gas," he recalls. "So, I walked down there to check it out. I looked inside and there was Ervin, sound asleep on the front seat, the sweat just runnin' off him. I remember there was pieces of an outboard motor scattered all over the back seat, but he hadn't brought so much as a change of clothes."

Ervin, who had arrived in the wee hours and had sweltered in his car so as not to disturb his old friend, was again in town to plug *Sweeter Than the Flowers*, and he asked Gene, now something of a Nashville insider, for help. So, after loaning Ervin a clean shirt and a pair of pants—"Luckily, we wore the same size," says Gene—the cowboy and the fiddler drove into Nashville to the Ryman, where they intended to do some mingling—a later generation would term it "networking"—backstage during the *Opry's* Saturday night broadcast.

"Ervin really wanted to get *Sweeter Than the Flowers* recorded; in fact, he was obsessed with getting it recorded," Gene says. "We thought the tune really fit Roy Acuff, so that's who we decided to try and see." *Sweeter Than the Flowers* did seem written to order for the King of Country Music, whose heartfelt, wailing vocals had made standards of metaphysical spirituals (*The Great Speckled Bird*), mournful ballads (*Wreck On the Highway*) and melancholy love songs (*Blue Eyes Crying in the Rain*).

Although Acuff was past his peak as a recording artist—Ernest Tubb and Eddy Arnold, among others, were more consistent hitmakers—the Maynardville, Tennessee native was an American institution; indeed, Japanese soldiers during World War II were said to have heckled their American counterparts with the cry, "To hell with Roosevelt, to hell with Babe Ruth, to hell with Roy Acuff!"

Just as important, Acuff had also become one of the industry's most influential businesspeople through his partnership with songwriter Fred Rose in Acuff-Rose Publications, which had become one of the nation's largest and most successful music publishers since its founding in 1942. The Nashville-based company was not only a country colossus but, through Rose's New York connections, it would eventually find even greater success placing its hillbilly copyrights with major pop artists. Hank Williams, for example, who was under a writing contract with Acuff-Rose, enjoyed a windfall when his songs became hits for the likes of Tony Bennett (*Cold, Cold Heart*), Jo Stafford (*Jambalaya*), and Rosemary Clooney (*Half as Much*). Certainly, Acuff would have been a stellar contact on a variety of levels for Ervin to have cultivated.

Backstage, Ervin and Gene found Acuff holding forth in one of two communal dressing rooms. "Roy knew who Ervin was because of *Orange Blossom Special*," says Gene. "So, Ervin played fiddle and I played guitar and we done *Sweeter Than the Flowers* for Roy. When we got finished, it just knocked him out. He said, 'Oh, man! I like that! I like that!'" On the strength of a handshake, Acuff agreed to record Ervin's tune—for which he undoubtedly also wanted the publishing rights—as soon as possible.

Elated, the duo returned to their room at the Tulane Hotel, which Gene describes as "the place where all the hillbillies, 'rasslers, and preachers stayed," with the intention of celebrating their triumph.

Likewise ensconced at the Tulane were Moon Mullican, a popular boogie-woogie piano player, and Sydney Nathan, owner of Cincinnati-based King Records, the label for which Mullican recorded. According to Gene, Nathan and Mullican had been also backstage at the Ryman, and had overheard *Sweeter Than the Flowers*.

Aubrey Wilson "Moon" Mullican, a native of Corrigan, Texas, presaged Floyd Cramer as a pianist who earned headliner status. But unlike Cramer, the rotund Mullican, who billed himself as "The King of the Hillbilly Piano Players," also sang, and had charted two Top 5 hits in 1947: *New Pretty Blonde (Jole Blon)*, a send-up of the traditional Cajun ditty that had recently scored for both fiddler Harry Choates and Roy Acuff; and its derivative followup, *Jole Blon's Sister*.

Mullican, however, was at a career crossroads; assuming he did not plan upon commemorating Jole Blon's mother, aunts, and cousins, it was apparent that he needed a new tune—perhaps something of a more somber nature—that would showcase his versatility while maintaining his momentum. Nathan, described by one musicologist as " a cigar-chomping tyrant; loud, abrasive, argumentative, crude, willing to take huge risks but always looking for an edge," apparently thought that a sentimental weeper such as *Sweeter Than the Flowers* would fit the bill nicely, Ervin's previous commitments to Acuff notwithstanding.

Perhaps the most telling insight into Nathan's method of operation is related in Nick Tosches's irreverent *Country: The Twisted Roots of Rock 'n Roll* (Da Capo Press). According to Tosches, Nathan would send recording artist Lloyd "Cowboy" Copas from Cincinnati to Nashville for the purpose of buying songs. Upon his return, Nathan would publish the acquisitions under his subsidiary, Lois Music, while Copas would record them, taking an author's credit as well.

Following one such trip, Copas told Nathan that he had turned down a tune called *Tennessee Waltz* because writer Pee Wee King wanted an outrageous twenty five dollars for it. "All it is, is a copy of Eddy Arnold's *Missouri Waltz*," Copas explained, "and I don't want people going around saying I'm copying Eddy Arnold." Nathan agreed, but suggested that "for superstitious reasons," perhaps Copas should buy the song anyway the next time he was in Nashville.

Nonetheless, the following month Copas reported that he had again passed on *Tennessee Waltz* "because the bastards put the price up to fifty dollars." Nathan reassured Copas that he had done the right thing, adding, "There ain't a song in the world worth fifty dollars."

It is a good story, but Nathan was no fool; King Records, founded in 1943, would grow to become one of the most successful independent labels of the post-war era by concentrating on "the music of the little people," which in Nathan's parlance meant southern whites and African-Americans. At various times during its twenty-five-year run, King's roster included, in addition to Copas and Mullican, the Delmore Brothers, Grandpa Jones, Clyde Moody, Wayne Raney, Reno & Smiley, and the Stanley Brothers along with rhythm and blues artists Earl Bostic, Little Willie John, Hank Ballard & the Midnighters, and James Brown.

And, in addition to operating its own publishing company, King boasted its own recording studio, its own distribution system, and its own record-pressing equipment. By eliminating the proverbial middle-man, Nathan made money every step of the way.

Ervin was no match for this savvy operator, who had been a pawn-shop manager and a professional wrestling promoter before finding his niche in the music business. Gene says that he left Ervin alone briefly, and returned only to find their room empty. About an hour later, he located his inebriated friend, along with Nathan and Mullican, together in Mullican's room. "Ervin looked up at me and said, 'Gene, Moon's gonna do my song!'" he recalls. "They had got to drinkin', and it was 'old buddy' this and 'old buddy' that. Pretty soon, Ervin had promised that Moon could have *Sweeter Than the Flowers*. I said, 'Ervin, remember we give Acuff our word.' But he didn't care who done it, or who got it first."

Almost immediately thereafter, Nathan published and Mullican recorded *Sweeter Than the Flowers*, which entered the *Billboard* charts on May 15, 1948, and eventually rose to No. 3. Then, in November of that year a displeased Acuff cut *Tennessee Waltz* and, despite Ervin's duplicity, used *Sweeter Than the Flowers* on the B side. Acuff's release, which peaked at No. 12, thereby provided an unexpected and perhaps undeserved free ride for Ervin's doleful tune. "Next time I saw Acuff, he acted sort of cold, like he thought I had somethin' to do with all that," says Gene, who recognized the disadvantages inherent in drawing Acuff's ire. "Hell, I was as pissed off as he was."

Granted, Moon Mullican did make a national hit out of *Sweeter Than the Flowers*, and there is no reason to assume that an Acuff release would have fared much better—at least in the short term. Acuff would notch only one more Top 10 hit in his career, and then not until 1958. Nonetheless, he was *Roy Acuff*, the man who would become first living member of the Country Music Hall of Fame in 1962; the man who would remain the *Opry's* most dominant personality until his death in 1992.

Conversely, Mullican—although he would chart several additional solo hits and co-author *Jambalaya* with Hank Williams—was all but forgotten by 1960, and was dead by 1967. "It was a hit for Mullican, but it could have been another *Great Speckled Bird* for Acuff," says Gene.

Worse, in casting his lot with Nathan and Mullican, Ervin had given away most of his creation; Nathan, Mullican, and Lois Mann, who ran Lois Music, had each taken a writer credit, with Mullican using the pseudonym Morry Burns.

That Ervin had made a bad deal would become even more apparent in subsequent years, when *Sweeter Than the Flowers* was covered by Hylo Brown, June Carter, Wilma Lee and Stony Cooper, the Franklin Brothers, George Jones and Gene Pitney, the Louvin Brothers, Reno and Smiley, the Stanley Brothers, Carl Story, Kitty Wells, Mac Wiseman, and Slim Whitman, among others.

Three-quarters of the royalty income generated by these and other recordings went to "co-writers," meaning that Ervin pocketed relatively little for composing a song that had reportedly sold more than a half-million copies in 1948, and had continued to sell, albeit at a less torrid pace, as new versions were released.

Then, in 1971, *Sweeter Than the Flowers* was born again, so to speak, as a gospel song called *I Know*. Songwriter LaVerne Tripp, now a staple on the Christian Broadcast Network, borrowed Ervin's melody and composed new lyrics proclaiming the certainty of eternal salvation. *I Know* was subsequently recorded by the pre-secular Oak Ridge Boys, along with the Dixie Echoes, the Gaither Brothers, and other popular gospel performers. Nonetheless, the impact on Ervin's bank account was negligible; including Tripp, royalties were now split five ways instead of four.

"It was just terrible about *Sweeter Than the Flowers*," says Louallie. "Ervin was obviously not competent to make decisions when he gave most of it away. I think he could have done something about it legally, but he never bothered." Still, his family can take some solace in the fact that Ervin did not sell the tune outright, which Nathan had undoubtedly urged him to do.

"The only other song [besides *Orange Blossom Special*] that I make any royalties on is the one about my mother, *Sweeter Than the Flowers*," Ervin told the *Miami News* in 1977. "I didn't make much on it, but enough to brag a little."

BOUYED BY HIS NASHVILLE BREAKTHROUGH, Ervin decided the morning after Mullican agreed to record *Sweeter Than the Flowers* that he wanted to try again to get to Hollywood, and to break into the movies. "He said, 'Gene, let's go out to California and get in them damn pictures,'" Gene recalls. "I said, 'Ervin, we don't know nothin' about pictures.' But somehow, he talked me into it. So we took my car—I wasn't about to let Ervin drive—and we started out."

That Ervin had a wife and three small children at home in Miami appears not to have been a major concern; in his view, as long as he was sending some money home, he was adequately fulfilling his marital and parental obligations.

Gene owned a massive Lincoln Zephyr; a used luxury sedan of the type favored by traveling hillbillies prior to the ascendancy of tour busses. Its trunk was big enough to swallow a full compliment of musical instruments, while a lanky man could sleep without too much difficulty in its wide, pillowy back seat. But these vintage land barges were not known for their fuel economy, so Ervin employed the same technique to wheedle gasoline that Claude Casey had observed a decade earlier.

"Now, this is an example of how Ervin done things," Gene says. "Just outside Memphis, I told him we was gonna have to stop and spend some of our money on gas. And he said to find a gas station that's got some folks hangin' around. So, we finally found one of them old-timey grocery stores that had gas pumps out front. There was eight or ten fellas out there, sittin' on benches, and we got out and started talkin' to 'em. Finally, one of 'em asked, 'Where you boys headed?' I said, 'We're goin' out to California to see how them movies are made.' Then, after we talked a little while longer, Ervin asked, 'Do you folks like good pickin' and singin'? Would you like to hear some?'"

The two supreme buskers then presented a mini-concert, and collected about twenty dollars in tips from the store's patrons. "We made enough money to fill up the tank, and had plenty left over," Gene says. "Today, that seems kind of embarrassin'. But back then, we didn't think nothin' of it."

Ervin and Gene arrived in Memphis by about 4 p.m., and quickly decided that the city's rowdy juke-joints provided further opportunities to replenish their coffers. "By eleven o'clock we'd made a hundred dollars," says Gene. "That was damn good money, and it was all from people who hadn't seen us or heard of us before. So, we decided keep on goin' west as long as we could."

Exhausted, the duo finally stopped to spend the night near Little Rock, Arkansas, and the following morning tuned the car radio to a local country station, KTHS, on which they heard a disc jockey name Tommy Trent.

"We decided to go see that fella and try to get some work," Gene says. "We found the station, and I left Ervin in the car and went inside. I told Tommy Trent who we were, and asked him to listen to us. He agreed, and I went out and got Ervin and our instruments. Then, we did our usual routine—that's all you could do with Ervin—and Trent said, 'Boys, you've got a hell of an act; but I just can't use any musicians right now.'"

Trent did, however, offer to make a telephone call on their behalf to some politically connected friends in Hot Springs, where a fiercely contested local election was under way. Perhaps, Trent said, his friends could use a couple of crack hillbilly show-men to draw crowds.

Hot Springs, promoted as a resort destination for its stone and brick spas along Bathhouse Row, was then one of the most decadent and corrupt cities in the nation; a center for graft, gambling, and prostitution. Because local elected officials and law enforcement officers were receiving ample kickbacks, including a "pleasure tax" collected from houses of ill repute, efforts to clean the town up had been fit-ful and futile.

In 1946, however, returning veterans had led a "GI revolt" against the status quo, forming the Government Improvement Party (GIP) and electing one of their own, Sid McMath, to the post of prosecuting attorney for the 18th judicial district, which encompassed Garland and Montgomery counties. "We finally broke the shackles [of organized crime] in Little Rock and set the stage for government to be run honest and clean," says Jacob King, who was then chairman of the Garland County Democratic Central Committee and a GIP activist. McMath, who would later be elected governor of Arkansas, adds, "We'd just been overseas fighting for freedom, so it seemed like we ought to have it at home, too."

However, it was not the GIP with which Ervin and Gene aligned themselves; instead, it was with the Progressive Businessmen's Association (PBA), which was backed by gambling interests. In the summer of 1948, these diametrically opposed organizations were each running slates of candidates for three important posts: prosecuting attorney—McMath, a candidate for governor, did not seek re-elec-tion—along with Garland County sheriff and tax collector. Also at stake was con-trol of the Democratic Central Committee, which had heretofore been dominated by PBA sympathizers.

Ervin and Gene had no knowledge of, or interest in, the history behind this holy war for the soul of Hot Springs; they were merely offering their services to whomever would pay enough to finance their California trip. "We went down to [PBA] headquarters, where Trent had told us to go, and I asked 'em if they could use some entertainment," says Gene. "We didn't know or care what the election was about. They said, 'Okay, let's see what you can do.' Then, I went out to the car and got Ervin, and we auditioned. Well, they hired us on the spot. I said, 'Look, we ain't got no damn money and no place to stay.' So, the fella give me a twenty-dollar bill and they set us up in hotel there in town."

The two stayed in Hot Springs for six weeks leading up to the July 2 primary elec-tion, performing at perhaps five political rallies daily from the back of a flatbed truck. (As if to further accentuate the stark contrast between the PBA and the GIP, the reformers employed a gospel group, the Stamps Quartet, to provide music at their gatherings).

Yet, despite the many unsavory diversions a city such as Hot Springs offered, Gene says that he and Ervin generally behaved themselves and saved their money, making weekly trips to the post office to send a share of their earnings back to their respective homes. "We'd just walk around town, check out the pawn shops, things like that," says Gene. "We never went in one of the spas, even though our hotel was right across the street from one."

As for womanizing, it strains credulity to suggest that such a free-spirited pair would have remained entirely chaste while exploring this modern-day Sodom. Still, Gene viewed his marriage vows with a gravity atypical of his profession, while Ervin, who may or may not have harbored moral qualms about adultery, became hopelessly befuddled and tongue-tied when confronted offstage by members of the opposite sex.

"One thing I liked about Ervin was that he didn't chase women," says Louallie. "His brothers told me that after performances, when women would approach them, he'd get out of there as fast as he could." Although this assertion may have been influenced by wishful thinking, it is nonetheless safe to speculate that heavy drinking, if not their only indulgence, would have been the primary recreational activity pursued by Ervin and Gene during their brief foray into politics.

Finally, when the election was held and the votes were counted, only the PBA candidate for tax collector won—he would later be convicted of pocketing poll tax receipts—while twenty-four PBA delegates to the Democratic Central Committee were ousted by GIP challengers, thereby giving the reformers a majority. However, Gene's recollection is that PBA officials were not discouraged by the results—indeed, the reform movement would be short-lived—and wanted the duo to remain in Hot Springs.

"They said, 'Boys, if you stay around, we're gonna take good care of you,'" Gene says. "But Ervin said, 'Our work's over; let's go on to California.' I argued with him about it. I said, 'Let's wait and see what these people are gonna do for us.' But Ervin was obsessed with going on. We both got teed off, and finally Ervin said, 'You do what you want; just take me to the bus station.'" After putting his stubborn friend aboard a westbound Greyhound, Gene returned to Tennessee.

Ervin, not surprisingly, never made it to California; instead, in a reprise of the truncated 1941 cross-country journey with Louallie, Gordon, and Carrie, he apparently ended up in San Antonio. While there, Ervin performed for perhaps a month with a cowboy singer whose name Gene could not recall. "When Ervin got back to Miami, I just remember seeing pictures of him and some fellas dressed in western outfits," he says. In fact, the singer was undoubtedly Ervin's old friend, Red River Dave. "I'd been concerned about Ervin, goin' off by himself," Gene says. "He was kind of gullible in some ways. But he told me he'd had a good time, even if he didn't get to California."

Back in Miami, however, Ervin's struggling family had not shared in the merriment. Gordon had begun supplementing his income by mowing lawns, while Louallie, frequently sick with asthma and allergies, had begun to seriously contemplate leaving, taking the children, and rebuilding her life without Ervin.

A devout Christian, she had prayed for her husband's redemption—but sometimes it must have seemed as though even the good lord himself wanted no part of the devil's box.

The Bluebird label (above) released the Rouse Brothers' version of Orange Blossom Special in 1939, but the recording failed to catch on. The only surviving photograph of Ervin T. Rouse as a child vaudevillian (right) shows the youngster, probably at about nine years of age, demonstrating a standard trick in his repertoire: making music by sliding his fiddle up and down a bow tucked between his knees.

Ervin and his older brother, Gordon, frequently performed as a duo. In these photographs, probably taken around 1930, Ervin performs two of his favorite fiddle tricks: coaxing bird sounds from the strings while playing Listen to the Mockingbird (above) and the old reliable bow-between-the-knees routine (right). The Rouses often appeared in hillbilly garb and combined music and cornpone humor.

Ervin and Gordon (above left and above right) could play it straight, but they had no difficulty putting on their rube faces. Gordon, in particular, "could make the dumbest face you ever saw," according to his wife, Carrie. These publicity photographs were taken in 1939.

From the same 1939 photo session, Ervin poses solo, looking surprisingly dashing. However, few who knew Ervin in his later years, after drinking and illness had taken their toll, would associate this handsome young fiddler with the rumpled, ruined figure who played for tips in such out-of-the-way hangouts as the Gator Hook.

"Irvin" (sic) Rouse displays one of his more highbrow stage costumes in this 1938 publicity photograph.

The Rouse boys (minus oldest brother Jimmy) flank patriarch Ernest at the funeral of Eloise Rouse. Shown are (left to right): Durwood, Gordon, Earl, Hayward, Ernest, Paul, Guy, Ervin, and Herbert. Inset are the Rouse girls (left to right): Mabel, Bettie, Eloise, and Gay. Jimmy (far right inset) is shown shortly before his death. He missed the funeral because of a performing engagement, which would have been perfectly understandable to "Miss Ella."

By the late 1970s, Ervin certainly did not give the appearance of a man who had might have written one of the world's most familiar songs. These photographs of Ervin accompanied his Miami Herald obituary, which stated that the musician was "frequently penniless."

This remarkable photograph of Ervin performing at the Gator Hook (above) appeared in National Geographic. A writer and photographer researching a story on the Big Cypress Swamp found themselves more fascinated by the eccentric fiddler than by the nature preserve where he kept a ramshakle second home. Although he could always please a crowd, Ervin's act never changed. Even in his fifties (right), he was performing the same fiddle tricks that he used on the vaudeville stage as a child.

At Ervin's funeral (above) family members flank a train-shaped floral arrangement sent by Johnny Cash. Cash first heard about Ervin through Maybelle Carter (right, with daughters Anita and Helen). Cash asked the legendary Mother Maybelle, who would soon become his mother-in-law, if she knew who wrote Orange Blossom Special . Maybelle remembered the Rouses fondly, although how they originally met is unclear, and Cash was intrigued enough to seek the obscure fiddler out.

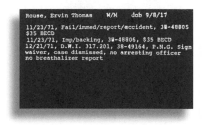

Ervin's only arrest was for drunken driving, but he escaped punishment when the arresting officer failed to show up for a court date. Throughout his life, Ervin was terrified of uniformed authority figures.

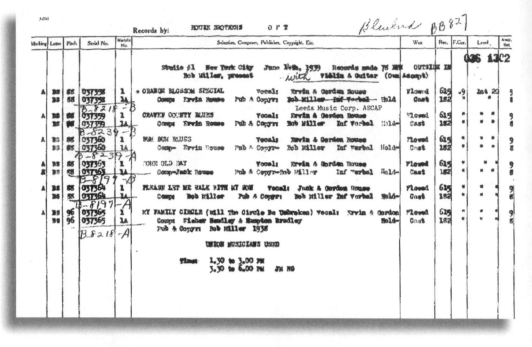

The session sheet from the Rouse Brothers' 1939 Bluebird recording session, which was arranged by their musical mentor, Bob Miller.

Old pals: Gene Christian (above), a former Blue Grass Boy, was Ervin's closest friend and protector for more than thirty years. Benny "The Big Tiger" Martin (right) fiddled for Flatt & Scruggs and sometimes called himself "Mr. Orange Blossom Special" because of his no-holds-barred version of the tune. Martin is shown performing at the Black Angus in Miami, where Christian led the house band. Ervin was in the audience, but was too debilitated to join his friends onstage.

Fiddlers three: The only known photograph of Ervin (left) and Chubby Wise (center) together. Gene Christian is on the right. The photograph was taken in the late 1940s at Ervin's Miami home.

Robert Russell "Chubby" Wise and Geneva Kirby as newlyweds in 1932. Geneva, the sweet-natured daugher of a respected Lake City farmer and church leader, was taking a risk by marrying Chubby, whose parentage was uncertain and whose desire to earn a living playing music precluded him from holding a steady job.

Chubby (above right) prepares for a radio broadcast with the Georgia Peach Pickers, with whom he played briefly before joining Bill Monroe's Blue Grass Boys. Shortly after hooking up with Monroe in 1943, Chubby appeared on Nashville's WSM (below) playing "the sweetest sound this side of Heaven."

Monroe and his troupe (above) traveled for a time in a 1941 Chevrolet airport limousine. Shown are (left to right): Howard Watts, Chubby, Monroe, and Lester Flatt. Chubby usually drove, as he would later for Hank Snow. After leaving Monroe, Chubby became a fixture on the Washington, D.C., country music scene. Enjoying a night on the town are (below, clockwise from foreground): Tommy Jackson, Rossi Wise, Paul Howard, Chubby, country star Ray Price, and Price's wife, Janie.

Children often compared Chubby to Santa Claus, and the similarity is easy to see. The fiddler is shown (right) with step-grandson Jason Case and (top) with an unidentified young admirer at a bluegrass festival.

Hank Snow (right) was known as the Singing Ranger to his fans. But to Chubby, he was the Little Chief, an imperious taskmaster with a barely discernable sense of humor. Chubby traveled the world with Snow, and played concerts in such far-flung locales as Kobe, Japan, where Mac Yasuda snapped the two men together onstage (below).

Chubby and Bill Monroe (left) spoke to one another for the first time in years at this chance meeting at a bluegrass festival in Columbus, Ohio. Monroe died shortly after this photo was taken. Toward the end of his life, Chubby recorded several well-regarded albums for Orlando, Florida-based Pinecastle Records. American Original (below) demonstrated that age had not robbed the old fiddler of his mastery.

Chubby and Rossi Wise (below): their unorthodox union endured numerous obstacles, including Chubby's drinking, Rossi's disdain for Chubby's family, and infidelity on both sides. "But for the last twelve years of his life, Chubby was perfect," Rossi says.

Chubby (above) is all smiles during a 1984 visit to Lake City, where he was inducted into the city's Hall of Fame, served as grand marshal of a parade in his honor, and (right) helped cut the ribbon opening a Civil War museum. Despite his harsh life there as a youngster, Chubby always recalled Lake City fondly.

Columbia Records placed a full-page ad in Billboard *magazine touting Cash's new album. It was an unorthodox collection that included three Bob Dylan songs and a Dylanesque "protest" song called* All God's Children Ain't Free *in addition to the title tune. By the mid-60s, Cash had positioned himself as more of a folksinger than a mainstream country artist.*

ORANGE BLOSSOM SPECIAL

Words & Music by ERVIN T. ROUSE

MCA MUSIC
A DIVISION OF MCA INC.

Johnny Cash had a hit record with the world's most famous fiddle tune. But the Man in Black's version of Orange Blossom Special *featured a harmonica and a saxaphone, not a fiddle. For the next three decades, Cash performed the tune in virtually every concert appearance and on numerous television programs.*

Cash and Chubby (above) appeared onstage together once, during a concert in Lake City, where they performed Orange Blossom Special. *Cash was careful to introduce Chubby as a man "who plays a great version" of the song, not as the man who actually wrote it. While in Lake City, Cash, who had just been released from the Betty Ford Center, addressed the local Rotary Club on the dangers of drug abuse. Cash's host, Judge Vernon Douglas (left), said the singer did not specifically mention the authorship controversy during his visit.*

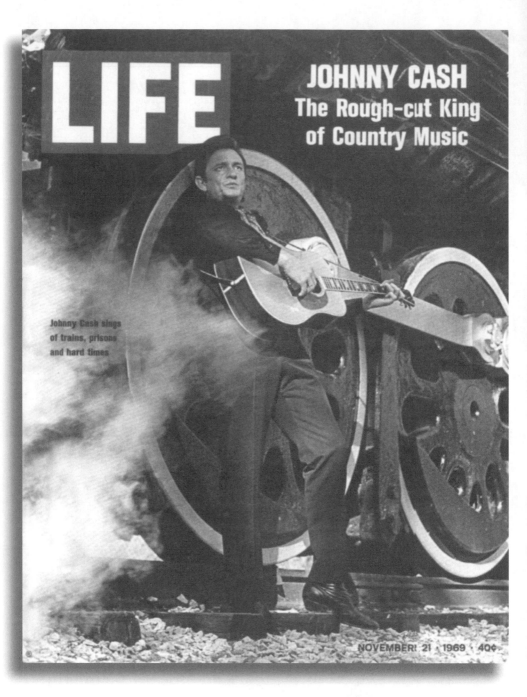

LIFE

JOHNNY CASH
The Rough-cut King
of Country Music

Johnny Cash sings
of trains, prisons
and hard times

NOVEMBER 21 · 1969 · 40¢

By November 1969, when this edition of Life *magazine appeared, Cash was at the peak of his fame.
And he had further fattened Ervin's bank account by including* Orange Blossom Special *on his
landmark 1967 album,* Live at Folsom Prison. *The album went platinum and is today generally
regarded as one of the most powerful live recordings ever made.*

Before the advent of the diesels, steam engines (above) carried the Orange Blossom Special's plush Pullman passenger cars. The train offered what was then considered to be the ultimate in luxurious travel accomodations. But by 1938, sleak and powerful diesel locomotives (below) sheared two hours and fifty minutes off the Special's New York to Miami run. Photos courtesy of ACL and SAL Railroads Historical Society.

The original hand-written sheet music for Orange Blossom Special, *as submitted by Gordon Rouse to the Library of Congress copyright office. The reciept stamp clearly indicates that the song had been written prior to the train's exhibition tour stop in Jacksonville, thus damaging Chubby's claims of co-authorship.*

Cartoonists lampooned Henry Ford's obsession with fiddle music, which was considered lowbrow by many. But Ford's fiddle contests gained widespread publicity for the eccentric automaker and amateur social engineer, who said he was "trying in a small way to help America take a step, even if it is a little one, toward the saner and sweeter idea of life that prevailed in the [pre-war] days."

VIII

Moving On: Chubby Wise
and the Singing Ranger

*You tell the Little Chief if he fools around with me this morning
there's going to be some bear walking around this lobby. Tell the
Little Chief I'll come when I'm good and ready.*
    Chubby Wise, responding to
    a summons from Hank Snow

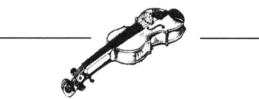

In early January, 1948, Chubby Wise was nearing the conclusion of his historic
tenure with Bill Monroe and the Blue Grass Boys, and was booked for two
weeks with the group at an American Legion-sponsored tent show at the Florida
State Fair, then held in Miami.

Between shows, Chubby was sitting at a table near a concession stand eating a
hamburger when a striking redhead asked if she and her two children could join him.
"I liked what I saw," said Chubby, who rarely wanted for feminine companionship
when traveling. "Of course, in those days, I'd have made love to a bush if I'd have
thought there was a bird in there."

As it turned out, however, Rossi Truell Case, a registered nurse, was a Lawrence
Welk aficionado, and was present at the show only because she was working
temporarily at a nearby child-care center. Additionally, she was married—as was
Chubby, albeit nominally—and had come to Miami from her home in the
Washington, D.C., suburbs to obtain a divorce from her husband, Ralph.

Yet, despite the fact that Chubby's music was not her style—she had only the
vaguest notion of who Bill Monroe was—Rossi was entranced by the extroverted
fiddler's seemingly guileless demeanor, and by his all-consuming desire to please.

Chubby was not, by most definitions, a handsome man; he was short, pudgy,
balding, and walked with a pronounced limp as a result of his childhood injury. Yet,

his deep brown eyes twinkled when flashed a magnificent smile—the teeth were not real, but the sentiment was—and he effectively employed the sheer force of his personality as compensation for any physical shortcomings. "He was so sweet and kind that I guess it was love at first sight," Rossi says. "We got to talking and he asked me for a date. I said yes. I was going to meet him that night, but I stood him up."

The following evening, however, she returned to the fair, and to Monroe's tent. "Me and a girlfriend, we were talking to the other boys in the band," Rossi says. "Then, here comes Chubby, limping down the aisle. He said, 'You stood me up last night, but you're not standing me up tonight.'"

What followed was ten days of intensive "partying" that culminated when Chubby proclaimed that he had fallen in love, and promised to pursue the budding relationship regardless of distance. Rossi may or may not have believed this typically hollow vow, but Chubby was serious; he returned to Miami just days later. "I was living with my roommate, and she had a little boy," recalls Rossi. "I also had my two boys. So, we sat there on the bed until two or three in the morning, and when it was bedtime, he had to sleep with the kids. It like to have killed him."

Frustrated but infatuated, Chubby returned to Nashville. Rossi followed her new paramour and rented a small apartment. Geneva, busy caring for a teenaged daughter and fretting over her husband's increasingly prolonged absences, was unaware of the budding romance. "I used to go to the *Opry* when Chubby was playing with [Monroe]," Geneva recalls. "My mother had come to stay with me, and we'd both go to the shows. I later realized that Rossi used to sit right behind us. And when Chubby would be smiling toward us while he was onstage, he was really smiling at her. I didn't know any of this. And if I had—well, I would have fought a circle-saw when I was younger."

Chubby left Monroe in late January 1948, and moved with his family to the Washington, D.C. area to join country music entrepreneur Connie B. Gay's Radio Ranchmen. The group, which broadcast over WARL in Arlington, Virginia, also featured fellow Monroe alumnus Clyde Moody and accordionist Pat Patterson.

The innovative Gay, a masterful promoter known as "The Hick from Lizard Lick"—his hometown was Lizard Lick, North Carolina—nurtured a thriving, multi-media musical empire in the nation's Capitol through his *Town & Country* television, radio and live stage shows, which drew from an impressive roster of talent that included Billy Grammer, Grandpa Jones, Hank Penny, Patsy Cline, Roy Clark, George Hamilton IV, and Gay's breakthrough star, Jimmy Dean. Chubby later recalled seeing both Dean and Cline perform—on the same evening—at a tiny tavern called Little Miller's Covered Wagon located across 14th Street from the Greyhound station. Conveniently, the newly divorced Rossi was now living in nearby Baltimore, Maryland, and moved shortly thereafter to D.C., where she and Chubby dated "on the sly." Rossi's children, in the meantime, had moved in with their father.

"It was the golden era of country music here," said steel-guitarist Marvin Carroll, once a member of Jimmy Dean's Texas Wildcats, during a 1987 interview. "From the time I came here in 1949 through the 1960s, all you had to do was open a door, put a country single on the jukebox and you had a crowd. It was booming."

Demographics played a large role in this phenomenon; by the late 1940s, the city of eight hundred thousand was populated by significant pockets of white, working-class Southerners who had migrated from the eastern Appalachians in search of better lives. Anxious to retain some vestige of home, these displaced hillbillies found comfort in the sound of fiddles, steel guitars, banjos, and nasal vocals.

Among the hundreds if not thousands of musicians who called the Capitol area home was Earl Rouse, who had divorced, remarried, and fathered four more children. "I loved ballads," says Elaine Rouse, Earl's daughter from his first marriage. "So, when Daddy found out that I could sing, we formed an act and hit all the clubs in D.C. Daddy played the fiddle, and I knew about three chords on the guitar. I'd do pop songs like *Cry* and *Little White Cloud*, and the people really loved us. We were pulling in about a hundred dollars a night."

Those who saw Earl and Elaine perform remember their act as a lively crowd-pleaser, largely because Earl was savvy enough to push his pretty offspring out front. Certainly, he knew from experience that a precocious youngster with a flair for showmanship was far more likely to attract significant tips than a middle-aged hillbilly.

In any case, Earl and other buskers working the D.C. clubs enjoyed fringe benefits above and beyond an all-cash income source. The Capitol was brimming with young, single, and decidedly independent women who had left their hometowns to seek employment in the burgeoning federal bureaucracy. On their own and feeling frisky—or perhaps lonely, since many had been widowed in World War II—they haunted the bars and flattered the musicians, offering their favors to anyone able to carry a guitar or a tune.

Those who were intrigued by handsome Earl sometimes eyed teenaged Elaine with suspicion. "I remember at one club, this Indian woman, a girlfriend of Daddy's, tried to trap me in the ladies' room," she recalls. "She was going to kill me because she didn't believe I was really his daughter. She thought it was all a cover-up."

Yet, despite the Capitol's obvious appeal for those whose interests included performing, womanizing, and drinking—not necessarily in that order—Chubby and Moody left the Radio Ranchmen after little more than a year, moving with his family to Durham, North Carolina, and landing a daily radio program.

According to Rossi, Chubby would finish a noon show, borrow a car, and drive three hundred miles to D.C. for trysts that he described to a suspicious Geneva as "fishing trips." At least once, Rossi rushed to Durham at the behest of Moody, who reported that Chubby, ensconced in a rooming house, had drunk himself into a nauseated stupor, and had vowed to continue bingeing until she arrived.

But Rossi, who says she never encouraged Chubby to leave his wife, grew weary of her seemingly dead-end role as a mistress, and was initially reluctant when the fiddler called one evening to plead for bus fare. "He said, 'I love you and I can't do without you,'" Rossi says. "I studied about it for a while, and said he could come. Then, when I picked him up at the bus station he had one dollar and a pint of whiskey in his pocket. I said, 'Chubby, Geneva may be happy with you running back and forth, but I'm not. You make up your mind right now what you want.' He said 'I'm staying.'"

That, in effect, was the end of even the pretense of a marriage between Chubby and Geneva. "Chubby left us, we didn't leave him," Geneva recalls. She returned to Lake City in 1949 and sought to rebuild her life, securing a job at a dime store to support herself and her daughter. She was granted a divorce in 1951, and shortly thereafter remarried a local farmer named Claude Meeks. Chubby, for all intents and purposes, was out of her life for good.

SHORTLY AFTER HIS RELATIONSHIP with Rossi gained quasi-official status, the restless fiddler found himself back in Nashville, rejoining the Blue Grass Boys in the fall of 1949. Although this second tour of duty lasted less than a year, Chubby did play on Monroe's final Columbia recording session—his first in Nashville—held October 22, 1949 at the Tulane Hotel's Castle Studios.

It was not a pleasant experience. Monroe was angry that Columbia had signed the Stanley Brothers, whom he regarded as crass imitators, and was fulfilling a contractual obligation before bolting to Decca. One memorable tune resulted: *Can't You Hear Me Callin'*, which was said to have been written about Monroe's girlfriend, Bessie Lee Mauldin.

Chubby left, he says, because of Monroe's erratic pay schedule: "Bill would come in and say, 'Can you get by on ten dollars, Chubby?' 'Can you make it on fifteen dollars?' The other part never did come." In fact, as the 1950s dawned Monroe's career was in decline; he and the Blue Grass Boys were playing to sparse crowds at schoolhouses and movie theaters, usually for a percentage of the gate. It would be years before the world rediscovered the Father of Bluegrass Music.

In mid-1950, Chubby, this time joined by Rossi, took a bus to Detroit, where he joined the Kentucky-born York Brothers, best known for their skillful country covers of rhythm and blues songs released on Syd Nathan's King Records. However, this association survived a scant six months before the couple left the Motor City to reunite with Chubby's old bandmates Lester Flatt and Earl Scruggs—now separated from Monroe and fronting the Foggy Mountain Boys—on WVRK in Versailles, Kentucky.

Although this promising stint was also unseemingly brief, Chubby did participate in a May 1951 Columbia recording session that produced six Flatt & Scruggs sides, including the classic *Jimmy Brown the Newsboy*. Leaving Kentucky, the couple returned—apparently with great reluctance—to the D.C. area, where Chubby formed a four-piece band and played a circuit of local clubs, or as he termed them, "beer joints."

Why did a fiddler of such renown find it so difficult to remain gainfully employed? Undoubtedly, like many super-sidemen, Chubby hoped one day to have the spotlight to himself; a goal that was unreachable as long as he toiled in Monroe's huge shadow. It is also possible that he was weary of rigidly structured bluegrass, and saw little opportunity for a fresh creative challenge with Monroe disciples Flatt & Scruggs.

Although these considerations surely came into play, Chubby was rootless by nature; his entire life had been a series of upheavals, and he knew no other way to live. He was also a prolific drinker, making it likely that alcoholism, not art, contributed mightily to this puzzling series of hasty departures.

In any case, with no other options immediately apparent, he unenthusiastically made the rounds of downtown hotspots such as Boondocks, Captain Guy's, the Famous, the KitMar, the Ozarks, the American Bar, the Rendezvous, and Vinnie's. In pre-gentrified Georgetown, he played the Shamrock, the B&J Tavern, the Potomac Tavern, and Pete's Tavern. When the bars closed, Chubby and other musicians working the area would congregate at Turner's Arena (now Capitol Arena), from which Gay's *Town & Country Jamboree* was televised live on Saturday nights over a network of stations in D.C., Virginia, and Maryland. "Everyone was pretty well loaded by the time they got there," Carroll recalled.

Still, Chubby's musical prowess remained undiminished. Among those inspired by his Capitol performances was a talented but troubled teenaged fiddler named Scott Stoneman, son of seminal country recording artist Ernest V. "Pop" Stoneman and member of the Stoneman Family, a lively hillbilly combo that combined down-home music with uninhibited showmanship.

The band, fronted by Pop on vocals and guitar, at various times also included daughter Donna on mandolin, daughter Patsy on autoharp, daughter Veronica (Roni) on banjo, and son Jimmy on bass. Matriarch Hattie played fiddle and clawhammer-style banjo, while other siblings and spouses rotated in and out of the family enterprise as needed. "Scotty loved and admired Chubby," says Donna, who now devotes her energies to evangelism. "They took pocketknives and carved their names on each other's fiddles. That alone ought to tell you the kind of mutual respect they shared."

Scott warrants further attention in large part because many bluegrass aficionados insist that his 1962 recording of the *Special* remains unsurpassed. No less an authority than Marty Stuart, who backed Lester Flatt and Johnny Cash before embarking upon a successful solo recording career, contends that "Scotty had the ultimate version; it's a spiritual event that leaves you breathless." But Scott, like Chubby and Ervin, was as tormented as he was brilliant. "Oh, Lord yes, Scotty was such a heavy drinker," says Rossi. "But Chubby was his idol, and you can hear a lot of Chubby in Scotty's playing."

The Stonemans, originally from Galax, Virginia, lived in Carmody Hills, a shabby, working class neighborhood in Prince George's County, Maryland. They performed regularly at Armstrong's Restaurant and Tavern, the Wagon Wheel, the Club Hillbilly, and other nightspots, supplementing their modest salaries by passing the hat. In 1947, after winning a talent competition sponsored by Gay and WARL, the family appeared for twenty-six weeks on *Gay Time*, a local television program broadcast from Constitution Hall.

Yet, despite their growing local renown, the Stonemans led a hand-to-mouth existence throughout the late 1940s and early 1950s. Decades later, Patsy described the family's often dire circumstances in a song called *Prayers and Pinto Beans*:

> *When the times were gettin' hard,*
> *and things were goin' bad,*
> *we always called upon the ones we knew.*
> *Mama fed our souls with the Bible and her prayers,*
> *then pinto beans and music saw us through.*

Scott, arguably the most gifted Stoneman, had in his teens begun to accumulate various "championships" through participation in fiddle contests, besting such savvy old-timers as Curly Fox. He also mastered other stringed instruments, and taught his siblings how to play them. Nonetheless, the young fiddler's personal deportment could sometimes be bizarre, foreshadowing a self-destructive bent that would culminate in disaster.

According to Ivan Tribe, who wrote about the musical clan in his book *The Stonemans: An Appalachian Family and the Music That Shaped Their Lives* (University of Illinois Press), "[Scott] drank some from his mid-teens, but tended more in the direction of such activities as upsetting outhouses or tying two cats together by the tail and throwing them over a clothes line. In one notable instance, he defecated in the neighbor's piano. He hated pianos and horn music, sister Roni says."

In his early twenties, Scott toured as a sideman with bluegrass vocalist Mac Wiseman, and played on records with mandolinist Buzz Busby and country singer Pete Pike. In 1956, he founded a group called the Blue Grass Champs, which held forth six nights weekly at The Famous, and quickly emerged as one of the region's biggest draws. "Everybody and everything came into The Famous," says Rossi. "There were always a lot of queers and prostitutes hanging around. It was a real circus."

The combo, which included sister Donna and brother Jimmy along with a guitar-player named Jimmy Case and a banjoist named Porter Church, even appeared on the popular CBS-TV program *Arthur Godfrey's Talent Scouts*, winning the nationally televised competition with a performance of the bluegrass standard *Salty*

Dog Blues. (Patsy Cline would launch her ascent to stardom two years later via appearances on Godfrey's broadcasts).

Subsequently, the Champs weathered personnel changes and Scott's increasingly erratic behavior to become regulars on *The Don Owens T.V. Jamboree*, a local program broadcast weekly on WTTG-TV. Eventually, other Stoneman Family members, including Pop, also became Jamboree fixtures. And, while the youngsters usually performed popular hits, Pop enjoyed resurrecting tunes that he had recorded for Ralph Peer and Okeh more than three decades earlier, including chestnuts such as *The Titanic* and *The Face That Never Returned.*

This exposure ultimately attracted the attention of urban folk-music fans, who came to realize that Mother Maybelle Carter was not the only living link to commercial country music's genesis. Consequently, in 1957 folk scholar Mike Seeger traveled to Carmody Hills to record ten traditional songs featuring Pop, along with Hattie and a handful of other family members. The resulting album, *Old Time Tunes From the South*, was released on the Folkways label, and was much praised by scholars.

The Blue Grass Champs, now including youngest brother Van on guitar, also recorded for several small labels, but the resulting sides had little impact beyond the D.C. market.

In the winter of 1962, the Stoneman Family—the Blue Grass Champs had ceased to exist as a separate entity—appeared on the *Grand Ole Opry*, where Scott stopped the show with his trick fiddling and a lightening-fast rendition of *Orange Blossom Special.* (Ivan Tribe writes that Hank Snow was not amused when encores for the Stonemans cut into his stage time.) That summer, the group recorded an album for Nashville-based Starday Records called *Ernest V. Stoneman and the Stoneman Family: Bluegrass Champs*. Although sales were disappointing, the Stonemans could at least celebrate the fact that they were finally affiliated with a mainstream record label. With any luck at all, a hit record would come in time.

Heartened but cash-strapped, the family returned to D.C. and resumed working clubs. They also competed at the 1962 Warrenton [Virginia] Jaycees National Country Music Contest, held at Whippoorwill Park. There, Scott took top fiddle honors for the eighth consecutive year while another combination of family members won "best band."

The following year, seeking to capitalize on their genuine backwoods appeal, the Stonemans performed at folk festivals sponsored by Lamar University and the University of Illinois. The approving narrative of a student reviewer at Illinois indicates how campus intellectuals, who customarily cheered cardigan-clad folk acts such as the Kingston Trio, responded to an unabashed hillbilly presentation:

> The high point of the action was no doubt the performance
> of the fiddler, Scott, who spent the first part of the evening
> playing the part of the village idiot, skulking about the stage,

dispensing corn-fed humor and generally trying to make a shambles of his kinfolks' efforts. He really stole the stage, however, when he gave a classic example of trick fiddling— holding the bow between his knees and moving the fiddle over it, lying on the floor and arching his back while he played the fiddle under his 'bridge,' playing the instrument while holding it behind his back.

The whole performance was both entertaining and significant. The Stonemans, making only their second appearance before a college audience, had made no effort to remodel their efforts into "folk music." They simply presented the same act with which they entertained audiences in their native Appalachians.

In the fall of 1963, the Stonemans returned to Nashville to record a second album for Starday. The resulting compilation, titled *The Great Old Timer at the Capitol*, featured Scott's now legendary rendition of the *Special*. Although the album was no commercial blockbuster, it did solidify the Stonemans as a viable folk act, and increased the fervor of Scott's growing hipster fan base.

So, the family continued to tour, packing trendy West Coast clubs such as the Troubadour in Hollywood and the Golden Bear in Huntington Beach. Scott, however, frequently found himself banished from the group because of drinking and unreliability.

"My brother had so many problems [with alcohol] that sometimes we'd lose him," recalls Donna. "One time, we were playing a club date in California without Scotty. But the people kept yelling for *Orange Blossom Special*. It's like they were getting mad at us, so I started getting mad right back. I said, 'Okay, if they want *Orange Blossom Special*, then I'll give it to them on the mandolin.' I'd never played the song before, but I was mad enough to give it some speed. Well, when I finished we got a standing ovation, and people were hollering for encores. From then on, that song became a big part of our show—with or without Scotty."

Although they would never have a career-making hit record, the Stonemans would go on record fifteen albums for major and near-major labels, and to headline their own syndicated television program. They would become the toast of Printer's Alley thanks to a highly successful long-term engagement at Nashville's Black Poodle nightclub, and would win a Country Music Association (CMA) Award for Vocal Group of the Year in 1967.

Scott, however, drifted in and out of the band as personal problems and alcoholism overwhelmed him. He died, apparently after consuming shaving lotion for its alcohol content, in 1973. "Chubby was so upset to hear about Scotty," Rossi recalls. "But he was on the road somewhere when it happened, and he couldn't get back for the funeral. You know, that's the way it is with musicians. They care about each other, but they've got to be out making a living."

IN SEPTEMBER 1951, WHILE still languishing in D.C., Chubby received documents confirming that, after eighteen years of marriage, Geneva had been granted a divorce on the grounds of desertion.

"After he got those papers, Chubby threw his arms around me and said, 'Honey, will you marry me?'" recalls Rossi. "I said, 'Lord, yes! I thought you'd never ask.'" With two friends present to act as witnesses, the couple wed at a small Baptist church in Rockville, Maryland, thereby beginning a rocky and at times unconventional union that would, somehow, endure for forty-four years.

Precisely how unconventional became apparent one week following the ceremony, when Chubby joined a retinue of performers organized by Gay to entertain at military bases in Trinidad and Puerto Rico. "When he went overseas, I said, 'Chubby, you do anything you want to do or are old enough to do, because you may never get the chance to do it no more,'" Rossi recalls. "I said, 'What you do two hundred miles away or two thousand miles away won't hurt me.'"

So, having been granted carte blanche to carouse, Chubby, along with singers Betty Bean, Smitty Smith, Jimmy Dean, Billy Grammer, and Smokey McClenny, spent two wild weeks in the Caribbean. Also traveling with the troupe was Gay, his secretary, Jane Trimmer, and, oddly enough, Rossi's first husband, Ralph Case, a friend of Gay's who operated the public address system.

Chubby, at least, enjoyed the islands' many attractions, including their exotic women. "One of them Puerto Rican gals called me 'Chobby,'" he said. "She wanted to come home with me. Rossi had told me that I could do anything I was big enough to do, and friends, I did." Upon the tour's conclusion, the bawdy Rossi even bragged to friends about the "new techniques" her husband had apparently learned while overseas.

Back in D.C., Chubby resumed "spotting clubs" with bassist Red Seal; work he continued to find demeaning and unrewarding. However, he did play an unforgettable engagement on January 1, 1953, as an added attraction on a Richmond, Virginia package show headlined by Red Foley. Earlier in the day, it had been announced that Hank Williams, twenty-nine, had died enroute to show dates in Charleston, West Virginia and Canton, Ohio. "It was so sad," Chubby recalled. "Everyone was heartbroken. Red Foley came out and sang *Peace in the Valley*, and there wasn't a dry eye in the house. It looked like a bunch of white flags waving around in the audience when people pulled out their handkerchiefs."

Shortly thereafter, Chubby and Rossi enjoyed a belated honeymoon in Miami, where Rossi snapped a photograph that is now a minor treasure; her husband, looking typically cherubic, is draping his pudgy arms over the shoulders of a stone-faced Ervin and a grinning Gene at Ervin's home in Alapatta. The couple then headed north to Lake City, where they visited daughter Marvelene and members of the Wise clan, including Barbara and even Bob.

Unfortunately, Chubby did not elaborate on what must have been a satisfying, if ultimately bittersweet, homecoming. Although his career seemed temporarily stalled, this unwanted, illegitimate street urchin had overcome profound obstacles to become Lake City's most famous former resident. It must have been sorely tempting to boast, but his friends insist that Chubby would never have flaunted his long overdue good fortune, even to those who had treated him badly.

So, now that his personal life was in order—at least to the extent that "order" might be defined in Chubby's universe—it was time to concentrate on his career, and to make another run at the big time. That process was accelerated in March 1954, when a telegram arrived from a dour, Canadian-born singer whose harsh early life rivaled even Chubby's Dickensian upbringing: the Singing Ranger, Hank Snow.

CLARENCE EUGENE "HANK" SNOW, one of country music's most important stylists and prolific recording artists, was born in Brooklyn, Nova Scotia, on May 9, 1914. One of four children—three were sisters—Hank's parents divorced when he was eight years old.

The youngster was then sent to live with his paternal grandparents, although he frequently ran away to his mother's home, where he taught himself to play guitar while listening to recordings by Vernon Dalhart and Jimmie Rodgers. However, his mother soon remarried, to a violent and abusive man about whom Snow later said, "I took many beatings from him, and still carry scars across my body that were left by his hamlike hands."

With nowhere else to turn, the unfortunate twelve-year-old signed on for a three-year stint as a cabin boy aboard a North Atlantic fishing trawler, where he entertained the crew by singing and playing the harmonica. Determined to succeed as an entertainer, Snow was hired by a Halifax radio station in 1933, billing himself as "Hank, the Yodeling Ranger."

His popularity gradually increased and, by the late 1930s, Snow rivaled Wilf Carter—known in the United States as "Montana Slim"—as Canada's most renowned home-grown country singer. He even had a sponsor—Crazy Water Crystals—and had released a series of well-received original tunes such as *Blue Velvet Band, Galveston Rose,* and *My Blue River Rose* for Bluebird, which operated a Montreal-based satellite office.

Snow, however, was anxious to conquer the far more lucrative American market. A modestly successful stint on *The Big D Jamboree* in Dallas brought Snow to the attention of fellow Rodgers devotee Ernest Tubb, who intervened on his behalf with the *Grand Ole Opry.* Tubb's cajoling finally won Snow an audition and an *Opry* slot; however, his Ryman debut, in January 1950, was eminently forgettable. "I don't mind telling you that I bombed," Snow said in the mid-1960s. "The people just sat there while I sang. And sat. No applause, no nothing, almost. Just sat."

Then, in the summer of 1950, Snow released what would become his signature song, *I'm Moving On,* for American Victor. This rambunctious recording, which would later be covered by the Rolling Stones, topped the *Billboard* Country &

Western charts for twenty-one consecutive weeks, and would ultimately rank as the most popular country record of the decade. Two more No. 1 hits followed in quick succession: *The Golden Rocket* and *Rhumba Boogie.*

By March 1954, when Snow contacted Chubby about replacing fiddler Tommy Vaden, the anti-charismatic Canadian, who once teetered on the brink of dismissal from the *Opry*, had notched eighteen Top 5 records, and was arguably the institution's hottest star.

Chubby, anxious to escape what he had come to regard as musical purgatory, was concerned that Snow may have pigeonholed him in the bluegrass genre. Therefore, for his audition tape, Chubby fiddled while Herbie Jones, a member of Jimmy Dean's Texas Wildcats, sang Snow's recent hit, (*Now and Then There's) A Fool Such as I*, a love ballad that featured several melancholy instrumental breaks.

Three anxious days after sending the recording, Chubby received a telephone call from Snow asking him to fly immediately to Miami, where he joined the Rainbow Ranch Boys for a show at the Miami-Dade County Auditorium. The engagement went well, and Chubby was offered a permanent job—as Snow's fiddler and driver—at a salary of a hundred dollars per week. "Chubby was thrilled," recalls Rossie. "He was so disgusted by those clubs, and by having to deal with all the drunks."

Gratefully, Chubby and Rossi packed their bags, hitched their mobile home to Chubby's Oldsmobile, and headed to Music City, beginning an association which, aside from one eighteen-month interruption and several shorter splits, would endure until 1970. Once in Nashville, Rossi found employment as a nurse at St. Thomas Hospital, and Chubby went on the road again. "You didn't sit still with Hank Snow," Chubby said. "Even if you had to take a dog sled there, we went and played."

If the king of the bluegrass fiddlers was seeking a creative change of direction by joining Snow, then he surely found it. Although his style was firmly rooted in traditional genres, the Singing Ranger—a new stage moniker had been adopted when his deepening voice made yodeling a challenge—was musically conversant in jazz, blues, gospel, and even the mambo. His resonate, quaintly accented baritone—a bit like Ernest Tubb's, but on pitch—was instantly recognizable, as was his distinctive, exacting guitar work.

Backing the versatile Snow, Chubby was free to experiment, as was evidenced during the making of a 1955 Jimmie Rodgers tribute album. Producer Chet Atkins, who then managed Victor's Nashville studio, was dissatisfied with Chubby's rendering of *Way Out On the Mountain.* "He'd say, 'Chubby, do it this way,' but I just couldn't feel it," Chubby said. "I bet we cut that thing fifteen times, and we couldn't get a take. Finally, Hank went to Chet and said, 'You're going to have to let Chubby play what he feels; if he don't feel it, he ain't gonna to play it.' Then Chet come in and said, 'Chubby, forget what I told you. You go on and play what you feel.' There was one more take, and that was it."

If Snow's musical approach differed from Monroe's, his personality was remarkably similar. Like Monroe, Snow was a perfectionist who did not suffer fools gladly, and was frequently described as aloof, pompous, and humorless. Nonetheless, he was instantly enchanted by Chubby's relentlessly upbeat disposition, and even allowed the fiddler to address him as "the Little Chief" with impunity.

In his 1994 autobiography, *The Hank Snow Story* (University of Illinois Press), the Country Music Hall of Famer devotes the better part of a chapter to Chubby's adventures, writing: "I believe that the two gentlemen I had the most fun with during my career were Bill Davidson [a previous fiddler] and Robert 'Chubby' Wise."

Of course, *Orange Blossom Special* was added to Snow's repertoire when Chubby joined the Rainbow Ranch Boys and, as always, it proved to be a show-stopper around the world. With Snow, Chubby took the *Special* to the Far East—including Viet Nam—as well as to a dozen European countries and Canada. He also played it on the *Opry's* nationwide radio broadcasts and at Snow's numerous stateside concert appearances, thereby introducing the tune to an audience well beyond Monroe's bluegrass partisans.

So, when Chubby told Snow his increasingly familiar version of how the *Special* was written—apparently all but eliminating Ervin from the narrative—a sympathetic Little Chief opined that a court of law might well rule favorably if he were to seek a share of the royalties. "Hank told Chubby that he'd help him [with legal expenses] if he could find a way to prove to a judge that he co-wrote the song," says Rossi. "Chubby wouldn't do it. The only person who could have confirmed [the story] was his first wife, because she was there. But Chubby said he'd caused her enough trouble when they were married, and he didn't want to put her through any more." In fact, Chubby probably realized that he had overplayed his hand, and was relieved when Snow let the matter drop.

As time passed, Chubby became something of a resident court jester for Snow and the Rainbow Ranch Boys—and not always voluntarily. "Any time anything unusual happened to anybody in the band, it was Chubby," wrote Snow in his autobiography. "It seemed like trouble came looking for him."

For example, prior to a mid-summer *Opry* appearance in the late 1950s, Chubby was standing onstage behind the Ryman's heavy curtain, which was mechanically raised and lowered as a single unit instead of parting. When the massive, red-velvet drape began to ascend, the leg of Chubby's pants somehow became entangled with a horizontal rod that anchored the skirt, pulling the surprised fiddler off his feet and lifting him toward the rafters. Luckily, before he was elevated to dangerous heights, Chubby's pants ripped and he tumbled unceremoniously to the stage floor, bruising himself but saving his fiddle from damage.

"Chubby's outfit was a mess," wrote Snow. "He didn't have another stage suit to change into, and he looked like a hobo. A lot of people were scrambling around trying to find a pair of pants to fit him, but all we could find was an old mackinaw in one of the back rooms, which was actually a thick winter jacket." With no choice, Chubby donned the woolly, three-quarter-length coat to hide the tear in his pants, and sweltered through Snow's set as the band stifled giggles and the audience looked on in puzzlement.

Other times, Chubby brought trouble on himself—usually as a result of his drinking. The phobic fiddler dealt with his fear of flying by getting drunk before boarding an airplane, and by remaining drunk throughout the trip. "Chubby would start drinking about six hours before flight time," wrote Snow. "Sometimes I wondered whether we'd get him through the gate check and on to the aircraft when he was so tipsy— and there were several times we almost didn't make it." But, the combination of liquor and jitters usually made the normally outgoing Chubby even more vivacious, and the reserved Snow always enjoyed watching the merry minstrel chat up his unsuspecting seatmates.

Unfortunately, this otherwise endearing quality proved dangerous in some foreign locales. "In strange cities, regardless of what country we were in, [Chubby] would go out at night and wander around the streets," wrote Snow. "If you happened to pass by a bar, you might see him sitting on a stool having a beer and perhaps talking to a sailor, soldier, salesman, or just about anybody. Wherever he was, he treated everybody as if he'd known them all his life."

However, not everyone reciprocated in kind. In Wiesbaden, West Germany, for example, Chubby wandered away for an after-dinner stroll and was gone all night, prompting Snow and the other Rainbow Ranch Boys to fear for his safety. "We wondered if he had drunk too much and had fallen asleep somewhere," wrote Snow. "Knowing Chubby, that was a reasonable explanation. About 7 a.m., one of the boys went to the lobby [of the Klee Hotel] to check, but still no Chubby. About that time, I happened to look out the hotel's front door, and I saw a taxicab, and the cab driver was pulling Chubby out. He had his two hands under Chubby's arms, pulling him with his feet dragging on the ground. The driver got Chubby into the hotel, and several of us in the lobby carried him upstairs to his room. He wasn't hurt, but he was still pretty well stoned—and his wallet was missing."

Then, in Naples, Italy, Chubby was mugged again. According to Snow, the fiddler related the story this way: "As I was walking down the street, some young kids walked up to me and asked me for a couple of cigarettes. As I reached for the pack of cigarettes, they grabbed me from behind. They took my wallet, my cigarette lighter, and the ring off my finger. They even took my little shaker of false-teeth powder I use to hold my false teeth in. Two of those little bastards yelled with delight when they saw this white stuff. They probably thought they'd hit the jackpot and had found cocaine. I hope that powder glues their nostrils together."

Chubby also used his predilection for mishaps as a cover when explaining alcohol-induced behavior. Back in West Germany, following a show at an NCO club, Chubby, who was wearing a new and painfully ill-fitting set of dentures, got drunk and decided that the best way to eliminate the problem was to eliminate the teeth. "I took them teeth, rolled down the window [of the car], and threw 'em just as hard as I could," Chubby said. "After I kind of sobered up, I thought, 'Well, what in the hell was I thinkin' of? What am I gonna tell Rossi that I done with my teeth?'"

Bassist Jimmy Widener had a solution: Chubby should claim that he had been robbed of his choppers by a toothless mugger, and then beaten senseless when the scoundrel realized that they did not fit. Since Chubby had fallen earlier in a gravel parking lot, he was already appropriately bruised, adding further realism to the account. Coming from anyone less accident-prone, such an explanation would have been dismissed as ludicrous; coming from Chubby, however, it seemed entirely plausible.

Occasionally, when Chubby was "tipsy"—to borrow Snow's dainty euphemism—he could be stubborn and disagreeable with his boss and his co-workers. The morning after a show in Halifax, Snow and the band, joined by Cowboy Copas, sat waiting in two cars parked outside the Lord Nelson Hotel while Chubby dallied in the lobby, loudly haranguing guests with jokes and stories. Snow, his patience ebbing, finally summoned a bellboy and said, "You go back in there and tell Chubby I'm giving him five minutes to get his butt out here and in the car, or we're going to leave without him."

Shortly thereafter, the boy returned bearing this reply from Chubby: "You tell the Little Chief if he fools around with me this morning, there's going to be some bear walking around this lobby. He better stay where he is. Tell the Little Chief I'll come when I'm good and ready."

Chubby did emerge, "in his own good time," according to Snow, and pointedly chose to ride—not drive—to the next engagement with Copas. "They told me that Copas stayed doubled up with laughter as he listened to Chubby all the way to our destination," wrote Snow. "That night, after about a gallon of black coffee, Chubby sobered up, and as usual he did a fine job."

In his book, Snow does not mention the time that his toupee was snatched from his head by Chubby's errant fiddle bow—a possibly apocryphal incident that Chubby delighted in relating—nor does he make reference to his own misbehavior. "It was okay for Hank to get drunk whenever he wanted, but Chubby wasn't allowed to drink before a show," Rossi says. "When Hank was drinking, he was hard to get along with, and he and Chubby mixed it up sometimes."

On at least one occasion, says Rossi, an inebriated Snow—who was not particularly jolly even when sober—apparently uttered a derogatory comment about her, prompting the normally passive fiddler to threaten his boss with a punch in the nose. "They had some problems," says Rossi of her husband's relationship with Snow, whose libations of choice were scotch and vodka. "They were drinking buddies, but there were some things Chubby resented."

Of course, Chubby was not the only sideman ever to tipple, nor was Snow the only headliner ever to exempt himself from his own code of conduct. Life on the road promoted substance abuse—mostly booze and pills—while large egos in close quarters enkindled conflict.

Therefore, to promote a degree of equanimity, Chubby agreed to stay sober long enough to drive the car between engagements, and to refrain from drinking immediately prior to performances. In return, Snow offered Chubby steady employment, a solo segment for *Orange Blossom Special,* and the freedom to be himself, for better or for worse. It was an increasingly shaky pact, but it seemed to work as well as could be expected, considering the divergent personalities involved.

During this period, Chubby and Ervin enjoyed several brief reunions. In 1958, when Snow played the Miami-Dade County Auditorium, the two old buskers held an impromptu, backstage jam session as Carl Dees watched. "Snow was standing nearby, and when they got through playing, Snow said to Rouse, 'How would you like a job?'" recalls Carl. "Rouse just looked at him and said, 'Man, I wouldn't work for you for a thousand dollars a night.'" Why Ervin was so instantly hostile to Snow is difficult to say; perhaps he interpreted the Singing Ranger's compliment as an intentional slap at Chubby—which perhaps it was—and took offense. More likely, he was simply drunk and in an ornery mood.

Chubby, however, was never in any danger of being replaced. As a studio musician, he was in demand more than ever, both for Snow's RCA Victor sessions and, when time allowed, for those of other artists. In May 1954, Chubby played fiddle with Flatt & Scruggs on one song, *Foggy Mountain Breakdown*, and soon thereafter appeared on recordings by Flatt & Scruggs protégés Hylo Brown and Mac Wiseman.

He likewise backed Jimmy Martin, and in 1961 recorded an instrumental album with the Rainbow Ranch Boys called *Tennessee Fiddler*. Chubby also had an eye for new talent, and arranged for Snow to hear Jacksonville-based musician Kayton Roberts, who played rhythm guitar, steel guitar, and fiddle on a local television show. Roberts became Snow's steel man, and subsequently enjoyed a long career as respected session player.

Still, Chubby seemed at times eager to sabotage both his career and his marriage. In 1959, he abruptly quit Snow's band and returned to D.C., where he took up residence with a female companion. Rossi, in turn, obtained a divorce, prompting Snow, who wanted his wayward fiddler back, to engineer a reconciliation. "Hank called me and got Chubby's telephone number [in Washington]," Rossi says. "He called him and asked him to come back, and Chubby said yes. Later, he called me again and said, 'Rossi, I want you to come out to my house. I want to talk to you.' So, I went out there, and we were talking about Chubby and different things. And Hank called every hotel and motel in Nashville to see if Chubby had gotten in yet. I said, 'Hank, there's no telling where he is because he's got a girlfriend, and he's probably with her.'"

Finally, at about 4 a.m., Snow's doorbell rang. "Hank went to the door," Rossi continues. "Then he came back and said, 'Rossi, I ordered a case of beer and I don't have the money to pay for it. Will you go to the door and pay for the beer?' So, I went to the door with my little pocketbook in my hand, and there stood Chubby, grinning. He grabbed me, and I grabbed him. We were both tickled to see each other." The reunited couple rented a home and moved in together, although Rossi at first refused to consider another try at matrimony. "I said, 'We've been married once, and that's enough,'" she recalls. "But Chubby said, 'I'm not going to live with you unless you marry me again.' I had no other choice."

Although the volatile couple may have been too preoccupied to notice, times and tastes were changing. By the late 1950s, the popularity of rock 'n' roll had caused many radio stations to abandon the country format—there were only eighty-one stations playing country music as of 1960—thereby triggering a slump in record sales.

The industry fought back by softening country music's hard edges with lush arrangements and polished vocals—the so-called Nashville Sound—and by abandoning the once-ubiquitous twang. Crooners such as Eddy Arnold, Jim Reeves, Ray Price, and Marty Robbins began to score with silky-smooth ballads appealing to both pop and country fans, while hip, urban audiences embraced the quirky genius of Roger Miller and the stark originality of Johnny Cash.

Concurrently, traditional country artists were falling by the wayside; even Snow's records were no longer automatic Top 10s. Still, the Singing Ranger notched a chart-topper in 1962, the rapid-fire travelogue *I've Been Everywhere*. Then, two more substantial hits followed—*The Man Who Robbed the Bank at Santa Fe* and *Ninety Miles an Hour (Down a Dead End Street)*—before the inevitable slump set in. Snow would continue to place records on the charts until 1980—a remarkable testament to his longevity—but he would reach the Top 10 just two more times: with *The Wishing Well (Down in the Well)*, in 1965; and with *Hello Love*, a surprise smash in 1974.

By early 1963, Snow's diminished cash flow had prompted him to slash the salaries of the Rainbow Ranch Boys to seventy-five dollars per week. Consequently, Chubby and several other band members, including bassist Ralph Jernigan, angrily took their leave.

But for Chubby, money was not the only issue. He had grown weary of the constant travel, and had gradually come to believe that Snow viewed him less as a fellow artist and more as an amusing chauffeur and valet. "I'm never carrying anybody else's guitar or anybody else's luggage again," he vowed to Rossi, who had her own reasons for hoping her husband would quit. "Chubby's drinking had become real bad on the road, and there were so many temptations," Rossi says. "Plus, he'd gamble. He'd stash gambling money away at home before leaving on tour, and I'd find it. He'd say, 'Did you take my money?' And I'd say, 'I sure did; I'm not going to stay home working to try and pay our bills while you gamble away what you make.'"

But life without Snow proved professionally difficult for Chubby—in part, Rossi claims, because a vindictive Singing Ranger had blackballed him in Nashville, prompting several headliners to renege on previous job promises. So, while his wife remained in Nashville, Chubby drove to Miami to visit Gene Christian, and to investigate career opportunities in southern Florida. But the fiddler, who had a history of bleeding ulcers, became seriously ill shortly after his arrival.

"Chubby was sleepin' on my couch one night, and I heard him coughing and gagging," Gene recalls. "I come runnin' out and almost slipped and fell because of the blood he'd coughed up on the floor." When Chubby refused to go to the hospital, Gene's physician step-father, M.H. Tallman, was summoned, and agreed to provide medical services gratis. "My step-dad came over just about every day and doctored on him." Gene says. "Chubby ended up stayin' at my house for a couple of weeks before he was well enough to be up and around." Rossi says that Gene's wife, Helen, called to tell her that Chubby was sick, but assured her that he was under a doctor's care, and was in no immediate danger.

After recuperating, Chubby returned briefly to Nashville, and then traveled to Maryland, where he found work in a band called The Kentuckians, fronted by mandolinist Frank Wakefield and guitarist Red Allen. (Scott Stoneman also fiddled with the group on occasion). "Chubby had been away for about a week when he called me [in Nashville] and said, 'Sell everything we've got and get up here,'" recalls Rossi. "I said, "I haven't got time to do that.' So he said, 'Alright, just give it away.'" Anxious to rejoin her husband, Rossi sold their mobile home for a hundred dollars, packed a few personal effects, and set out for the Old Line State, where the couple bought a small house—the first house they had ever owned—in Capitol Heights, just southeast of D.C.

Soon thereafter, Chubby began a year-long stint with the String Dusters, the house band at Hunter's Lodge, a Fairfax, Virginia nightspot that hosted Nashville acts such as Ray Price, Faron Young, Johnny Paycheck, Bill Anderson, and others. He was also hired by Patsy Stoneman, who had left the family band to headline a country-bluegrass revue called The Patsy Stoneman Show.

"Scotty had introduced me to Chubby," recalls Patsy. "Those two had a real mutual admiration society going on. They'd pat each other on the back and steal from each other at the same time. I'd heard about the drinking and all, but a lot of musicians were that way. I had to keep three or four extras around all the time so I'd have enough who could perform. Chubby, though, was always reliable with me, and he never gave me any back-lip."

Nonetheless, Rossi, who had found nursing work at Prince George Hospital, was not surprised when her rambling husband announced that he was anxious for yet another change of scenery. "Chubby was just restless by nature, which I knew when I married him," Rossi says. "He wanted to go back to Miami, and to try it again down there. I always supported whatever he wanted to do, so we went." She vividly remembers the date they departed D.C.: July 31, 1964—the same day crooner Jim Reeves was killed in an airplane crash.

Back in southern Florida, Rossi was hired at Baptist Hospital and Chubby played for whomever would listen, sometimes busking with the Rouse Brothers and sometimes joining Gene, who was then engaged by the Black Angus restaurant chain to perform nightly at its Miami, Hialeah, and Cutler Ridge outlets.

In early 1965, Rossi injured her back while helping to lift a patient, and was in traction when Chubby visited her hospital room to deliver some news. "He said that we needed to talk," Rossi recalls. "I asked him what it was about, and he said 'I got a telegram today.' Well, naturally I was worried that it was going to be bad news. Chubby liked to tease me that way. I said, 'What's it about?' Then he just smiled and said, 'Hank wants me to come back to Nashville.' I said, 'Okay, then get me out of here.'"

Despite Snow's personality quirks, and despite Chubby's desire to someday strike out on his own, the lure of a steady paycheck—$110 per week this time—and the chance to re-establish himself in the Nashville mainstream proved too tempting to resist. Besides, Chubby noted with more than a hint of pride, Hank had approached him—not vice-versa.

For the next five years, Chubby again toured the world with Snow. He also resumed womanizing—if, indeed, he had ever really stopped—and began receiving amorous letters and telephone calls, many of which were intercepted by Rossi, from his numerous, far-flung conquests. "I let it go because, listen, why worry yourself?" Rossi says. "I knew he wasn't sitting in no motel twiddling his thumbs. He had time on his hands." But, when Chubby began acquiring Nashville girlfriends, a rather nebulous line was crossed, resulting in yet another rancorous separation.

Still, the estranged couple moved in the same social circles and, on one potentially disastrous occasion, crossed paths at a party in the Germantown area in north Nashville. Chubby, who was with another woman, immediately asked his wife to dance, while his compliant companion agreed to dance with a friend. "I was dancing with Chubby, and she [Chubby's date] bumped into me," Rossi says. "I told Chubby, and it was loud enough for her to hear, I said, 'You tell that old whore over there that if she bumps into me again, I'm going to take a beer barrel and knock her in the head with it.'" Not surprisingly, Chubby's new sweetheart quickly decided to pursue less risky relationships. "I broke up romances of his and he broke up romances of mine," says Rossi. "We must have been meant for each other. We'd separate over nothing and go back over nothing."

Among Chubby's many professional admirers during this period was Merle Haggard, who had become a working-class hero in 1969 with his anti-hippie anthem, *Okie From Muskogee*. Yet, the brooding, complex Haggard was far more than a redneck messiah; he was one of country music's most gifted musicians and perceptive songwriters. "Chubby could have worked for Merle Haggard whenever he wanted to," says Carl Dees. "Haggard thought he was the greatest fiddle player around."

In fact, Chubby did appear on a hugely successful 1970 Haggard album, *The Fightin' Side of Me*, which was recorded live before ten thousand cheering fans at

Philadelphia's Civic Center Hall. On the album, Chubby is introduced by name, and fiddles the old Bob Wills hit *Corrine Corinna*. Interestingly, however, his fiddle is silent when Haggard mimics a stoic Johnny Cash rasping *Orange Blossom Special*. (The Bakersfield, California-bred superstar also delivers credible impressions of Marty Robbins, Buck Owens, and the Singing Ranger himself).

Chubby had also been making solo recordings for the tiny Stoneway label, based in Houston, Texas and owned by insurance executive Roy Stone, a Wise acquaintance originally from Live Oak, Florida. In 1969, one of Chubby's Stoneway releases, a new version of Bob Wills' *Maiden's Prayer*, unexpectedly caught on, reportedly selling forty thousand copies in the Houston area alone. The tune's popularity, in turn, ignited demand for Chubby as a solo act, particularly in east Texas, where his jazz-tinged fiddle style was widely revered.

"Maiden's Prayer gave Chubby a chance to go out on his own again," Rossi says. "But he was getting a steady paycheck with Hank, and was nervous about leaving. I told him, 'Okay, if you want to be a sideman, then you'll stay a sideman. If you don't want to be sideman, then let's go.'" Roy Stone also offered encouragement, and based upon the success of *Maiden's Prayer,* agreed to release a series of fiddle albums.

Hesitant but hopeful, Chubby informed a dubious Snow of his decision: He would move to east Texas, where he had a small but supportive record label and a growing fan base. "Hank didn't want Chubby to go, and he asked me if I'd be happy listening to bluegrass," Rossi says. "He knew I didn't like banjos. He said, 'You think you're gonna be happy listening to all them banjos plunking?' Then I said, 'I'll tolerate it.'"

Chubby explained his decision to Vassar Clements by borrowing a line from Snow's biggest hit: "Vassar, I think I've just been movin' on for too long."

IX

"Hello, I'm Johnny Cash:" *The Special* Gets On Track

He had the kind of magnetism that makes you turn around and look, and everyone did. There was something else about the man, though—his humbleness, and the way he stood in a corner out of everyone's way...His rugged, tanned face and arms gave him the appearance of an athlete, but his snow-white hair showed that he was well past thirty-nine.

Johnny Cash, describing Ervin T. Rouse

A s the 1950s dawned, Ervin and Gordon resumed their busking routine, although they also parlayed the popularity of *Sweeter Than the Flowers* into a handful of paid engagements. They frequently appeared at the Holiday Drive Inn in Opa-Locka, where advertisements touted "the Rousch (sic) Brothers, Writers of the Famous Song That Sold Two Million Copies, 'Sweeter Than the Flowers,' and Many Others."

Yet, despite the tune's success, it did little to advance their careers, and Ervin's royalties, dispersed as they were among Syd Nathan, Moon Mullican, and Lois Mann, were not sufficient to elevate the family's standard of living. Plus, Ervin was spending more time at home—which was often not a happy arrangement for his wife and children.

Eloise, the couple's only daughter, remembers her father as an enigmatic figure; at times affectionate and loving, but more often distant and prone to outbursts of temper, almost always directed at Louallie. Now living in Bowie, Maryland, Eloise, not surprisingly, harbors conflicting feelings about this gifted but unstable man, who was quite unlike any other daddy on the block. "My dad always had trouble sleeping," Eloise recalls. "I vividly remember the nights he'd stay up writing, while I'd lie in bed and hear him singing—he had the sweetest singing voice—along with beautiful violin or guitar music."

However, equally vivid childhood memories involve Ervin's noisy frays with Louallie, which usually erupted over the fiddler's drinking and his general irresponsibility. "Sometimes, Daddy would have people over to the house—other musicians—and if they started drinking, my mother would throw them out," she says. "Also, my mother was very particular about some things; she disliked anyone using foul language, and she was very careful about her appearance. She always looked good, and she made sure that my brothers and I looked good, too. But Daddy became more and more unkempt, and he spoke to her in a very abusive way. I became very protective of her."

Most fathers, at some point, become embarrassments to their youngsters. But Ervin, with his disheveled wardrobe, sporadic hygiene, and unpredictable temperament, must have been particularly so. Eloise was apprehensive about inviting friends over when Ervin was present, not because she feared for their safety—he was typically gentle and passive with everyone except his wife—but because she could never be certain what inappropriate or inexplicable statements he might utter. "Of course, Daddy had mental illness, and that's why his behavior could be bizarre" she says. "He was in a world of his own, and was just unable to cope with everyday life."

However, Eloise wants it clearly understood that she remains proud of her father's talent and his accomplishments, and that regardless of his actions, she has never doubted his love for her, her two brothers, and her mother. Given the circumstances, she believes, Ervin was probably doing the best that he could.

As his domestic situation deteriorated, Ervin spent what royalty money he had accumulated for ten acres of land off Loop Road in the Big Cypress Swamp, an inhospitable, nine-hundred-square-mile wilderness sprawling from the western bank of the Everglades to the Gulf of Mexico. There he built a plywood shack and lived among a small community of outcasts and roughnecks whose inhospitable temperaments and suspicious occupations dictated a need for privacy, and a desire for neighbors who appreciated the importance of minding one's business.

Until completion of the Tamiami Trail in 1928, Big Cypress had been a virtually impenetrable quagmire of waist-high muck, palmetto thickets, and giant bald cypress trees, where alligators, snakes, and biting insects thrived. Then, as laborers hacked, burned, bulldozed, and blasted their way through the morass, Florida's east and west coasts were connected by a thirteen-million-dollar marvel of modern engineering described by one newspaper columnist as a perfect example of what was meant by the phrase "hell and high water."

Loop Road—today known as Florida Highway 94—is a twenty-three-mile-long, L-shaped strip of pock-marked asphalt and gear-shattering gravel that originates to the east on the Tamiami Trail at Monroe Station, then terminates to the west at the edge of the Miccousukee Indian Reservation, where the Naples-to-Miami throughway concludes a sharp, southerly drop.

Originally called Chevelier Road, Loop Road was constructed by the Chevelier Corporation on the mistaken assumption that Tamiami Trail access would make tracts of company-owned land appealing for development. Although a town called Pinecrest was platted, few expressed any interest in living there. Al Capone's cousin built a lodge which, until it burned in the 1930s, provided an appealingly low-profile getaway for gangsters.

But by the early 1950s, Pinecrest consisted of roughly two hundred scattered residents served by one grocery store, one gas station, and two taverns. As time passed, Ervin would become a fixture in the isolated community; perhaps the only place where he truly felt at home and at ease.

It was to this unlikely outpost that Bob Miller, armed with recording equipment, traveled in March 1953. On this brief trip, Ervin and Earl—Gordon, apparently, did not participate—along with a local steel guitar player named Jimmy Morgan recorded two sides: *Loan Me a Buck* backed by a new version of *Orange Blossom Special*. The tunes were released six months later on the Rockin' and DeLuxe labels, both subsidiaries of Syd Nathan's King Records, with the composer's credit ignobly reading "Erwin" Rouse. Although the tunes were favorably mentioned in *Billboard* magazine, they were not hits.

The circa 1953 *Special* is melodically identical to the 1939 Bluebird release, with crisp fiddling, competent guitar accompaniment, and tight, reedy harmony. However, the brothers add some falsetto scatting and some corny puns to the nonsensical dialogue between verses: ("Hey, lady, you'd better get aboard. And if you can't get aboard, then get a plank.") Inexplicably, they also make a curious lyrical change: instead of a second reference to "goin' down to Florida," they sing "or maybe California." The New York-to-Florida streamliner did not, of course, travel to the Golden State—at least not directly. South Floridians wishing to make a rail journey to the West Coast could ride the Special only from Miami to Jacksonville, where they boarded the Gulf Wind to New Orleans then the Sunset Limited to Los Angeles.

Yet, quibbling aside, the DeLuxe recording is every bit as much fun as its Bluebird predecessor, sounding even more spontaneous and capturing Ervin in fine form. *Loan Me a Buck* also boasts a catchy tune, but its forced cadences and tortured rhymes point up Ervin's glaring deficiencies as a lyricist:

> *Hey, buddy, I got a date with Susie,*
> *I promised I'd take her to the show.*
> *Please hurry, don't be late,*
> *I'll pay you back next Tuedsay.*

> *(Chorus)*
> *Hey, buddy, loan me a buck,*
> *I'll pay you back tomorrow.*

Good buddy, I need a buck,
Today and not tomorrow.

See good buddy, it's kind like this,
One dollar keeps life from being embarrassing.
It's so nice to feel in your fist,
And again it's so impressing.

Miller returned in October 1953, this time spending two weeks in southern Florida and recording ten traditional instrumentals with Ervin and Earl, including *Home Brew Rag, Flop Eared Mule, Up Jumped the Devil, Mississippi Sawyer, Down Yonder, Under the Double Eagle, Jackson Schottische, Rubber Dolly, Arkansas Traveler*, and *Varsouviana*. Five of these tunes—*Home Brew Rag, Flop Eared Mule, Under the Double Eagle, Jackson Schottische,* and *Rubber Dolly*—were released, all on DeLuxe.

Although Earl had written several new songs in the 1950s, Miller apparently deemed them unworthy of recording or publishing. For example, a bizarre patriotic number called *Freedom or Dictatorship* refers to a military invasion of Russia:

> *There's a warship on the ocean,*
> *that's waiting there for me,*
> *to take me to fight the Russians,*
> *across the deep blue sea,*
> *for I know they are too yellow,*
> *to come and fight with me,*
> *so it's time to get together,*
> *and prevent a World War Three.*

Miller, who was ill when the sessions were held and who would die two years later, told Zeke Clements that his time in the Big Cypress "was the strangest two weeks I ever spent." Unfortunately, the resulting tunes attracted no notice and, as far as can be determined, the Rouse Brothers never again recorded.

Louallie finally left Ervin in 1954, although not before he suffered another breakdown and was committed briefly to the psychiatric ward at Jackson Memorial Hospital. Ervin's family will not discuss what seemed to trigger the relapse, although Louallie says that it involved a dispute with one of his brothers. "After he got out [of Jackson Memorial] Ervin asked me, 'Why am I different?'" recalls Louallie. "I told him that I thought it was his life when he was young, traveling and playing music. He never learned what it took to make a real home. So, I knew that if our children were going to be raised properly, then I had to get them away from Miami. I also knew that Ervin loved me, and that he loved the children. Still, I felt that I had to leave."

Carrie supported Louallie's decision, saying that her sister-in-law's physical and emotional health was threatened. "Louallie was in bad shape when she finally left Ervin," says Carrie. "She looked like a walking skeleton. I don't know what might have happened if she'd stayed any longer." Agrees Gene: "Louallie done everything she could have done. She just finally got fed up, and there's nobody that could blame her."

Although the couple never divorced, they never again lived together; Louallie returned with the children to North Carolina, where she worked at a department store in Greenville, eventually becoming a buyer and a department manager. "I was proud of the fact that I could take care of myself and my family," Louallie says. "I never received any money from Ervin. I didn't want his money. I left him, so I didn't feel that I was entitled."

A chastened Ervin occasionally visited his family, but his stays were often awkward and sometimes sad. Futilely, he continued to hold out hope that his broken home could be restored.

"Sometimes Ervin acted like he and Louallie were still together," says Gene. "We'd be playin' somewhere, and women would come up and start lovin' on us, and Ervin never paid 'em no attention. He'd just brushed it off. In fact, I'd be willing to bet money that he never had a woman after Louallie left. I was with him nearly all the damn time, and I think I'd have known about it. He'd say, 'Gene, I can't do it; I've still got my Baby Doll.'"

WITH LOUALLIE AND THE CHILDREN gone, various Rouse siblings and their families, including Earl, Durwood, Guy, and Mabel, commandeered Ervin's Alapatta home. Carrie says that she and Gordon placed strict, two-week time limits on visiting relatives, but Ervin, who passively allowed open-ended stays, simply retreated to the swamp to find solitude. "He told me his family run him out of the house," says Gene.

Still, Ervin managed to hold himself together well enough to continue playing. Glen Odom, a country-music fan and owner of a Miami-based aircraft parts company, remembers meeting Ervin and Gene while they were busking at Huck's Bar, on the corner of Southwest 67th Avenue and the Tamiami Trail. "I was walking by and heard this music," says Glen. "Well, it was Ervin and Gene, playing and passing the hat. I went in, and I ended up staying for two or three hours and spending about fifteen dollars. I'll tell you what, they were great. I'd never seen or heard anything like it."

Tired of the constant travel, Gene had left Bill Monroe after little more than a year to front his own bluegrass band, Gene Christian and the Country Pals. However, by the mid-1950s, bluegrass music was in a commercial slump, battered by both rock 'n' roll and the pop-influenced Nashville Sound. "At that time, you couldn't give bluegrass away," says Gene. "A lot of musicians thought that buskin' was kind of low-rate, but I'll tell you this: Me and Ervin were makin' better money than they were."

Glen became friendly with both musicians, recognizing Ervin as a musical genius who was squandering his talent and ruining his health. "I set Ervin up in the lawn-care business," Glen says. "I bought him a mower, and the first yard he cut was mine. I told him, 'If you'll stay off the booze for ninety days, I'll send you to Nashville. You can go up there with Gene, and you can do something with your music.'"

Not surprisingly, Ervin was unable to stay sober for ninety days, and proved ill-suited for outdoor work. "Hell, I once saw Ervin try to drink sterno," says Carl Dees. "He was the greatest, but he just couldn't leave the whiskey alone."

So, Ervin continued busking—now more often with Gene than with Gordon—at joints such as the 7-11 Club, the Silver Spur, the Sweetwater Bar, Jimmy's Bar, the Whip Inn, and most notably at a popular nightspot called the Biscayne Club, located in south Miami on the Old Dixie Highway. "We played there for four or five months straight," says Gene. "Since his house was probably fifty miles away, Ervin moved into a hotel that was attached to the club. To tell the truth, even though I lived close by, I ended up staying there pretty often myself."

For Gene, at least, the proverbial big break finally arrived in 1955, when he and the Country Pals appeared on the CBS-TV program *Arthur Godfrey's Talent Scouts,* which was being broadcast from a downtown Miami movie theater. The combo performed *Salty Dog Blues,* the same tune that would win the competition for Scott Stoneman and the Blue Grass Partners a year later. Based upon the readings from a meter purported to measure the decibel level of audience response, Gene and his group took first place.

"Ervin and everybody was watchin' the program on TV back at the Biscayne Club," Gene says. "It was quite a night. After the show, I went on down to the club and Ervin and I played. He was real excited for me." Why, then, did Ervin not join his friend on *Talent Scouts*? "Well, he just didn't want to," Gene says. "Ervin wasn't no bluegrass musician. He wasn't what you might call a commercial musician. He did his thing, and that's all he wanted to do."

In the aftermath of his national exposure, Gene and the band moved to Little Rock where, with Godfrey's assistance, they established a base of operations at radio station KTHS, a CBS affiliate. However, neither Gene nor the Country Pals could long endure playing remote one-nighters, which frequently stretched into the wee hours, and then rising at dawn, exhausted and bleary-eyed, to host their morning broadcast. Consequently, after just six months Gene left KTHS to return to Tennessee, and finally to Miami. "The band didn't want to stay, and I didn't want to stay," Gene says. "Miami was always a damn good town for me, and I wanted to come back and get in a situation where I could work steady without all the travel."

Ultimately, he succeeded; by the mid-1960s, Gene had abandoned bluegrass for mainstream country music and, with his new band, the Nashville Gents and Girls, had landed a permanent engagement with Black Angus. "All the Black Angus restaurants had bars and dance floors, and we started playing dance music," says Gene, who would remain affiliated with the upscale steakhouses for twenty years. "I tried to get Ervin involved, but he just wanted to cool it. He was always around, and he'd play with us sometimes, but as far as anything permanent, he'd say, 'Gene, don't depend on me.' And I'd say, 'Ervin, it just don't work like that.'"

It was, perhaps, just as well. Ervin's drinking—and Gene's, for that matter—had worsened. Although Gene was rarely so impaired that he could not perform, Glen recalls an evening when he visited the Black Angus in Miami only to find that his guitar-picking pal, normally a consummate professional, was "obviously stoned," slurring his words and rambling. "I went up to the front and called him aside, and I said, 'Get off the stage, you damn drunk. You sound and smell like shit,'" says Glen, a teetotaler. "Gene thanked me for it later."

Drunk or sober, Ervin's performances were far more erratic. When Gene invited him onstage, the unpredictable fiddler might choose to galvanize the audience with a spirited rendition of *Orange Blossom Special*, or he might choose to deliver a puzzling, stream-of-consciousness monologue about his childhood, his career, and his travels. Such revelations would have been fascinating to a biographer—Ervin was never so forthcoming with friends or family—but Black Angus patrons wanted to hear music, not musing. "I'd sometimes kind of heckle him to get him started playing," says Glen. "Sometimes Gene would have to step in and get him on track." Obviously, Ervin's onstage verbosity was a form of self-administered therapy, and a psychologist could make much of this otherwise taciturn man's willingness to bear his soul before a roomful of strangers.

Ervin also continued writing, his most notable composition being *The Champion*, another lively train tune that was published in 1955 by Acuff-Rose and subsequently recorded by Grandpa Jones for RCA. Like all of Ervin's songs, the lyrics are secondary to the instrumentation; however, it is interesting to note the similarities between *The Champion* and *Orange Blossom Special*, both of which salute Florida-bound diesel streamliners:

> *All the people gathered 'round the station,*
> *going' southern bound, waitin',*
> *for the Champion comin' 'round the bend.*
> *Be ready to board the train,*
> *you can almost hear the people sing:*
> *Here comes the Champion.*

> *Buy your tickets while they last,*
> *this train goes mighty fast,*
> *high-powered diesels sure look good.*
> *If it's true we advertise,*
> *I'm glad that I got wise,*
> *I'll ride the Champion.*

Rocky Mount, I'll see you all,
may be 'round this comin' fall,
honey child, I hate to leave you now.
When I get there, I'll write a line,
I'll let you know I'm doin' fine,
I'm a 'leavin' on the Champion.

Tell your mama and your dad,
the best time I've ever had,
goin' down to see the coconuts.
Gotta go, hate to say,
Miami Beach, I'm on my way,
I'm a 'leavin' on the Champion.

Ervin also performed with Gordon, Earl, Stoney, and Carrie's teenaged nephew, Vernon "Bear" Hudson. Bear, now an Orlando contractor, still recalls the exhilaration of hearing his Uncle Gordon announce: "Okay, let's get Junior up here to do one; he sings just like Elvis!" The youngster enlivened the brothers' repertoire of old-time tunes with such Presley hits as *Don't Be Cruel.*

"They put on a great show," Bear recalls. "But Ervin could be kind of childish, and the other brothers would get frustrated with him. They'd be playing a song, and Ervin would turn his back on the audience and start fooling around with his fiddle. Gordon would kind of make a joke out of it and say, 'Well, folks, it looks like my brother wants to play something else.' But when Ervin got ready to do whatever he was going to do, they'd all step back and get behind him. You couldn't control him. But he was a real showman, and the brothers respected that."

Bear says that in the mid- to late 1950s, the brothers still did their usual vaudeville-style hillbilly act, complete with trick fiddling and familiar tunes. They wore their overalls and straw hats and rendered such standards as *Boil That Cabbage Down* and *Wildwood Flower*. Other than Bear's Elvis imitation and Earl's Hank Williams hits, there was little new to be heard. Still, the roadhouse crowds didn't complain. The show was funny, fast-paced, and even offered some poignant moments.

"A highlight of the show was when Ervin would do *Sweeter Than the Flowers*," Bear recalls. "He could never get through it. He'd choke up before he could finish, and Gordon would sing the rest while Ervin just sobbed. It was an unbelievable moment. People in the audience would be crying, too." At the opposite emotional extreme, the brothers would elicit bawdy hoots and guffaws performing the risqué old blues number, *Get 'Em From the Peanut Man (Hot Nuts):*

Nuts, hot nuts, anybody here want to buy my nuts?
Sellin' nuts, hot nuts, I've got nuts for sale.

You tell me that your nuts is night fine,
But I bet your nuts isn't as hot as mine,
Selling nuts, hot nuts, you buy 'em from the peanut man.

But the supreme showstopper—and the supreme moneymaker—was still the *Special*. While playing it, Bear says, the brothers would line up behind one another and chug-a-lug through the audience, train style, passing the hat as they snaked their way around the close-set tables. The tune could last ten or fifteen minutes—and it never failed to incite a frenzy. "Carrie came with us and would sometimes sing," Bear recalls. "But she also took care of the money, and she was all business. We'd come out of those places with three or four hundred dollars."

Throughout the 1950s and 1960s, Ervin traveled roughly twice yearly to North Carolina, where he called upon Louallie and the children, and granted interviews to longtime friend and announcer J.B. Ham at radio station WFTC in Kinston. "Ervin would always go by the station, and he'd talk and play for thirty minutes or so," recalls family friend Tull Jackson. "He was just a poor boy who had made good, so he was treated like a celebrity in this part of the country."

Jackson recounts a particularly memorable 1958 visit, during which Ervin attended a Grandpa Jones concert at the New Bern Recreation Center: "Ervin had on a white suit and a hat, and when he walked in and took his seat, people went to clapping. Everybody knew who he was. There was a local fiddler who opened the show, and he invited Ervin up on stage. Of course, the audience started hollerin' for *Orange Blossom Special*, but Ervin didn't play that one. Instead, he did his trick fiddlin' on *Pop Goes the Weasel*, holdin' the bow between his knees and even lyin' down on the floor. He was such a great showman."

Ervin later told Jackson that he had declined to perform the *Special* because he did not wish to "show up" a fellow fiddler: "Ervin said, 'I want that young man to do good in life; I don't want him thinkin' that I was tryin' to push him into the ground.'"

Guitarist Wayne Sullivan, who then fronted a popular, Kinston-based bluegrass band called the Carolina Partners, also recalls an unexpected mid-1950s performance by Ervin during a package show at the Hookerton School in Craven County. "I don't know how Ervin knew where we were playin', but he just showed up backstage," recalls Sullivan. "Of course, I'd knowed him since I was a young man, and I recognized him right away. But before I could call out his name, he put his finger to his mouth like he was tellin' me to keep it quiet. So, I just introduced him to the other boys as an old friend of mine who'd like to join us for a few numbers."

At first, neither the band nor the audience realized who the unidentified fiddler was. "But when he played the *Special*, everybody in the band and in the audience recognized that it was Ervin," Sullivan says. "There wasn't no way it could be anybody else. Well, he brought the house down with that tune. Then he did *Sweeter Than the Flowers*, and some trick fiddlin' on *Listen to the Mockingbird*. He played behind his head, then stuck the fiddle bow between his legs and played it that way. He was a one-of-a-kind entertainer, and when he finished the people was standin' and cheerin'. Ervin just bowed, real polite and dignified, then walked backstage and out the door. That was the last time I seen him."

During other North Carolina excursions, Ervin would visit tiny Cove City, essentially a wide place in the road between New Bern and Kinston, where Friday night jam sessions were—and still are—held in an abandoned service station. "Ervin wasn't one to brag," recalls Jackson, a guitarist who has been a Cove City regular since the early 1960s. "But when he'd come out, he'd be leadin' the group. He'd turn to me and say, 'Come on, Jackson, get that Martin [guitar] and just follow me.' Then he'd throw out that left foot and play the *Special*. And after he played, it, buddy, you knew it had been played."

Ervin also visited Nashville, and was occasionally hired by acts such as Bill Monroe and Flatt & Scruggs to appear as a featured attraction on short tours. While in Music City, he also met and became friendly with musicians who had heard tales of the mysterious, swamp-dwelling nonconformist and were anxious to make his acquaintance. Among them was the late Benny Martin, a hard-living fiddler who had recorded *Orange Blossom Special* in 1957 during a Stanley Brothers session for Mercury Records. Martin, known as "The Big Tiger," claimed that Ervin had tapped him as the *Special's* heir apparent, and occasionally wore tee-shorts proclaiming himself "Mr. Orange Blossom Special."

Thus, by simply being himself, Ervin had become a minor legend among country-music insiders. Yet, despite growing renown among his peers, Ervin's career remained stalled until 1961, when easy-listening maestro Billy Vaughn discovered *Orange Blossom Special* and recorded the first orchestral arrangement of the fiddle tune for Dot Records.

Vaughn was the most popular orchestra leader and arranger of the 1950s and 1960s, releasing numerous best-selling instrumental albums while serving as musical director for labelmates Pat Boone, the Fontane Sisters, and Gale Storm. Known within the industry as "the man who never met a song he didn't cover," Vaughn's compilation *Orange Blossom Special and Wheels* entered *Billboard's* Pop Albums Chart in April 1961, and remained there for forty-three weeks, eventually peaking at No. 11.

Vaughn's recording finally exposed the *Special* to an audience beyond bluegrass fans, and generated Ervin's first significant royalty checks. He purchased a new Cadillac, made some improvements on his ramshackle Big Cypress retreat, and began accumulating an unsightly collection of junk cars and noisy airboats, on which he poked and prodded when not fishing, trapping, or haunting local taverns. "Ervin didn't know how to work on anything with an engine," says Gene. "He'd do more harm than good, but he loved tinkerin'." (Somehow, a belief that the mechanically impaired fiddler had actually invented the airboat, and then failed to patent his design, came to be accepted in some circles. In fact, "swamp buggies" had first been used during construction of the Tamiami Trail.)

Not surprisingly, the suddenly prosperous fiddler harbored little notion of how to handle money; he had, after all, worked most of his life for tips and, like many survivors of the Great Depression, he was uncomfortable dealing with banks. "At first, Ervin carried around a lot of cash," Gene continues. "He said he just wanted to feel of it. Then, when he finally opened a bank account, he'd carry around big books of traveler's checks. Still, he'd blow it as fast as he got it—buyin' crazy things that he didn't need, settin' the house up with drinks, things like that."

Also, much to the dismay of his relatives, Ervin began impulsively giving money to strangers. Earl's daughter Elaine recalls one such incident, which occurred as her father and her uncle played their fiddles on the porch of Ervin's Alapatta home: "Uncle Ervin said, 'The next person that walks by the house, I'm gonna give him fifty dollars.' Well, we needed that money so bad. But sure enough, he saw somebody coming down the sidewalk, and just gave it away."

MEANWHILE, ON JULY 25, 1964, a rangy, black-clad singer named Johnny Cash took the stage at the Newport Folk Festival in Newport, Rhode Island. Cash, racked by amphetamine addiction and seemingly bent on self-destruction, was still Nashville's most creatively adventurous recording artist and, arguably, its most charismatic personality.

After viewing his festival performance, *New York Times* music critic Robert Shelton wrote that "Johnny Cash, the Nashville star, closed the gap between commercial country and folk music with a masterly set of storytelling songs."

Following his performance, Cash and Columbia labelmate Bob Dylan ensconsed themselves in a motel room and spent the night swapping songs with Joan Baez and her sister and brother-in-law, Mimi and Richard Farina. The protest-era icons were enthralled by Cash, a performer whom they considered to be an authentic folk balladeer in the tradition of Woody Guthrie. After all, Dylan, Baez, and the Farinas were the products of comfortable, middle-class homes; their friend fellow Cash admirer Ramblin' Jack Elliott (real name: Elliott Adnopoz) was the son of a Brooklyn physician. This farm-hardened Arkansan, however, had actually lived his music.

Cash was just as interested in the folkies as they were in him. He had begun a correspondence with the Dylan after hearing his 1963 album, *The Freewheeling Bob Dylan*, which featured soon-to-be classics such as *Blowing in the Wind, A Hard Rain's A-Gonna Fall; Masters of War; Don't Think Twice, It's All Right*; and *Girl from the North Country*. Cash had also ventured into Greenwich Village to perform in such hipster venues as the Gaslight Club, and had befriended such folk-scene fixtures as Ramblin' Jack, Peter Lafarge, and Ed McCurdy.

Invigorated by his growing counterculture cache and intrigued by the chance to take his music in a new direction, Cash had begun recording material that would solidify his folk credentials while maintaining his commercial viability. For his upcoming Columbia album, he planned to include three Bob Dylan compositions— *Mama, You've Been On My Mind; Don't Think Twice, It's Alright;* and *It Ain't Me Babe*, which had already been a hit single as a duet for Cash and June Carter. He also planned to include a self-penned protest song called *All God's Children Ain't Free*.

Still, he needed a title cut; something apolitical, so that reactionary country disc jockeys would not shun it, yet something that was also different, authentic, and rooted firmly in the folk tradition. Then, he recalled an old train song—a bluegrass number that featured a hair-raising fiddle—and asked Mother Maybelle Carter if she was familiar with *Orange Blossom Special*. "In those days, everybody who recorded the song claimed the arrangement because no one knew who wrote it," said Cash in 1994. "So I asked Mother Maybelle, 'Do you know who really wrote *Orange Blossom Special*?' And she said, 'Sure I do. Ervin Rouse and his brother, Gordon.' And I said, 'Where are they?' She said, 'Last I heard, they were in Florida.' It was the only clue I had."

IF JOHNNY CASH HAD ASCENDED to Hillbilly Heaven in the mid-1960s—as it was widely assumed that he would, given his excesses—then he would still be ranked among the most influential artists in the history of popular music. But Cash—unlike Hank Williams and Jimmie Rodgers—survived, and his unprecedented career stretched into the millennium. Indeed, the 1990s saw the old renegade, paired with hip-hop producer Rick Rubin, playing to packed houses, earning more Grammys, and reemerging as a hero among youthful trendsetters, who endorsed *Rolling Stone's* contention that, "Wherever he is, whoever he's with, Johnny Cash is always the coolest man in the room."

And Cash's already monumental presence loomed even larger after his death in 2003. A Hollywood film about his life earned critical raves and an Oscar for Reese Witherspoon, who played June Carter Cash, and his posthumously released album, *A Hundred Highways*, reached No. 1 on both *Billboard's* Top Country Albums and Top Pop Albums charts. It was Cash's first No. 1 pop album since *Johnny Cash at San Quentin* in 1969.

One explanation for the Man in Black's longevity was his willingness to take creative risks, as he did in early 1964 by releasing *The Ballad of Ira Hayes*, a denunciation of the treatment accorded Hayes, a Native American hero of World War II who ultimately drank himself to death on an Arizona reservation. When country radio stations were at first reluctant to air the controversial indictment, penned by Peter LaFarge, Cash bought a full-page ad in *Billboard* skewering the industry for its cowardice.

Because of—or, more likely, in spite of—the singer's stridency, *Ira Hayes* was a respectable hit, rising to No. 3 on Billboard's *Top Country Singles* chart. *Bitter Tears*, the riveting concept album that contained *Ira Hayes* and other unvarnished explorations of Native American history, further enhanced Cash's credibility as a voice for the downtrodden. Writing about Cash in *Sing Out*, a grateful LaFarge floridly described his hard-living friend as being "a-crawl with nerves, charred by his own poetry, leaving a mighty wake and singing down great storms of beauty."

But dealing with Johnny Cash in the early to mid-1960s was a risky proposition; the singer had begun to miss engagements, or to arrive unable to perform. "It's incomprehensible to me how I kept walking around," Cash wrote thirty years later, describing himself as "nothing but leather and bone; there was nothing in my blood but amphetamines; there was nothing in my heart but loneliness; there was nothing between me and my God but distance."

Still, his undiminished drawing power ensured that some promoters would be willing to roll the dice. Among the gamblers was "Cracker Jim" Brooker, a disc jockey on WQAM in Miami, who booked the Johnny Cash Show for Saturday, October 15, 1964, at the Miami-Dade County Auditorium. By then, Cash's high-powered troupe included the second incarnation of the Carter Family—Mother Maybelle and daughters June, Helen, and Anita—as well as the Statler Brothers, a folk-country quartet later to rank among the most popular acts in country music.

Mother Maybelle had told her future son-in-law about the unforgettable Ervin and his musical siblings, and Cash, who had always displayed an affinity for underdogs and outcasts, must have been intrigued by the notion of plucking such an unconventional character from obscurity. Therefore, he asked for Brooker's help in locating the elusive fiddler.

Said Cash: "I asked Cracker Jim, 'Did you ever hear of Ervin Rouse?' And he said, 'Aw, I know Ervin. He lives with the Seminoles out in the swamp, and he makes swamp buggies for a living.' I said, 'You got any idea how I could talk to him?' And he said, 'Sure. I'll announce it on the air.'"

Actually, this exercise was pure hype; Ervin had a telephone, and his number was listed in the city directory. But bogus or not, the "search" was a wonderful promotional gimmick. On his afternoon program, Booker broadcast his appeal: "Rouse Brothers, come out of the woods, come out of the swamps, come out wherever you are; Johnny Cash wants to meet you!" Carrie heard the program, as did Ervin, who called Brooker and was given Cash's telephone number. "It wasn't an hour until Ervin Rouse called me from some little settlement in the swamp," Cash recalled. "I said, 'Ervin, I happen to be coming to Miami on tour. Would you come to my show and do *Orange Blossom Special* with me?'"

Not surprisingly, accounts of the resulting Cash-Rouse encounter have varied. The most detailed version—and the most widely circulated—comes from Cash himself, on the liner notes of his *Orange Blossom Special* album. Cash, however, writes as though Ervin had wandered backstage unbidden and unknown:

> The gentleman quietly walked into our dressing room
> during intermission at our show in Miami a few years ago,

five years to be exact. (Wrong; Cash recorded the *Special* just two months after he and Ervin met). He had the kind of magnetism that makes you turn around and look, and everyone did. There was something else about this man, though—his humbleness, and the way he stood with his hat in his hands, waiting to be acknowledged, and I spoke to him. The face wasn't familiar, but there was a distinction about him that commanded attention. His rugged, tanned face and arms gave him the appearance of an athlete, but his snow-white hair showed that he was well past thirty-nine.

After I stood and introduced myself, I was very embarrassed when he called me "Mr. Cash." I usually can cover my embarrassment by replying, "Mr. Cash is my daddy." This time, I was afraid it might sound disrespectful. His name, he said, was Ervin Rouse, and he hesitatingly went on to say that a few years ago, he had written some songs himself, but that I had probably never heard them. I felt the name should ring a bell, and offering him a chair, I asked what songs he had written.

He honestly tried to avoid answering by saying they were just a bunch of old tunes. I asked him again what songs he had written, and he replied in a beautiful Southern seaboard dialect that a Southerner such as myself enjoys hearing. He finally said that probably his best number was a fiddle tune. I sensed his honesty and finally asked him point blank: "What fiddle tune, Mr. Rouse?" Evidently, people had not believed him in the past when he mentioned his songwriting, so he reluctantly said, "Well, I guess my biggest one was the *Special*." I didn't raise my eyes when I asked politely, "You mean *Orange Blossom Special*?" This time, his answer was a question, and everyone in the room knew, as I did, that this man was sincere. That question was: "Did you ever ride on the Atlantic Coast Line? I've been up and down it many times, and even out west on the Southern Pacific, but I'm pretty well settled in the sandy land now."

He went on to say that that night, or rather that day, he had traveled for miles across the Everglades in a machine he built and called a "swamp buggy." Then, somewhere near Miami, he borrowed his sister's bicycle and rode about ten miles to our show. The second half of the show was about to begin, and Mother Maybelle Carter was tuning her guitar to go onstage. He turned to her and said: "Mother Carter, I know you may not remember me, but I met you years ago and worked a show with you in Virginia. My name is Rouse, ma'am. I used to sing a little, and play the *Special*—the *Orange Blossom Special*, that is—and probably the only other one of mine that most anyone ever heard was a little tune I wrote for my dear mother called *Sweeter Than the Flowers*. Of course she remembered, as did all of us sitting around listening. He added, "The *Special* belongs to everyone now, I guess, but it used to be my best number."

I asked Mr. Rouse to be my special guest on the show that night. The house was packed for two shows, and when he did *Orange Blossom Special* they tore the house down. It was hard to coax him to encore, and when he did, I asked him to sing *Sweeter Than the Flowers*. At first, I thought he was going to flatly refuse. He said, "It's just too sad and hits too close to home, and I'm not in the mood for it." However, the audience wouldn't let him stop. His sincerity and his magnetism automatically commanded complete attention throughout the auditorium as he sang *Sweeter Than the Flowers*.

The customers in the coffeehouses in New York and other big cities haven't seen Ervin Rouse. The tidal wave of discoveries of folk-music performers missed this man...Since that night, I have seen the man many times and spent many hours talking to him and listening to him sing. He's probably past sixty (actually, the hard-living Erin was just forty-eight years old in 1965) and I don't think he would mind telling you so, but his voice is as clear now as it must have been thirty years ago.

Either Cash had forgotten that Ervin was backstage at his behest, or he had decided that the unexpected appearance made a better story. In any case, most other aspects of the narrative ring quite true: Ervin's shyness, his tendency to give obtuse answers to straightforward questions and, most of all, his reluctance to perform without being prodded. But where was Gordon? He is not mentioned in the liner notes, although Cash recalled in subsequent interviews that both Ervin and Gordon were present and performed.

Cash may well have remembered it that way, but it was Gene Christian, not Gordon, who accompanied Ervin to the Miami-Dade County Auditorium—and they arrived together in Gene's car, thereby negating the admittedly more colorful swamp buggy and bicycle yarn. "Ervin and Gordon had gotten into it, and Gordon didn't want to go," says Gene, whose story is detailed and credible. "I took Ervin to the show. I picked him up at his home in Alapatta."

According to Gene, Brooker did not want "local talent" sullying his promotions—and he was particularly disdainful of Ervin, whom he regarded as no more than a small-time, honky-tonk busker. "So, when we come to the backstage door, me with my guitar and Ervin with his fiddle, this cop told us that he had orders not to let anybody in," Gene says. "Just about that time, Mother Maybelle walked by and seen us standing there." Country music's reigning matriarch immediately recognized Ervin, whom she had been expecting, and instructed the security guard to allow him and his partner inside.

Then, after a nostalgic rehash of bygone days, Mother Maybelle escorted the duo to a crowded dressing room, where they were introduced to an atypically lucid and focused Cash. "He seemed real interested in us, and in what we were doin'," Gene recalls. "We were standin' up against the dressing' room wall so we wouldn't get in the way, and I think we did three or four songs. Of course, Cash wanted to hear the *Special*. You know, that song has a talkin' part in the middle, and me and Ervin, we'd usually just say whatever came to our minds when we played it in bars and other places. It was all ad libbed. So, when we played it for Cash, Ervin said somethin' like, 'Hey, boy, ain't you worried about gettin' your nourishment in New York?' Then I said, 'Well, I don't care if I do-die-do-die-do-die-do.' It was nonsense; didn't mean a thing. But damned if that ain't the way Cash recorded it."

Impressed with the impromptu performance, Cash asked for a transcription of the *Special's* lyrics exactly as they had just been sung. "I wrote the words down on a napkin," Gene says. "It's all that was lyin' around."

During the show, the Man in Black brought Ervin and Gene onstage—much to the annoyance of a fuming Cracker Jim, who dared not interfere—where they received extended standing ovations following renditions of *Sweeter Than the Flowers* and the *Special*. "I thought we done damn good for a couple of lost-lookin' hillbillies," Gene says. "Of course, I done most of the talkin', because Ervin was a rambler."

Cash later recalled that the performance "absolutely killed [the audience]. At the end of the song, [Ervin] literally got down on his knees. He was such a sweet, humble man." (In this telling detail, Cash's memory is correct: Ervin's distinctive bow, which he had used since vaudeville, involved dropping to one knee with a theatrical flourish, and tilting his head forward toward the applause.) Says Gene: "After the show, Cash told us what a good job we done, and indicated that he was interested in Ervin's material—particularly the *Special*."

Gene, however, was not convinced that Cash truly intended to record the tune. "I said that I didn't think the song fit him," he recalls. "I told Ervin, 'Hell, he ain't gonna cut that. That ain't no Johnny Cash song.'" In fact, the *Special*—at least as it had been interpreted to that point—did seem an odd choice for a brooding folksinger with rockabilly roots. But the innovative Cash, who had added a brass section to *Ring of Fire* after claiming to have heard mariachi trumpets in his dreams, concocted an arrangement to fit his singular style.

On December 20, 1964, Cash and the Tennessee Three—Luther Perkins, lead guitar; W.S. "Fluke" Holland, drums; and Marshall Grant, bass—were joined by Boots Randolph on saxophone and Charlie McCoy on harmonica in Nashville's Columbia Studios. Alongside these renowned session players was a man named Ed Grizzard, a custodian and courier whom the unpredictable Cash had recruited as his dialogue partner. (Some Cash completists have long believed that the record's unidentified second voice belongs to Roebuck "Pop" Staples, the legendary blues singer and patriarch of the Staple Singers. While Staples and Cash were friends and Columbia labelmates, it is the unheralded Grizzard who is heard on *Orange Blossom Special*.)

There, under the supervision of longtime producers Don Law and Frank Jones, this eclectic group cut the ultimate fiddle tune with nary a fiddle in sight. More remarkably, they did so with little or no preparation and with no musical score to follow. Indeed, McCoy and Randolph were not even told what song Cash was scheduled to record until they arrived at the studio. "We just knew we were hired for a Johnny Cash session," McCoy recalls. "We didn't know what he was going to do. But that wasn't unusual in those days. A good studio musician was expected to know all the old songs, and to be ready to play them on the spot. There was no sheet music, and no real rehearsal. Boots and I just worked out our parts there in the studio, then we let it lose."

Because of the harmonica's tonal limitations, McCoy immediately realized that he would need to use two instruments tuned to different keys, and to alternate them quickly during the instrumental breaks. "I'd heard the tune all my life," he says. "It didn't take long to figure out what I needed to do."

The Cash version is indeed a strange one, opening with the singer hooting a few ragged railroad whistles as Perkins and Grant lay down a lazy, looping beat. On the snare drums, Holland mimics the train's clickity-clack. The instrumental breaks, where a fiddle would normally be heard, feature McCoy and Randolph. Cash, who is noticeably hoarse, sings the first, second, and third verses essentially as they were written, and engages Grizzard for the dialogue:

> Grizzard: *Hey man, when you goin' back to Florida?*
> Cash: *When am I goin' back to Florida? I don't know, I don't reckon I ever will.*
> Grizzard: *Ain't you worried about gettin' your nourishment in New York?*
> Cash: *Well, I don't care if I do-die-do-die-do-die-do...*

His destructive and irresponsible road behavior notwithstanding, Cash's recording sessions were usually businesslike affairs, with the singer in total control of the proceedings. Such was the case during the recording of the *Special*. "John knew what he wanted, and he called the shots at his sessions," McCoy says. "We got it in just a couple of takes." The harmonica wizard says that he knew the resulting cut would be an important one. "This was one of those sessions where I had a certain feeling," he recalls. "I've felt it from time to time over the years. I felt it when I backed [George] Jones on *He Stopped Loving Her Today*. I knew it was going to be big."

After laying down the final take, McCoy gave his harmonicas to Cash and showed the singer how to approximate the solo for use in live performances. (Although his playing never advanced beyond rudimentary, for the next thirty-five years the Man in Black compensated for his lack of technical skill through showmanship, making a production of switching harmonicas and then tossing the instruments to audience members upon the tune's conclusion. In the 1970s, Cash even landed an endorsement contract with Hoener Harmonicas—a remarkable feat considering the fact that he could competently play only one song.)

For McCoy, the *Special* became a signature tune as well. He continued his career as a top session musician, becoming undoubtedly the most recorded harmonica player in history. Then, beginning in the early 1970s, he recorded a series of solo harmonica albums for the Monument label, eventually charting sixteen singles. His 1973 version of *Orange Blossom Special* peaked at No. 26 on *Billboard's* Hot Country Singles chart, and even dented the pop listings at No. 101.

"I've recorded the *Special* seven times in all," McCoy says. "But I recorded it again in '73 just because I'd gotten so much better at playing it. On the Cash cut, it's a little slower. Of course, with the limitations of the human voice, a harmonica will never be as fast as a fiddle. But I'd refined the tune over the years, and I wanted the newer version out there."

Just a week before Cash's version of the *Special* was released, the singer debuted it on ABC-TV's *Shindig!*, a prime-time program that normally spotlighted rock acts, alongside Herman's Hermits, the Righteous Brothers, and Paul Petersen ("Jeff" from *The Donna Reed Show*). It was a debacle; Cash was drunk, and perhaps annoyed at the notion of dressing in a hobo costume and cavorting with a gaggle of prancing teenaged dancers. He botched the *Special's* lyrics and stumbled about the stage, growling and groping.

Backed by the Statler Brothers, Cash also performed the gospel song *Amen*. But despite the fact that the lyrics consist primarily of one word, "amen," he was lost. "We were horrified because we all idolized Johnny," said host Jimmy O'Neil in a 1991 interview. "It took us almost three hours to get a useable take."

Despite the *Shindig!* embarrassment, the *Special* debuted in *Billboard's* country rankings on January 20, 1965, peaking five weeks later at No. 3 (it reached No. 80 on the pop charts). The *Orange Blossom Special* album, released in March, peaked at No. 3 on the country charts and No. 49 on the pop charts. The cover photograph is of a grizzled Cash, again in hobo garb, sitting atop a boxcar. As usual, the fact that the title song was actually about a passenger train catering to an affluent clientele was overlooked.

Meanwhile, Ervin did little to capitalize on the priceless opportunity Cash had granted him. Accompanied by Gene and sometimes Gordon, he continued to perform at local bars and to immerse himself in the solitude of Big Cypress. His teeth were gone, his wiry hair was unkempt, and his ever-present, two-day stubble was gray and scruffy.

More ominously, his health had begun to fail; despite full-blown diabetes, he had continued to consume sweets and alcohol, thereby bloating his body, lining his once-handsome face, and irreversibly damaging his heart, liver, and kidneys. No wonder Cash had mistaken him for an old man.

Still, the Man in Black, who would temporarily conquer his demons and achieve unprecedented popularity by decade's end, was not yet finished with *Orange Blossom Special*—or with Ervin. In 1966, cognizant of the fact that even the savviest songwriters could be duped by the Byzantine accounting practices of record companies, Cash asked his friend Charles "Chuck" Glaser to meet with the fiddler, and to make certain that his composer royalties were being distributed in a timely fashion.

Glaser certainly knew the business: he and his brothers, Thomas Paul (Tompall) and James William (Jim), performed together as the Glaser Brothers—the trio had toured with Cash for a time—and owned a music publishing company, Glaser Publications. In the 1970s, their now-legendary recording studio would serve as unofficial headquarters for Nashville's so-called outlaw movement, offering refuge to shaggy nonconformists such as Waylon Jennings and Willie Nelson.

At Cash's behest, Glaser sent Ervin a bus ticket and an invitation to visit his busy 19th Avenue offices. John Hartford, a Glaser Publications songwriter who worked nights as a disk jockey at Nashville radio station WSIX, was present when the rumpled fiddler, outfitted in a heavy trench coat despite the searing summer heat, arrived and introduced himself.

Hartford's wife, Betty, worked as a Glaser Publications secretary, giving the Missouri-born musician a convenient excuse to linger in hopes of catching Glaser's ear. (The following year, he would succeed in doing so with *Gentle On My Mind*, which would become a huge hit for Glen Campbell and a country-pop standard.) But the versatile Hartford was also an extraordinary fiddler, and was surprised and thrilled to meet the man who had written perhaps the greatest fiddle tune of all time. Recalled Hartford: "Chuck took me aside and said, 'Me and Johnny Cash are trying to get Ervin some royalties on his song, but I can't have him hanging around here all day. Would you take him around town and keep him company?'"

Hartford happily complied, squiring Ervin along Music Row and listening as the old-timer delivered a nostalgic commentary about his younger days. "He was just a good old fella, but you could tell that he'd been rode hard and put up wet," said Hartford. "He looked like a rummy old fiddle player; big red nose, wide-set eyes.

But he told these great stories about him and his brothers, riding trains from one town to the next. He said they'd get off the train, find a bar, and play for tips before they moved on. No dates scheduled in advance. To him, that was how you worked the road." (Although Ervin accurately described the tried-and-true Rouse Brothers busking routine, he fudged when naming their preferred method of transportation; the well-traveled siblings would never have squandered money on train fare when they could have packed themselves and their gear into a battered Chevy.)

Later, Hartford, whose WSIX shift began at 4 p.m., returned his talkative charge to Glaser Publishing, grateful that he had met the enigmatic Ervin T. Rouse but rueful that the pair had been unable to swap tunes. "He didn't bring a fiddle with him and I didn't have a car, so we couldn't go and get one of mine from home," said Hartford.

That evening, the Glasers took Ervin to The Black Poodle, a Printer's Alley night-club at which the Stoneman Family appeared nightly. The group had been engaged at the behest of maverick producer "Cowboy" Jack Clement, who was seeking a venue at which to showcase his protégés for Nashville record company executives and other industry notables. "That whole district had been going to pot," recalls Patsy Stoneman, who would assume leadership of the group upon Pop Stoneman's death in 1968. "But, after they brought the Stonemans in, things started to change."

Indeed they did; within weeks, the once moribund nightclub had become the hottest spot in Music City. "Nothing has ever had the effect at 'the Poodle' that the Stonemans had," enthused *Music City News*. "They literally captivated the audience, and as word spread even die-hard pop fans and local founding fathers came to see what the ruckus was about. Presently, even Monday, Tuesday, and Wednesday nights have SRO crowds."

The night Ervin visited, errant brother Scott, who had rejoined the group after what had been politely described by his sisters as "a year's leave of absence," recognized the old fiddler and called him to the stage. What followed was an explosion of music and mayhem, as arguably the two best improvisational fiddlers of their day swapped tunes and tricks before launching into an extended version of *Orange Blossom Special*.

Perhaps sensing that they were witnessing a magical moment, audience members were on their feet, applauding, shouting, and dancing as the two masters scorched their strings, each trying to outdo the other. "Ervin just blew everybody out the god-damn door," said Hartford. "That performance was one of the great, undocumented moments in country music history. People are still talking about it thirty-five years later." As old-timers might have said, "It was regular monkey show."

For Ervin, however, the glory was fleeting. The next morning, having galvanized Printer's Alley just hours before, he boarded a Greyhound bus bound for Miami. Still, the trip had been productive; Glaser had successfully identified royalties owed and, according to Ervin, payments were made promptly from that time forward.

Yet, why did Cash, who had problems of his own, take such an active interest in Ervin's well-being? Most likely, Cash saw something of himself in the gifted but maladjusted musician and thought, "There, but for the grace of God, go I."

Back in Florida, the freeloading Rouse siblings and in-laws had scarcely noticed Ervin's absence, and at least one family member was planning his own rise to national prominence. Older brother Guy, who had moved with his wife, Helen, to Ervin's increasingly crowded Alapatta home, declared his intention to seek the Republican nomination for President of the United States—a quixotic quest that even Ervin seemed to regard as ill-advised. Guy, however, was deadly serious; he noted that the 1968 Republican convention was slated for Miami Beach, so he would be conveniently situated in case the delegates called.

A deadpan profile of Ervin's delusional brother appeared in the August 1, 1967 edition of the *Miami Herald* under a headline reading, "He's Planning a Big Move: To 1600 Pennsylvania Avenue." The *Herald* describes Guy as "a jack-of-all trades in the building business, until a crushed hand and a couple of automobile accidents put an end to that." Guy confesses that he has only a fourth-grade education, but adds that "my daddy used to read me the Bible, and explain it as he went along." Supportive Helen then interjects that Abe Lincoln, a simple Illinois rail-splitter, was an effective president despite a lack of formal schooling.

In retrospect, Guy's political platform seems remarkably sensible: "First thing I'd do is call off the war [in Viet Nam]," he tells the *Herald*. "I see we got our boys bein' killed by their own battalions; droppin' bombs on women and little children over there. I think it's an awful shame. Puttin' all these different things together and seein' how dangerous it was, the sound of it, I decided to do somethin' about it."

The story further reports that younger brother Ervin, "a burly man in a straw hat with whom the Rouses live," apparently supports the family. "Ervin don't have to do anything," Guy says. "He gets royalties on his musical compositions. *Orange Blossom Special* is goin' real strong right now. Ervin's one of the best fiddlers in the U.S."

Still, Guy adds, he is not dependent upon Ervin alone to finance his campaign. "Helen and I have sent letters to twenty-six rich people askin' for donations," he states. "Nobody has contributed yet, but nobody has refused to, either."

IN THE MEANTIME, A RELATIVELY clean and sober Johnny Cash, who had just recorded a soon-to-be-released album called *Johnny Cash at Folsom Prison*, was preparing to tape a television special for the Canadian Broadcast Corporation (CBC) called, somewhat audaciously, *The Legend of Johnny Cash*.

The special was part of series of programs originating from the O'Keefe Centre (now the Hummingbird Theatre for the Performing Arts) in Toronto. Cash got the high-profile gig only after Hank Snow, who had starred in two previous O'Keefe broadcasts, declined and producer Stan Jacobson suggested the Man in Black as a replacement.

CBC executives—and even Jacobson—were nervous. After all, in 1966 a stoned and incoherent Cash had to be removed from the O'Keefe Centre stage before he ever sang a note. Indeed, his reputation as an unreliable, self-destructive hellraiser had been well-earned, and his bookings had suffered as a result. Although the CBC special offered a priceless chance at redemption, could an entire, hour-long program be built around this charismatic but troubled character and his touring troupe?

The Legend of Johnny Cash aired on March 24, 1968, preempting Canada's No. 1 program, *Bonanza*. And the star was in superb form, opening the show with *John Henry* and delivering a powerful program of chart-toppers along with gospel numbers and historical ballads. When the ratings were tallied, Cash's effort had topped a National Hockey League Stanley Cup playoff game. Even more impressive, it built upon the numbers typically posted by the top-rated western that it had replaced.

Mark Steilper is a Cash confidant whose soon-to-be-published book is called *The Johnny Cash Show: Triumph, Tribulation and the Making of a Legend*. In it, he traces Cash's seminal ABC-TV show—and his subsequent status as a cultural icon—directly to the success of the CBC's experiment:

> Sol Holiff, who had managed Cash from his London (Ontario) apartment since 1961, went to work. In those pre-VCR/DVD/DVR days, it was not all that easy to get your hands on a copy of a TV show. But finally, through Jacobson, now a hero, he was able to score a copy of a videotape. His plan was to strike while Cash was hot, and to shop the Canadian triumph and its attending ratings bonanza (so to speak) to the U.S. networks. But he needn't have gone to all the trouble. Canada is actually part of North America, and news tends to make it across the border fairly easily. NBC and ABC, the number two and three networks, had both felt the Nielson earthquake at about the moment it hit. The wheels were already turning.

Suddenly, Cash was everywhere. *Johnny Cash at Folsom Prison* became a full-fledged phenomenon, selling more than two million copies, winning the Country Music Association's Album of the Year award, and spawning a revival of Cash's 1956 hit, *Folsom Prison Blues*, which again topped the country charts and entered the pop Top 40. One of the historic album's most electric moments comes when Cash blasts a jarring train whistle on the harmonica, and the audience of five hundred noisy miscreants cheers in recognition of *Orange Blossom Special*. "I can switch harmonicas faster than I can kiss a duck," Cash quips to the whooping cons.

ABC-TV quickly moved ahead with plans to offer the singer a weekly network television program replacing *Hollywood Palace* for the summer.

"Of course, when we first talked about doing [a television series], I heard grumblings," Cash said in 1996. "I heard, 'We're not going to have so-and-so on this show in Nashville.' And I heard Pete Seeger's name mentioned. Pete's a friend of mine. I've sat in his cabin in New York and played rhythm while he played fretless banjo for many hours. So, I told them, 'If I do a weekly show, I insist on Pete Seeger being one of my guests, as well as Bob Dylan, if I can get them.' There was grumbling, there were heads huddled, and finally I had to say, 'It's either my way or the highway. I'm gone.' So, they went for it."

Additionally, Cash wanted his own entourage—including his old Sun Records labelmate Carl Perkins (*Blue Suede Shoes*) as well as the Carters, the Statlers, and the Tennessee Three—backing his solo numbers and on occasion performing their own music. June Carter, whom Cash had married the previous March, would also have a featured role. Jacobson, architect of the CBC triumph, came along as director, and would replace Bill Carruthers as producer in the second season.

To accommodate guest artists needing more lush accompaniment, an excellent staff orchestra was assembled by conductor Bill Walker. This top-notch ensemble subsequently worked with performers as diverse as Louis Armstrong, Chet Atkins, Ray Charles, Roy Clark, Judy Collins, Cass Elliot, Jose Feliciano, Arlo Guthrie, Phil Harris, John Hartford, Burl Ives, Peggy Lee, Jerry Lee Lewis, Rod McKuen, Melanie, Liza Minnelli, the Monkees, Rick Nelson, Odetta, Charley Pride, Linda Rondstadt, Marty Robbins, and Tony Joe White while never overpowering the raw power of Cash's own bare-bones sound.

Most importantly, Cash insisted that the show be taped at the hoary Ryman versus a generic, boxy studio in Los Angeles or New York. The creaky but revered Mother Church of Country Music, nearing a century old, was unairconditioned—temperatures onstage routinely soared above one hundred degrees during the summer—and was woefully ill-equipped for television. However, Cash believed—and rightly so—that its down-home ambiance would enhance the show's gritty authenticity. Likewise, he eschewed the predictable variety-show trappings—no Johnny Cash Dancers, for example—in an effort to replicate as closely as possible the look and the feel of a live, no-nonsense concert appearance during which the emphasis was on music.

It was a different and a daring approach; but, in the summer of 1969, the network needed Johnny Cash—who had reportedly sold 6.5 million albums during the previous twelve months—more than Johnny Cash needed the network. Consequently, the powers-that-be acquiesced, albeit reluctantly and temporarily, and taping began on Wednesday, April 15, 1969.

The first program to be aired, on Saturday, June 7, featured a rare television appearance by Dylan, along with fellow folkie Joni Mitchell, fiddler Doug Kershaw, and comedienne Fannie Flagg. However, the first program to be taped featured Glen Campbell, whose frothy but popular *Goodtime Hour* had debuted the previous year on rival CBS-TV, along with country songstress Jeannie C. Riley, rhythm and blues great Joe Tex, and comedian Ron Carey. Also on the bill: a special appearance by the Rouse Brothers.

"I talked with my producers about really doing it right, about giving the people an original country show, something nobody had seen on network television," Cash said in 1980, when reflecting upon his decision to book the Rouses. Certainly, the opportunity was an incredible one for Ervin and Gordon, who along with Carrie and brother Earl spent a heady two weeks in Nashville as guests of Columbia Screen Gems, the show's production company. (Although they were offered airfare, phobic Ervin insisted that the trip be made by car.)

"I don't know why Ervin asked Earl to come along," says Carrie. "Earl didn't have anything to do with *Orange Blossom Special*. But he sort of controlled Ervin around that time. He lived in Ervin's home, and he was able to get up and go whenever Ervin wanted. Gordon had his lawn business, and couldn't do that."

During their time in Music City, the Rouses were guests at an intimate dinner at Mother Maybelle's home. "Mother Maybelle fussed all over [the brothers] like a big old mother hen," Carrie recalls. "She called them 'her boys.' She said she was so proud of her boys." The group also attended rehearsals, saw the sights, and met some of Ervin's music industry cronies.

Because the Cash show was the first network television program since a 1950s *Grand Ole Opry* series to originate from Nashville, it was extensively covered by the local media. Interestingly, however, the stories invariably focused more on the unheralded Rouses than on the entertainment industry heavyweights who were also in town.

For example, the *Nashville Banner* published front-page a story headlined "Cash Show Filmed Here By ABC-TV," which was flanked by a three-column photograph not of Cash, but of the grinning siblings, decked out in white cowboy hats, string ties, and intricate Seminole Indian jackets.

Reporter Red O'Donnell, seeking an unusual angle, focused his piece on the colorful Floridians. It is riddled with minor inaccuracies, many of them supplied by Ervin, but is indicative of the unaccustomed attention the trio received:

> The best known *Orange Blossom Special* has nothing to do with a bridal bouquet—though there could be some romantic dissenters—or a fancy, potent concoction—though some imbibers may think otherwise. It is a frequently sung and played railroad song.
>
> And Irving (sic) Rouse, who composed the tune, was in Nashville Wednesday night, April 16, with his brothers Gordon and Earl, to perform it on the initial taping of the Johnny Cash ABC-TV Show, at the Grand Ole Opry House, a fifteen-segment package and the first (sic) network series to be produced in Music City, USA.
>
> *Orange Blossom Special*, written more than thirty years ago, has become a standard—an evergreen, as they say in

the music trade. It has been recorded in all idioms: Johnny Cash and Jimmy Wakely did it country style; Billy Vaughn and Lawrence Welk made it a million-seller in the pop field and Chet Atkins and Arthur Fielder included it in their semi-classical Boston Pops album, to mention only a few of the dozens who have put it on wax.

Irving, now fifty-two, and his brothers were up from Florida's Everglades country to do the TV show, which will air on Channel 8 Saturday night, July 5, although the series actually begins June 7. TV series programs are prepared far in advance and not necessarily in the order they'll be shown. For instance, the premier is not scheduled to be taped until May 1.

Orange Blossom Special—as the lyrics describe—was a crackerjack, fast-running train on the old Seaboard Air Line (now the merged Seaboard-Coastal Lines) running to and from New York and Jacksonville (sic). "I wrote it in 1936 (sic), the day the train was dedicated," Rouse recalled, as he mingled with other special guests on the show—Jeannie C. Riley, Joe Tex, June Carter Cash, and comedian Ron Carey (Glen Campell's segment was taped separately). "We were driving from Miami to New York for a recording session (sic). We were a pretty big attraction then—vaudeville and all that—but haven't been too active lately.

"Our late manager, Lloyd Smith, suggested that I write a song about the train. I wrote it as we rode along in the car. We didn't record it. Arthur Smith did the first recording (sic)."

The train that inspired the song is no more. It was discontinued about six years ago. Ironically, Irving Rouse, who immortalized the train in story and song, never rode on it.

Music City News, a monthly fan-oriented publication, also highlighted the Rouses, sending writer Everette Corbin to interview the brothers at a hotel coffee shop. "Of course, I was familiar with the song, and had been hearing it for years," Corbin says. "I remember I met with the three of them, and that Ervin did most of the talking. They were very excited about appearing on the show, and really appreciated the fact that Johnny Cash had remembered them, and that he'd gone to the trouble to track them down. My overall impression was that the Rouses were just wonderful country people; as country as could be."

Corbin's article likewise recounts Ervin's version of the *Special's* genesis, and presents the trio as colorful and unpretentious. Clearly, even the most creative press agent could hardly have conjured up such an embraceable story.

Finally, however, it was showtime at the Ryman. Because of the space required for bulky television cameras and other production paraphernalia, the auditorium's relatively small stage was extended out over the floor seats, which meant that the performers played mainly to the balcony. Nonetheless, the boisterous spectators, seated on austere wooden pews and waving fans to fend of the stifling heat, were an integral part of the presentation, cheering, whistling, stomping their feet, and stepping up to snap photographs with their Brownie-Hawkeyes.

Because of fits and starts typical of television, the brothers' segment was not taped until nearly 11 p.m. But when their names were called, Ervin, Gordon, and Earl were wonderful—or horrible.

Carrie, who was in the audience, says the brothers brought down the house with an incendiary, seven-minute version of the *Special*. "Gordon had to sing bass because all Earl could sing was tenor," recalls Carrie. "But they were great. They got a standing ovation." Agrees Donna Stoneman, who was also there: "The crowd loved the Rouse Brothers. When they finished playing, Ervin got down on his knees and bent all the way to the ground, his face almost touching the floor. He seemed like such a humble man."

Others strongly disagree. Joe Byrne, vice president of programming and specials for ABC, says that allowing Cash to host the Rouses was an indulgence that turned out badly for all involved. "John wanted Irving (sic)," says Byrne. "He said he was 'different,' and he wanted 'different' on the show. But these guys were off the charts different. It got so we had to insulate John from people after a while. He couldn't say no. But Irving is an example of John not making the best decisions."

Production Manager Tom Trbovich says he sensed trouble when he first laid eyes on Ervin, who he says arrived at the Ryman "smelly and disheveled; he was pitiful, old, and senile." Jacobson agrees that Ervin was "drunk, falling all over the place." He says that after seeing the Rouses perform, he knew their segment could not possibly air. And he believes Cash knew it, too. "John knew Rouse wasn't going to make the cut," Jacobson contends. "He had to know. It was awful."

Nonetheless, the Rouses apparently felt as though they had achieved a major career breakthrough. The jubilant brothers remained in Nashville through Saturday night, when they returned to the Ryman stage for an *Opry* broadcast. Once again, according to Carrie, the *Special* brought the audience to its collective feet, and earned warm kudos from other *Opry* performers. Among the spectators, she says, was a polite but reserved Hank Snow, who approached Gordon backstage and asked him about the song.

"I was standing right there with Gordon when Hank came up," says Carrie. "He said to Gordon, 'Tell me something. I've heard all these different stories, and I'd like to know the truth. Who really wrote *Orange Blossom Special*?' Gordon said, 'Me and my brother Ervin wrote it,' and he told the whole story. Hank nodded and was very businesslike, and said something like, 'Well, I just wanted to verify that.' And then he fired Chubby Wise that same day."

Actually, Chubby remained with Snow for another year, and when he left the parting was fairly amicable. The Little Chief, regardless of what he was told by Gordon or anyone else, always stood by his fiddler's version of events. Jacobson, for example, says he asked Snow about the authorship controversy when the two were drinking together at a Nashville bar. "Later we drove out to Hank's house in Madison," he recalls. "It was about three in the morning, but he insisted on calling Chubby. He got him on the phone and said, 'Chubby? This is the Ranger. Did you or did you not write the *Special*? You did? Okay.' Then he hung up."

Also while in Nashville, Ervin donated his fiddle to the Country Music Hall of Fame Museum during ceremonies attended by Earl, Gordon, and Carrie along with Hall of Fame officials. A press release indicates that the fiddle, "which shows years of wear and travel but is in excellent condition," is the instrument on which Ervin composed *Orange Blossom Special*. However, this contention appears doubtful. Ervin rarely kept fiddles for long; he either hocked them, lost them, or gave them away.

In any case, the battered artifact is no longer on display and, like many hillbilly musical relics, it is remarkable only because of its owner's renown. It is an amber-varnished replica of an Amati—a violin used by Italian masters in the 18th and 19th centuries—with a two-piece back made of maple and a top made of spruce. It has a wooden chin rest, ivory tuning pegs, and an ebony tailpiece. When new, it probably sold for fifty to seventy-five dollars.

"The *Opry* people wanted us to stay in town, so that Ervin, Gordon, and Earl could be on the show again the following Saturday," says Carrie. "But Ervin just got ready to go. He said, 'No, let's head back to Miami.'"

Years later, Cash contended that he had his first run-in with the network brass over the Rouse Brothers. "They said [to Ervin], 'Thank you very much,' paid him and he went back to the swamps," Cash said in 1994. "He kept writing and writing, wanting to know when he'd be on. And when they edited the show, this was really when I got an education on what TV's all about. Ervin Rouse was not on the show—and I was the one who had to call him and tell him."

If Cash did call, and it is doubtful that he had the heart to do so, Ervin never relayed the bad news to his brothers; Carrie and Gordon were watching the July 5 broadcast at their home fully expecting that the Rouse Brothers would appear. "Well, we were just devastated," says Carrie. "Think of what that appearance could have meant. I finally reached [Saul Holliff, Cash's manager], and he said that he was very sorry—but there were never any guarantees that the performance would be used."

Were the Rouses really as bad as all that? It almost seems as though members of the audience and members of the production team must have watched different performances, so divergent are their opinions. Undoubtedly, the brothers were every bit as unpolished as Byrne, Trbovich, and Jacobson remember. And it would have been surprising, given his history, had Ervin *not* been drunk. Still, although the Rouse

Brothers may have been small-time, they were at the very least consummate professionals. No tape of the performance is known to exist, but it seems likely that the trio
would have delivered the *Special* with their usual verve.

So what was the problem? The Rouses were unadulterated hillbillies, and entirely unknown to boot. Would sophisticated and demographically desirable urbanites
find the trio entertaining, or would they simply change the channel? Ultimately,
someone up the corporate ladder must have concluded that it was a chance not worth
taking. "That was about my first fight with network TV," Cash said. "It was about
my last one, too. I was determined from then on that I wouldn't stick my neck out;
that if I was going to do TV, I didn't own the networks, so I'd have to do it their way."

How would an appearance on *The Johnny Cash Show* have impacted the Rouse
Brothers? It is impossible to know for certain, particularly given Ervin's peculiarities
and his penchant for squandering opportunities. However, it is safe to speculate that
the exposure almost certainly would have resulted in opportunities to record again,
perhaps for a major label, and might well have ignited interest in the brothers as
live performers.

Of course, they were far too old-school—if not far too old, period—to have
become mainstream stars in their own right; yet, they would have made a potent
opening act, and would have been well-suited for folk-music clubs and for the
emerging bluegrass festival circuit.

Indeed, another unorthodox fiddler, Doug Kershaw, saw his career soar after
appearing on Cash's show. Following his network debut, the gyrating native of Tiel
Ridge, Louisiana, was inundated with television, recording, and film work, attracting
hoards of youthful fans with his other-worldly demeanor and his uninhibited playing.
Of course, Kershaw and his brother Rusty—unlike the Rouses—had enjoyed modest
success as recording artists, reaching the Top 10 with *Louisiana Man* in 1961. Still,
the "Cajun Hippie's" breakthrough demonstrates that, network timidity notwithstanding, television viewers often respond favorably when confronted with something "off
the charts different," as Jacobson had described the Rouses.

The brothers were not invited back during the subsequent two seasons of *The
Johnny Cash Show's* ABC-TV run. However, Cash compensated for the slight by performing the *Special* almost as often as his signature hits, *I Walk the Line, Ring of Fire,*
and *Folsom Prison Blues*. In fact, on *The Johnny Cash Show's* inaugural broadcast,
he opened with a medley that included the *Special*, then trotted it out as a stand-alone
on July 26. During the 1969-1970 season, Cash revisited the *Special* on January 21,
January 28 (during a medley with Glen Campbell), and April 29; during the 1970-
1971 season he showcased the now-familiar twin harmonicas on September 23 and
January 20.

He likewise boosted the *Special* on numerous other nationally televised appearances, and even re-recorded it in 1975, adding new vocals over the 1964 instrumentation for inclusion on an album called *Destination Victoria Station*, distributed as a

promotional item through a restaurant chain. Most importantly, the *Special* became a highlight of virtually every Cash concert appearance around the world for more than three decades, often accompanied by grainy video footage of hoboes, freight trains, and head-on collisions.

In 1997, after Cash was diagnosed—misdiagnosed, as it turned out—with a rare neuromuscular disorder, he ceased touring and subsequently contracted double pneumonia. As he lay near death, writers dusted off their obituaries while the Nashville music establishment, which had never embraced him in life, prepared to mark his passing with appropriate pomp and circumstance.

But they were premature. Again confounding expectations, Cash survived and was well enough to attend an all-star, Turner Network Television-produced tribute at New York's Hammerstein Ballroom.

There, performers from virtually every musical genre paid homage to the Man in Black by singing his most famous songs. Opening the show, which aired to impressive ratings on April 18, 1999, was fellow outlaw Willie Nelson and rock singer Sheryl Crow, who teamed for an unorthodox medley of *Jackson* and *Orange Blossom Special.*

When Cash finally did meet his maker on September 12, 2003, much of his catalog was repackaged and rereleased, and the *Special* reappeared on countless top-selling compilations.

"Man, Johnny picked me up right out of the ditch, me and some of the other writers he recorded," Ervin said in 1977. "He was the greatest thing that ever happened to poor people."

X

The End of the Line:
Legends and Legacies

Brother Chubby was an extra special person; he was all the time talking about the Lord.
Rev. Leslie Thomas,
MacClenney Christian Fellowship,
on his most famous parishioner

Daddy said he liked Jimmy Swaggart because he was a good performer.
Eloise Rouse Drennan,
Ervin's daughter,
on her father's religious beliefs

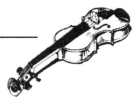

"Texas lives its clichés," wrote poet Andrei Codrescue. "It's big, it's rude, it's stormy. There are real men there. They wear their boots to sleep in the back of their pickups. They get their seventy-two-ounce steak free if they can eat it in one hour. They dance to real cowboy songs like *Orange Blossom Special*." So, it is not surprising that Chubby was warmly welcomed by music-loving Texans when he relocated from Nashville to Houston in the winter of 1970.

Determined to establish a solo career, the fiddler quickly parlayed the regional popularity of *Maiden's Prayer* into club dates throughout the Lone Star State. He also began recording albums for his friend Roy Stone, whose three Houston music stores subsidized the operation of Stoneway, a niche record label that also listed on its roster Leon McAuliffe, legendary steel guitarist for Bob Wills & His Texas Playboys; Kayton Roberts, Chubby's former Hank Snow bandmate; Howdy Forrester, veteran fiddler best-known for his stints with Bill Monroe and Roy

Acuff; and Gene Watson, an auto-body repairman with a soaring voice who would gain stardom in the 1970s with mainstream country hits such as *Love in the Hot Afternoon.*

Over the next decade, Stoneway would release at least twenty of Chubby's compilations, including *Cacklin' Hen* (Chubby's old childhood favorite learned from Bryan Purcell), *Chubby's Hornpipe, Chubby Plays Bluegrass, Chubby Plays Bob Wills, Chubby Plays Hank Williams, Daddy's Blues, Danny Boy, Down Yonder, Grassy Fiddle, Hoedown Number 1, Hoedown Number 2, Maiden's Prayer, Million Dollar Fiddle, Orange Blossom Special* (of course), *Precious Memories, Redwing, Stone's Rag, Sweet Bunch of Daisies, Three O'clock in the Morning,* and *Up a Lazy River.*

However, these efforts, which were primarily in the light country or western swing genres, did not please some bluegrass enthusiasts. Wrote Lance LeRoy: "Largely a potpourri of various styles of music—from concepts that were surely not his own—in many instances [the Stoneway albums] presented undistinguished examples of Wise's characteristically splendid work."

Chubby did appear as a sideman on several unadulterated bluegrass projects, including the Charlie Moore album *Legend of the Rebel Soldier,* released on the Wango label, and he collaborated with his old friend Howdy Forrester on two twin fiddle albums, *Sincerely Yours* and *Fiddle Tradition,* released on Stoneway. Yet, perhaps Chubby's most interesting project was a 1976 album called *The Good Ole Boys: Pistol Packin' Mama,* produced by the Grateful Dead's Jerry Garcia.

The album was the brainchild of Chubby's old friend Frank Wakefield and David Nelson, then playing lead electric guitar for The New Riders of the Purple Sage, a California-based country/rock band that had originally included a moonlighting Garcia on pedal steel guitar. "[*The Good Old Boys*] kind of came about on the spur of the moment," Wakefield recalled in an interview with Jim Moss, an archivist and fiddler who now backs Wakefield on tour. "I was out in Marin County, in California, staying at David's house and doing some shows with his band. Me and David were sitting around talking when I told David I'd like to do a record of me and him with Don Reno and Chubby Wise. At first, David thought I was kidding. When he realized I was serious, he said, 'Boy, I'd love to, but you can never get to talk to people like Don Reno and Chubby Wise.'"

But Wakefield, who had worked with both of the bluegrass veterans that Nelson so admired, felt he could persuade them to participate. So the pair pitched the idea to Round Records, the Grateful Dead's record company. Although President Ron Rakow had never heard of Chubby or Reno, he agreed to back the project. He even had a producer in mind: Jerry Garcia. "You know who Jerry is," Rakow explained to a puzzled Wakefield. "He's the guy who's been playing banjo with you." Wakefield did, in fact, know that the amiable hippie who occasionally sat in on his gigs with Nelson was named Jerry, but he did not know Jerry's last name—nor would it have mattered if he had. "I'd never heard of Garcia or the Grateful Dead,"

Wakefield said. "Whenever Garcia played with David and me, we'd have a full house. But I thought it was because of me."

Wakefield first called Reno, a banjo virtuoso who had replaced Earl Scruggs when Scruggs left Bill Monroe's Blue Grass Boys, and described the project to him. Reno, who later fronted the popular Tennessee Cut-Ups with Arthur Lee "Red" Smiley, had never heard of Garcia, Nelson, or The New Riders of the Purple Sage. But he agreed to come to California for eight hundred dollars and two airline tickets—one for him and one for his banjo. Chubby also agreed to the eight hundred dollar fee, but passed on the airline tickets. Instead, he and Rossi drove from their home in Texas to Garcia's San Rafael recording studio, a converted barn called Rolling Thunder, where they joined Wakefield, Nelson, Reno, and bassist Pat Campbell. "I'm sure Chubby didn't know who Jerry Garcia was," says Rossi. "I didn't know who he was, either. At first, Chubby didn't want to go. He only agreed because I'd never been to California, and I wanted to see it."

No stranger to acoustic folk music, Garcia had played hard-core bluegrass since the 1960s, and had previously fronted an all-star string band called Old & In the Way, which featured Peter Rowan on guitar, David Grissam on mandolin, John Kahn on upright bass, and Vassar Clements on fiddle. The short-lived group played only a handful of engagements before disbanding, but *Orange Blossom Special* highlighted each performance.

A recording of an October 1973 concert at the Boarding House in San Francisco captures the excitement of an Old & In the Way concert, and offers a fine example of Clements' exemplary fiddle work. The former Blue Grass Boy, who had just embarked on a solo career, plays the *Special* like a man possessed, and even embellishes the tune with a few notes from the *Dragnet* theme. Also of note is the improvisational interplay between instruments prior to the final stanza, showcasing the fiddler's jazz proclivities. (The Boarding House appearance was taped, and the resulting album, *That High Lonesome Sound*, is available on the Acoustic Disc label.)

Over a period of two days, with Garcia at the control board, the generation-spanning ensemble cut twenty-eight tunes, primarily country and bluegrass standards, along with one Wise original. "Chubby didn't have a name for the tune," recalled Wakefield. "I always called him 'Chubby Too Wise,' so I said, 'Why don't we call the song the *Too Wise Special*?' Well, that really tickled Chubby. When Chubby would start laughing with that big laugh of his, it would start his belly shaking all around. He said, 'That sounds mighty fine, Little Frankie!' Chubby would always call me 'Little Frankie.'"

Not surprisingly, mood-altering substances were prevalent during the sessions. "There was so much marijuana smoke [in the studio] that it almost made me sick," Rossi recalls. "Now, Chubby didn't use marijuana. But him and Don Reno had a fifth of whiskey they were passing back and forth. I'll tell you one thing: they all had a great time. Chubby was the life of the party wherever he went, and he kept everybody laughing." (Small wonder, given the amount of second-hand smoke that even non-participants would have ingested.)

The Good Ole Boys: Pistol Packin' Mama was released in March 1976. Although it is a delightful package still enjoyed by devout Deadheads and acoustic music traditionalists alike, it would mark Chubby's first and only counterculture adventure.

So, while Chubby had certainly not abandoned bluegrass, he had unquestionably become far more concerned with earning a decent living than with preserving a revered but narrowly focused art form. He even assembled a backup band, and briefly—very briefly—fronted his own group in an effort to attract more lucrative bookings. "That lasted for one engagement," says Rossi. "It was a dance, and the other musicians were drunk. Chubby was saying, 'Come on! Sober up! The show's starting!' Chubby was no leader. He found out he wasn't mean enough to be the boss."

This revelation, in hindsight, may have caused the happy-go-lucky rounder to view his own former employers, particularly Monroe and Snow, in a more sympathetic light. At the very least, Chubby found it difficult to enforce codes of behavior which, throughout his career, he had generally ignored. So, he continued club dates and backed Stoneway labelmate Gene Watson during a series of engagements at the Golden Nugget in Las Vegas.

Increasingly, however, Chubby was finding work—and, at long last, solo stardom—on the burgeoning festival circuit. Bluegrass festivals—which have been likened to religious revivals due to the fervor of the attendees—began in the mid-1960s as a spinoff of the folk-music boom, and are now held worldwide.

Promoter Carlton Haney staged the first large-scale festival on September 3-5, 1965, at Cantrell's Horse Farm in Fincastle, Virginia. The event, which featured Bill Monroe and His Blue Grass Boys, Jim Eanes, Benny Martin, Jimmy Martin, Clyde Moody, Don Reno, Larry Richardson, the Stanley Brothers, and Mac Wiseman, was so successful that it served as a template for hundreds of similar gatherings to follow, including the prestigious Bean Blossom Festival, founded in 1967 by Monroe himself and held each June in southern Indiana.

Haney's groundbreaking gathering culminated with a five-hour marathon called "The Blue Grass Music Story," during which Monroe was joined onstage by past band members spanning a quarter-century. Interestingly, neither Flatt & Scruggs nor Chubby attended, perhaps as a result of continuing animosity between the intransigent living legend and his former employees. Nonetheless, *Sing Out* magazine reporter Mayne Smith opined that the importance of the event "must finally escape expression in words."

Haney himself told Smith that, "The people know when you're transferring your mind through your hands to them, and that's when you're playing bluegrass. And that's what we did yesterday—to thousands, which has been my dream—and that's why we had the festival. I saw men crying; one time I had to leave the stage myself."

Writer Bruce Watson, dissecting the festival phenomenon for *Smithsonian* magazine, vividly described the scene at the 1993 Music in the Mountains hootenanny in tiny Summersville, West Virginia:

> From every state in the union they come, and from Canada, Norway, Japan, Germany and Australia. Rolling across the mountains in vans, campers and recreational vehicles larger than some houses in these hills, the guests "make themselves to home," all right. Parked cheek by fender with other monolithic RVs, they raise awnings and festoon them with brightly colored lanterns. On makeshift patios they set up folding furniture, welcome mats and redwood plaques carved with the family name and hometown.
>
> By Wednesday, the day before the start of this veritable bluegrass Woodstock, the Kitchen's [Edgar and Eunice, owners of the property and promoters] campground is a city of RVs hunkered down on hayfields. Then, late in the evening, about sundown, the guests open battered instrument cases, take out guitars and banjos and the pickin' begins. Whether in Tanglewood, Marlboro or Monterey, most music festivals are autocratic. The masters perform onstage, audiences listen, applaud and head home. But a bluegrass festival is democracy in the key of G. Here, fans take music into their own hands, making all the world a stage.
>
> Festivals draw flocks of zealots who drive for days, gorge themselves on banjo, fiddle, mandolin and Dobro (an acoustic slide guitar) then scatter, vowing to make it to next weekend's gathering in another dark holler some hundreds of miles hither.

For Chubby and many others, festivals became paramount to their financial well being. Most bluegrass musicians, then as now, recorded for small, independent labels offering spotty distribution and minimal resources for promotion. Likewise, country radio shunned all but a handful of bluegrass artists, meaning that festivals were the primary outlets through which performers were able to market themselves and their recordings. Therefore, in 1974 Chubby asked his wife to quit her job as a private duty nurse at Methodist Hospital, and to assume responsibility for his bookings. "He told me I could do a lot of good for him," Rossi says. "And I did."

Nonetheless, bluegrass stardom is rarely accompanied by significant paydays; although the hard-nosed Rossi says she was able to command three thousand dollars for some appearances, Chubby usually earned a third of that amount or less. "I paid

Chubby more than he got most places," says Tom Riggs, owner of Orlando-based Pinecastle Records and a festival promoter. "I told him he ought to raise his price. But he said, 'Colonel, if I do that I'm afraid nobody will hire me.' That was typical of a lot of musicians who grew up poor, and were afraid they might lose everything." Still, Chubby's attitude about money remained decidedly blasé: "The advice I'd give young people is to do what you love," he said. "The money, it ain't important. Money ain't what makes you happy."

In addition to booking Chubby's dates, Rossi's duties also included driving, loading and unloading equipment, and selling cassettes. Chubby, who had driven perhaps a million miles for Monroe and Snow, was at first nervous with his wife behind the wheel, joking to a friend that he would feel more secure being chauffeured by Ronnie Milsap, a blind country-pop singer. However, their constant proximity certainly discouraged additional infidelity.

"When Chubby got away from all that mess—Hank Snow, Nashville, and them fly-by-nights on the road—we had no more problems with us separating," Rossi says. "We had our ups and downs, but nothing big. It wasn't smooth sailing, but we had more consideration for each other. If he went, I went. We had a little difficulty every once in a while, but everyone does. That's human nature, you know. There wasn't but one perfect one, and that was Him."

In 1975, Chubby and Rossi relocated to Lake Livingston, Texas, a rural area located about seventy-five miles north of Houston, where they a rented a small home on a sprawling lot. "Our yard looked like a city park when I got done," recalls Rossi, who was more accustomed to occupying mobile homes and apartments throughout her tumultuous second marriage. "I loved working outside. But Chubby wouldn't lift a finger. He was a lazy musician. He'd always say, 'My hand don't fit that shovel.'"

In 1977, the couple moved again, to Colonial Beach, Virginia. There they stayed for six years before settling for good in Glen St. Mary, Florida, a small Baker County town straddling State Road 90, roughly midway between Jacksonville and Lake City. Three years earlier, Chubby had been badly shaken by the cancer-related death of daughter Marvelene, from whom he had been estranged, and was perhaps anxious to reestablish family ties. "Chubby made the remark that he was getting old, and that he wanted to die in Florida," Rossi says.

Chubby's grandchildren understandably harbored mixed emotions concerning the old fiddler's re-emergence in their lives. However, they saved most of their resentment for Rossi, whom they viewed as conniving and controlling. "Granddaddy showed up at the hospital the day before [Marvelene] died," says Rebecca Mangrum. "Rossi was with him, and we wouldn't let her in the room. She acted like we were beneath her. The few other times Granddaddy had visited, she'd just sit on the couch and drink and act bored. She didn't want him to have any kind of relationship with his family."

Still, Chubby and Rossi did their best to put down roots. After purchasing a lot and settling into a new mobile home, the couple rediscovered their faith at a local nondenominational church, the Mcclenney Christian Fellowship, at which a sober, born-again Chubby often provided music. "An evangelist had prophesied that celebrities would be coming to our church," says Brother Leslie Thomas, minister to the twelve-hundred-member congregation. "And he said that the celebrities would attract more people. That turned out to be true with Brother Chubby."

Church member Paul Johnson says that Chubby's renditions of traditional spirituals such as *How Great Thou Art* were moving and memorable: "When he stuck that fiddle up under his chin, his eyes looked like beacons; the sound would make chills run up and down your spine."

Apparently, Chubby's most notable addictions during his final years included nothing more sinister than inhumanly spicy chili—probably not what a doctor would have prescribed for a man with bleeding ulcers—and coffee so strong that it resembled hot tar.

Professionally, Chubby continued to work as much as he wanted—which was more than he should have   and to revel in the adoration heaped upon him by fans. "Chubby was always a crowd-pleaser," says Riggs. "Of course, he didn't have his own band, and in festival situations it's usually difficult to get other bands to back up a solo performer. But with Chubby, we'd have people standing in line wanting to play with him."

Even headliners felt privileged to share the spotlight with this rotund human dynamo, a consummate showman who, with his snow-white beard and ever-present suspenders, looked as though he had just stepped out of a nineteenth-century tintype.

After meeting him at an Oklahoma festival in the late 1970s, the Boys From Indiana backed Chubby at perhaps fifty appearances throughout the country. "It was always a pleasure and an honor for us," says Aubrey Holt, the group's guitarist and lead singer. "We'd do our set first, then we'd bring Chubby on. The people would always jump to their feet." Typically, Chubby and the group would open with several Hank Snow and Hank Williams tunes, followed by *Maiden's Prayer* and *Shenandoah Waltz*. Invariably, *Orange Blossom Special*—which most audience members assumed Chubby had composed—closed the show in grand style.

When logistics allowed, the Boys From Indiana invited the old fiddler to ride on their bus between engagements, and enjoyed hearing his anecdotes about Nashville stars and life on the road. "We got to know Chubby real well, and I can honestly say he was the most humble, sincere person I ever met," Holt adds. "He'd always sit up front in the captain's chair, and I'd ask him if he wanted to lie down in one of the bunks. I knew he was tired and feeling badly. But his breathing was so bad that he was more comfortable sitting up. I'll admit, there were plenty of times onstage with Chubby that I'd be holding back the tears. I never knew whether or not it would be the last time."

THEN, IN THE FALL of 1984, Lake City finally paid homage to the man who, six decades earlier, had limped along its streets selling pencils and oranges to survive.

Chubby Wise Day was the brainchild of E. Vernon Douglas, Chief Judge of Florida's Third Judicial Circuit, which encompasses seven primarily rural north Florida counties.

Unquestionably, the Lake City native and amateur fiddler was a man who could make things happen. In 1982, for example, the civic-minded jurist had led a community-wide effort to secure Johnny Cash's participation in a concert to raise funds for a proposed Columbia County Historical Museum.

Cash, a Civil War buff, had agreed not only to perform, but also to waive a portion of his customary fee as a gesture of support. The local daily newspaper, the *Lake City Reporter*, had heralded the singer's visit as "an historic moment," and the concert, held at Lake City Community College's Howard Gymnasium, had attracted a capacity crowd of two thousand. Most importantly, proceeds from the event, combined with donations and several state grants, had enabled the city to purchase and renovate the circa-1880 Perkins-Vinzant House, a once-proud Cracker classic in which artifacts from Columbia County's colorful past could be preserved and displayed.

During his 1982 visit and the negotiations leading up to it, Cash, a fiercely intelligent man with a wide array of interests, had enjoyed discussing concepts of justice with Douglas, and the two developed a bond. "Johnny told me how interesting it was to speak frankly and candidly with a judge about judicial philosophy," Douglas says. "He expressed concerns about judges legislating from the bench, and said he preferred [a constructionist] view of the Constitution. He also had concerns about mercy versus justice and strong beliefs about the equal application of laws to the oppressed."

Following the concert, Cash asked Douglas when he would be up re-election. Douglas told him it would be two years later, in 1984, and Cash said he would happily return at that time to perform again at Howard Gymnasium—and to offer Douglas an electoral boost. So, Douglas and other community leaders decided to hitch Chubby's proposed tribute to the Man in Black's return engagement. It certainly seemed logical to do so, particularly considering the serendipitous *Orange Blossom Special* connection.

In addition, Chubby Wise Day was bundled with a sacrosanct Lake City tradition: the annual reenactment of Florida's largest and bloodiest Civil War engagement, the Battle of Olustee, during which five thousand Union troops advancing west from Jacksonville were turned back by an equal number of Confederate defenders lurking in the Baker County pine forests.

As part of the weekend-long commemoration, held on February 17 and 18, a beaming Chubby was named Grand Marshall of a Civil War-themed parade and with Rossi at his side clattered triumphantly through downtown Lake City in a horse-drawn carriage. Then, flanked by a ragtag band that included a game but musically outclassed Douglas, Chubby fiddled briefly on the steps of the Columbia County

Courthouse before greeting several hundred fans, friends, and assorted well-wishers assembled in the picturesque town square.

"I'm not usually at a loss for words, but I really don't know what to say about this," said Chubby, obviously moved and humbled. "The good Lord not only smiled on me, He laughed out loud. But I promise you, none of this is gonna give me the big head. I'll still be the same old fat Chubby Wise that I've always been, and always will be."

In hindsight, perhaps the tribute should have concluded with those poignant and undoubtedly earnest sentiments. However, because of scheduling conflicts, Cash's show had been postponed to Friday, April 7, at which time Chubby had agreed to return to Lake City for another performance, and for his official induction into a museum-sponsored hall of fame.

Heady stuff indeed; yet, as events unfolded, the honoree came to view this obviously well-intentioned effort as a slight, and his wife came to regard the highly respected Douglas as a scoundrel who had traded upon her husband's good name. In fact, Douglas says he had been a fan of Chubby's for decades, and had been surprised to find that the pioneering fiddler, who was so highly regarded in music industry circles, had never been properly acknowledged in what was, for all intents and purposes, his hometown. "One thing you do when you get a little older is try to fulfill dreams," says Douglas. "I had always dreamed of meeting Chubby, and of finding a way that we could show our appreciation as a community for all he'd done. So, I started talking to members of Chubby's family, trying to come up with ways we could accomplish that. At the same time, we were digging up all this local history for the museum, and I certainly considered Chubby to be an important part of our heritage. It all seemed to come together very well. Unfortunately, though, I don't think we ever could have done enough in [Rossi's] view."

So it would appear. "He [Douglas] lied to us," says Rossi. "You can put this down. I done told him to his tooth. He told everybody this was a Chubby Wise concert. Well, Johnny Cash got thirty thousand dollars and Chubby got nothing. It was a Johnny Cash show. Johnny thought it was his concert because the judge had lied to him, too. He put Johnny on a pedestal. Went and got him in a limousine, and we came in my car."

Even the eternally laid-back Chubby seemed to share his wife's dismay, according to remarks he made in 1996. "Johnny Cash was supposed to be my guest," Chubby said. "Johnny was on my Chubby Wise Day. But I wound up doing about three [actually two] tunes with Johnny, and he directed the show. That's the way it turned out, and everyone was kind of disappointed."

Yet, a review of audiotaped planning meetings and promotional material related to the event reveals this assessment to be unfairly harsh, if not outright petty. Chubby clearly was invited to appear as a guest on Cash's show—not vice-versa—and he was promised only complimentary accommodations at a local hotel. During their discussions, organizers speak in reverent tones of Chubby's accomplishments, and repeatedly express a desire to "do right" by their native son. But Chubby Wise Day had come and gone, and if Chubby truly believed that he, not Cash, was to have headlined the April 7 concert, then he was deluding himself.

Nonetheless, Douglas graciously accepts responsibility for "a glitch in the timing" that may have cut Chubby's stage time shorter than anticipated. However, he notes, the homegrown fiddler had previously received public accolades at the museum, and had been grandly feted during his February 17 visit. "He got more attention from us in a short span of time than he'd probably gotten in his entire career," Douglas says. "We were only trying to honor a great man."

For Cash, 1983 had been a horrific year. He was again addicted to an array of drugs, and during a European tour experienced a hallucination in which he saw armies of phantom spiders skittering across a hotel-room wall. He badly lacerated his hand while trying to crush the imaginary arachnids, and was returned to Nashville for surgery. Cash later said that he barely remembered the ill-fated tour, although newspapers carried generally laudatory reviews of his work.

While in the hospital, doctors found internal bleeding and also removed Cash's duodenum and parts of his intestine, spleen, and stomach. Following the operation, the singer clandestinely stuffed a card of Valium inside the bandages covering his stomach wound. But the card melted into the wound and the Valium, when mixed with morphine and other drugs already being administrated by doctors, was very nearly lethal.

After an angry and tearful family intervention, Cash agreed in December to enter the Betty Ford Center in Rancho Mirage, California. The press was told that it was a "preventative" visit, to head off a relapse that the singer's regimen of prescription pain-killers might trigger.

Back Lake City, Cash seemed in good spirits, says Douglas, and much more relaxed than during his 1982 visit. Douglas had dinner at a local restaurant with Cash and his manager, Lou Robin, and says the singer spoke openly about his drug problem. "I asked, 'How bad was it?,'" Douglas recalls. "Johnny reached directly into a bowl of peanuts and grabbed a fistful. He then put them in his mouth and chased them with a Coke without chewing. He said, 'That's how I used to take bennies.'"

Later that evening, at the Holiday Inn where Cash and his troupe were staying, Douglas had a German chocolate cake, Cash's favorite dessert, delivered to the singer's suite. "I was with Johnny and June and Lou and Karen Robin, and we each had a slice of that cake," Douglas recalls. "Then Johnny says, 'Judge, cut me another large slab of that cake. There's nothing like a sugar rush to an old junkie.'" The following day, Cash spoke to the Lake City Rotary Club. His topic: "Dealing With Addictions."

In explaining the rationale behind Chubby's participation in the concert, Douglas had told Cash that "the man who helped Ervin Rouse write *Orange Blossom Special* is from Lake City." Cash certainly would have known Chubby by reputation, and Douglas notes that the singer did not correct his assumption that Chubby was the *Special's* uncredited co-author. However, Cash quietly dealt with the matter that evening, near the end of his crisp and energetic two-hour performance, when he summoned the fiddler from the audience.

"When Johnny called Chubby to the stage, I could clearly see a distance that Johnny put between himself and Chubby," Douglas says. "I also noticed that Johnny introduced Chubby without saying that he was the man who wrote *Orange Blossom Special*, but rather as a man who plays a great *Orange Blossom Special*. I definitely observed a distance and a friction between the two." Douglas, unaware of Cash's empathy for Rouse and unfamiliar with any authorship controversy surrounding the song, attributed the tension to a reluctance by either performer to share the spotlight.

Still, the pairing was powerful. Cash blew into a harmonica, shouted "Train time!" and intoned the immortal opening line, "Hey, looka yonder comin'…" The audience greeted *Orange Blossom Special* with a roar of approval and, as Cash and Chubby alternated harmonica and fiddle solos, two thousand sets of hands clapped in unison. When the tune concluded, the tightly packed crowd again stood and cheered as Cash turned and bowed in Chubby's direction, allowing the old trouper to savor the outpouring of affection. *The Special* was followed by a somber Cash reading of *How Great Thou Art*, on which Chubby played backup before exiting the stage.

Perhaps a cameo appearance was not the scenario that Chubby and Rossi had envisioned, but sharing the spotlight with a legend hardly rates as a slap in the face, either.

CHUBBY'S HEALTH BEGAN TO FAIL dramatically in 1987, when he contracted pneumonia and his bleeding ulcers flared up. After being admitted to Lake City Medical Center, doctors there told Rossi that a gallstone had passed into Chubby's bile duct, triggering infections and endangering his life.

Sadly, Chubby's dire condition also exacerbated the animosity between Rossi and the Wise clan, opening ugly psychic wounds that still fester among surviving family members. "Rossi always thought she was too good for us," says Pamela Wendel, echoing the feelings of Chubby's granddaughters and others. "She tried to keep Uncle Chubby at a distance."

Pamela, in particular, had grown close to Chubby after discovering a shocking secret related to her own parentage: Tennie Sweet, whom she had regarded as her mother, was actually her grandmother. Her mother, she learned, was the mentally retarded Patricia Sweet, whom she had regarded as her older sister. In 1961, at sixteen years of age, Patricia had been raped and impregnated, and Tennie, who had borne six biological children, had vowed that she would rear her disabled daughter's offspring as her own.

"Mama [Tennie] asked Uncle Chubby to talk to me," Pamela recalls. "I was twelve years old when I found out, and I had a hard time accepting it. But Uncle Chubby told me about his experience, and said that Tennie, the woman I saw when I looked up out of the cradle, was still my mama because she'd raised me and cared for me. He helped me so much, and after that talk, he was my idol."

So, when Tennie and Pamela—along with other family members—were told by Rossi that Chubby could not have visitors, tempers flared, particularly after an exception to the rule was made for Hank Snow. "My mama [Tennie] was so upset that she said she'd give me and my brother a hundred dollars if we'd go to the hospital and stomp a mudhole in Rossi's ass," Pamela says. "Those were her words. The whole thing upset her so much that she had a massive heart attack and died the next day. I blame her death on that incident."

Rossi further infuriated the Wises by indelicately hawking her husband's cassette tapes in the hospital lobby. "It was like, 'He's dying, so you'd better get your tapes now,'" Pamela says. "We just couldn't believe it."

Rossi, however, says that she limited access to Chubby's room "because he was there to get well; not to entertain or be entertained." The Singing Ranger was granted admittance, she adds, because he had driven all the way from Nashville, and because Chubby had asked to see him. Likewise, Rossi makes no apologies for selling tapes, insisting that she did so only after repeated requests from friends and fans.

More rancorous were insinuations that Chubby was ill primarily because Rossi was working him to death; a theory that fails to take into account Chubby's oft-stated contention that "as long as I can get that fiddle under my chin, I'll be cuttin' grass."

Clearly, Rossi had a mercenary streak, and was at times abrasive and tactless when dealing with her husband's family and others; yet, it is likely that her behavior during Chubby's illness was motivated as much by stress as by vindictiveness. Whatever her flaws, she, too, loved the old fiddler—and did not want to lose him. "When we traveled, I done everything I could to make Chubby comfortable," Rossi says. "We had a tent attached to our van, and Chubby would sit under there in a lawnchair when we were at festivals. If it was cold, he had a blanket and a heater. If it was hot, he had a fan. He loved to work, and my job was to make it as easy on him as possible."

When his organs began to shut down, a gravely ill and comatose Chubby was airlifted to Shands Medical Center in Gainesville, a state-of-the-art research hospital affiliated with the University of Florida, where he remained for more than a month, clinging tenaciously to life before gradually beginning to rally. "I never left the hospital the whole time he was there," says Rossi. "When Chubby was able to talk, we laughed and cried and had fun together." Rossi believes that God spared her husband's life, and allowed him to resume performing and recording.

But the effort required was supreme. Chubby also suffered from bronchial asthma, causing him to become short of breath after the slightest exertion, and eventually compelling him to sleep sitting up. Then, prior to leaving for the Peaceful Valley Bluegrass Festival in the Catskills, he suffered a fall, aggravating his childhood leg injury. Yet, despite pain and swelling, he and Rossi made the grueling Florida-to-New York drive.

"I was concerned about him," says Tom Riggs, who booked Chubby for Peaceful Valley and other festivals. "I took one look at his leg, which seemed about twice the normal size, and wanted to take him right to the hospital. But he said, 'No, I'm all right, I want to go on.' So, we drove him to the stage in a golf cart, and once he started to play, he seemed to drop fifteen or twenty years. He responded to those crowds like he'd gotten a shot of something."

Fans and fellow musicians certainly seemed to understand that Chubby Wise was, as his final recording would proclaim, "an American original." In Canton, Texas, Woodrow Pope recalls watching Chubby seated backstage, instructing a group of awestruck young players who would serve as his backup band just moments later. "He was giving pointers and telling each one what he would play on stage and how to do it," Pope says. "These young people were honored to play with Chubby, and he was giving them something they would remember for the rest of their lives. Also, he had a glow about him that I've seldom seen in anyone. I remember it because it was so bright."

That ethereal description is echoed by Andrea Lyn Todd, who described Chubby as possessing "a gentle, sweet, happy aura; the kind of spirit that just showed on his face." Even children sensed it; Edward Pollak recalls watching in amusement as Chubby was pushed through the lobby of a hotel in a wheelchair while a little girl chased along behind him yelling, "Santa Claus! Santa Claus!"

Chubby's solo recording career, however, was moribund. In fact, he had not been affiliated with a label since 1978, when Stoneway folded following Roy Stone's death.

There had, however, been some memorable one-shot projects; most notably a 1982 collaboration with Mac Wiseman on an album called *Chubby Wise and Mac Wiseman (The Original): Give Me My Smokies and The Tennessee Waltz*. The album was recorded live at Gilley's, a Houston nightspot then at the peak of its *Urban Cowboy* notoriety. Chubby and Wiseman were backed by veterans of Bob Wills' Texas Playboys, including fiddler Johnny Gimble (who also produced), steel guitarist Herb Remington, and pianist Curly Hollingsworth. The compilation, released on Gilley's in-house label, is a marvelous hybrid of traditional bluegrass, hard-core country, jazz-tinged western swing, and Chubby's trademark waltzes.

Then, in 1993 the old fiddler signed with Pinecastle Records, a company formed by Riggs with the original intention of showcasing young, emerging bluegrass artists. Chubby, however, was then seventy-seven years old; his place in musical history long since assured. "Still, signing Chubby was a great opportunity for us," Riggs says. "Even toward the end of his life, he had the same sweet tone that other performers his age had lost years before."

Riggs, perhaps realizing that time was short, envisioned Chubby's first Pinecastle release as a back-to-basics package showcasing the fiddler's musical roots. Therefore, the resulting compilation, *Chubby Wise in Nashville*, includes a seamless assortment of waltzes, breakdowns, hoedowns, gospel tunes, country tunes, and blues.

Chubby's polished fiddle is complimented by the "Pinecastle Hotshots"—Terry Eldredge (guitar), Gene Wooten (dobro), Larry Perkins (guitar), and Mike Bub (bass)—along with fiddler Jimmy Campbell, guitarist Ron McCoury, and mandolinist/producer Butch Baldassari. Also participating are bluegrass legends and Pinecastle labelmates Sonny and Bobby Osborne, better known as the Osborne Brothers.

The best cuts among thirteen gems include Bob Wills' *Trouble in Mind*, Floyd Jenkins' *Fireball Mail*, Rupert Jones' *Footprints in the Snow,* and Chubby's own *Cherokee Waltz*, along with new arrangements of traditional melodies such as *Waitin' on the Robert E. Lee* and *Carroll County Blues*.

Chubby Wise in Nashville, released to critical kudos in December 1993, was completed in three days at Studio 20, a converted home that had once been occupied by Patsy Cline. Each cut is a complete live take with no after-the-fact digital editing, demonstrating conclusively that the years had not diminished Chubby's musicianship. "I normally stay out of the studio," says Riggs. "But I was there when this album was cut because I was concerned about Chubby wearing himself out." However, the old man had come to play; despite a plethora of ailments, he simply outworked his younger compatriots, maintaining his habitual good humor throughout.

Riggs, however, bristled when a musician complained that he was apt to miss a rendezvous with a female friend because a session was running overlong. "That made me mad," Riggs says. "I told him to go ahead and go, because there were dozens of musicians in Nashville who would love to trade places and have a chance to play with Chubby Wise. Then Chubby took me aside and said, 'Well, Colonel, go easy on the boy; when I was his age, I was poking my rod anywhere I could.'"

Shortly thereafter, Chubby resumed touring and crossed paths with eighty-three-year-old Bill Monroe at a festival in Columbus, Ohio. Monroe, who had not mellowed with age, was known for nursing lengthy grudges, and apparently still held Chubby in contempt for having left the Blue Grass Boys forty-five years earlier. "Bill treated Chubby like a dog," Rossi says. "They hadn't spoken for years. Then, in Columbus, Bill walked right past where Chubby was sitting and didn't say a word. Chubby said, 'I'm just gonna go up and make him talk to me, whether he wants to or not.' Chubby caught up with Bill, and I saw them shake hands. I don't remember what Chubby said, but I do remember Bill's answer. He was talking about Heaven, and he said, 'Well, Chubby, I guess we're all tryin' to go to the same place, ain't we?'"

Having made amends, the two failing legends would never see one another again.

Chubby returned to Nashville in December 1994 for what would be his final recording session. *Chubby Wise: An American Original* was completed over a two-day period at Abtrax Studios, with Sonny Osborne producing and playing the banjo and the gitjo, a guitar-banjo hybrid. He was joined by brother Bobby on the mandolin, and by two other members of the Osborne Brothers' band: David Crow on guitar and Terry Smith on bass. Like *Chubby Wise in Nashville*, this sterling collection offers a mixture of waltzes (Bob Miller's *Green Valley Waltz*), gospel (Stuart Hamblen's *It's No Secret (What God Can Do)*), and country (Hank Williams' *I'm So Lonesome I Could Cry*) along with new arrangements of traditional hoedown fare such as *Cotton Eyed Joe* and *Little Liza Jane*. Chubby even ventures into ragtime with a bouncy rendition of *Stone's Rag*.

"Chubby was joking and having a good time, and everyone marveled at how well he was playing," says Riggs. "He sounded as good as ever." *Sing Out*, the folk-music journal, agreed, writing that Chubby's "bluesy, lyrical playing has always favored style over speed...this recording should be required listening for any aspiring bluegrass fiddler, and is recommended for anyone with a taste for instrumental bluegrass."

Riggs' liner notes explain how the album was named, and provide an affectionate remembrance of Chubby's joyful stage demeanor:

> Album titles come from the strangest places. At the 1995 Kissimmee Bluegrass festival, Chubby was on stage with three other fiddlers who also have releases on the Pinecastle label: David Crow, Jimmy Campbell, and Bob Kogut. It was a special set listed in the program as "The Pinecastle Fiddlers." It was a beautiful day, and the fans were into the music. David, Jimmy, and Bob were enjoying the opportunity of playing with the grand old man of bluegrass fiddlers, and Chubby, well, he was in his glory taking a verse or a chorus, signaling with his bow to one of the other three to take a verse, playfully swatting David and Jimmy (you know where), strutting a bit, and just generally having a ball. The fans were on their feet, applauding and demanding more. A veteran fan turned to me and said, "That Chubby, he's an original—an American original." Nuff said, we had our title.

Throughout 1995, Chubby and Rossi kept up a relentless pace, driving to festivals in Texas, Oklahoma, Kentucky, Virginia, New York, and California. In 1995, Brooks Judd saw Chubby captivate a West Coast crowd that had braved chilly, rainy weather to see him perform. Judd later wrote about the experience for the California Bluegrass Association's newsletter:

> Saturday night, Chubby Wise performs. It is cold, damp, and drizzly as my father and I huddle down in our chairs in front of the stage trying to stay warm. Chubby plays a great

set, and is called back for an encore. Then it happens. Chubby begins to play *How Great Thou Art*, and about one minute into the song something moves me to turn around and scan the audience.

As I slowly gaze through the rain and the mist at the faces partially hidden by coats, jackets, and blankets, I see that every face is transfixed on Chubby. No one is talking. In fact, most people are quietly singing along. It feels like I am in church. I watch Chubby make thiose big, long strokes with his bow and a shiver goes through my body. I close my eyes and tightly and feel the warmth the music brings to my body. I wonder if I am the only one experiencing this magic moment.

Chubby takes a bow, and slowly walks off the stage. I chide myself for getting so emotional over a song. Then [the emcee] strides onto the stage and says something that blows me away. "Folks, you have just been part of a religious/spiritual experience." I knew then that it was not just me. All of us who saw Chubby would have this memory to share.

The old maestro gave his final public performance in Myrtle Beach, South Carolina, before traveling to Upper Marlboro, Maryland, for a Christmastime visit with Rossi's sons and their families. While there, Chubby fell ill with pneumonia, and was hospitalized for ten days. Then, just hours following his release, he was stricken by heart failure and died at a son-in-law's home on January 6, 1996, at the age of eighty.

In addition to his Lake City relatives, he was survived by Geneva, Rossi, and three grandchildren whom he barely knew. Not unexpectedly, wire-service accounts of Chubby's demise invariably touted his unofficial status as the author or the co-author of *Orange Blossom Special* as his greatest claim to fame.

A winter storm had dumped three feet of freezing snow on the Capitol suburbs, so few outside Rossi's family were able to attend when Chubby was laid to rest at Lakemont Memorial Gardens in Davidson, Maryland—again enraging Wise family members, who had assumed that he would be interred in Lake City. "Being buried in Maryland was Chubby's request," Rossi says. "He changed his mind about Florida. He said, 'If we're buried down there, you know they won't take care of our graves.' But, oh, he hated snow so bad, and I didn't want to put him in that cold ground. So, we got two above-ground vaults; one for Chubby and one for me. That way, when I go, we'll be lying head to head. And I guess that makes sense, since we butted heads for forty-four years."

In October 1998, Chubby was posthumously inducted into the International Bluegrass Music Association's (IBMA) Hall of Honor—joining previous inductees

Lester Flatt, Earl Scruggs, and Bill Monroe, among others—during the association's annual awards program, held in Owensboro, Kentucky, at the Kentucky Center for the Arts' Whitney Hall. Honored along with Chubby was Carlton Haney, the promoter frequently credited with saving the bluegrass genre by popularizing the concept of outdoor festivals.

Rossi accepted on Chubby's behalf, and preceded her remarks by warning that she was a poor public speaker. Then, according to the *Louisville Courier-Journal*, she delivered the best speech of the night. "I was scared to death," she says. "I was praying for the Lord to give me the right words. I did wanted to do the best I could for Chubby. The main thing I wanted to get across was that he was a good man; for the last twelve years, he'd been perfect. I didn't go back any further than that, because the public knows that Chubby had drinking and gambling problems. But he overcame those problems and lived a clean, Christian life."

However, among the most moving of many tributes that Chubby received following his death is a poem written by Pete Gallagher, then a special projects writer for the Seminole Indian Tribe of Florida. Gallagher, who produced the Fire on the Swamp Bluegrass Festival at southern Florida's Seminole Indian Reservation, skillfully mixed standard country-music imagery with a dose Native American mysticism to mark the passing of his friend:

> *A twinkle in his eye,*
> *as the stubby fingers fly,*
> *rosin dust and beard are one before the bow.*
> *Lord a lonesome whistle cries,*
> *mourning Fiddlin' Chubby Wise.*
> *Only angels now will ever see his show.*

> *From* Peacock Rag *to* Old Joe Clark,
> *his music made the old dogs bark,*
> *and set wild mountain fires in the sky.*
> *On a Sunday afternoon,*
> *or from a blanket 'neath the moon,*
> *Chubby's fiddle brought to life the by and by.*

> *Though now the man is gone,*
> *his music travels on,*
> *each time the* Orange Blossom Special *rides the rail.*
> *Great god, he wrote a song,*
> *a great fiddle song,*
> *the one all fiddle players want to nail.*

I can see that old man now,
bearded mermaid on the bow,
riding headfirst into the wind and rain.
Precious fiddle in his hand,
clog dancing up the aisles of glory's train.

The Seminoles say this of death:
Fiddle man crossed over and now his breath,
is the wind and breeze that whips the clouds above.
The man, not the music, dies,
rest in peace Chubby Wise.
*In the key of D, boys...*Faded Love.

IT WAS LOOP ROAD AND THE BIG CYPRESS Swamp where Ervin returned following his non-appearance on *The Johnny Cash Show*. Sister Mable, brothers Earl and Guy, and sister-in-law Helen still occupied the Alapatta residence, and Ervin seemed content to let them remain there indefinitely.

Consequently, he began to spend more time visiting the handful of ramshackle taverns located near his rustic getaway, particularly the infamous Gator Hook, originally owned and operated by a retired Sweetwater policeman named Jack Knight.

The rowdy watering hole is no more, but it was not a place for the faint of heart; fistfights and even knifings were commonplace. "Everybody there wore sidearms," recalls Bear Hudson, Ervin's nephew. "People would walk in there like gunslingers. I can tell you, I wore a .357 whenever I went. But they'd quiet down for Ervin when he played."

Wilderness writer Peter Matthiessen, who set his 1998 novel *Lost Man's River* (Vintage) in the Everglades, includes a scene at the Gator Hook during which a drunk, one-armed gator pocher explains what might happen to a park ranger who dared to interfere with his business:

> Now I got nothin' personal against the ranger," the poacher says. "Might could be a real likeable young feller, just a-tryin' to get by, same as what I'm doin'. Might got him a sweet loving wife and a couple of real cute li'l fellers back home waitin' on him, or maybe just the sweetest baby girl, same as what I got. Ain't no difference between him and me at all! But if'n that boy tries to take my gators, well, I got my duty to my people, ain't that right? Got my duty to take care of my little girl back home that's waitin' on me to put bread on the table. Ain't that only natural?

So all I'm sayin'—and it would be pathetical, and I'm the first one to admit it—all I'm sayin', now, is if any such feller, and I don't care who, tries to keep me from my hard-earned livin' I surely would be sorry. 'Cause I reckon I'd have to leave him out there."

In addition to performing at the Gator Hook, Ervin was writing songs for the first time since the 1950s. The results, however, were decidedly mixed. In 1970, Glaser Publications accepted and published one tune, *Hey, Little Parakeet, Hey*, in which Ervin employs one of his campy trick-fiddling gimmicks: using the instrument to produce chirping bird sounds. However, the song is not only embarrassingly silly, it is also downright puzzling—in part because it is difficult to determine whether the awkward lyrics are merely childish or overtly sexual:

> *Hug little parakeet, hug little parakeet,*
> *hug-ya-luv-ya-luv-ya-luv-ya-luv.*
> *Tweet tweet it's time to eat,*
> *parakeet wake up from sleep,*
> *come closer and kiss me sweet,*
> *parakeet please eat your treat.*
>
> *You must be in love,*
> *who are you thinking of?*
> *I'll go back to the place I got you,*
> *get your true love, you're in love.*
> *Then you can lay and lay,*
> *lay eggs all the day,*
> *then at night, you'll both feel right,*
> *make love, love all night.*

On the evening of January 13, 1971, perhaps Ervin's worst nightmare came to pass when he was stopped by a police officer while driving erratically along State Road 90, about four miles west of Carnestown in Collier County. According to arrest records, a Florida Highway Patrol trooper named Graves cited the fiddler for driving under the influence of alcohol. "Ervin was terrified," says Carrie. "If you were wearing a uniform, all you had to do was walk up to him and he'd just about pass out." Unfortunately, the booking report offers no insight into Ervin's composure; it indicates only that he gave his occupation as "musician and songwriter," and that he named Gordon as his closest living relative.

Apparently, however, Ervin did not phone his long-suffering brother seeking bail. Instead, he spent a restless night in the Collier County Jail before being released, shaken and ill, the following morning. Later, he described his traumatic ordeal in melodramatic tones to Gordon and Carrie. "Ervin kept saying, 'They put me in jail! They put me behind bars!'" Carrie says. "It's like it was the worst thing that had ever happened to him, and considering how scared he was of policemen, it might have been."

Ultimately, the DUI charge was dropped due to a technicality; a breathalyzer test, routine under the circumstances, had inexplicably not been administered at the time of the arrest. Still, from that point forward, Ervin drove only when absolutely necessary. More often, he peddled around Alapatta on an old bicycle equipped with a wire basket for hauling groceries and other supplies.

Occasionally, he would take bus trips to visit family members. Elizabeth Rouse Walters, Jimmy's daughter and Ervin's niece, was working at an insurance agency in downtown Roanoke, Virginia, when her uncle arrived unannounced. "One of the agents came in the office to tell me that the dirtiest looking man he'd ever seen had just gotten out of a taxi downstairs and was asking about me," Elizabeth recalls. "He said the man had long gray hair and skin so dark that he looked like an Indian. I said, 'That's my Uncle Ervin.'"

Before coming inside, Ervin walked to a nearby haberdashery and purchased a bizarre ensemble highlighted by a thick, plaid overcoat. Then, he found a barbershop and had his matted locks shorn, thereby exposing irregular patches of white skin across his otherwise reddish-brown forehead, neck, and ears. "Well, Uncle Ervin came into the office with his new haircut and wearing that overcoat," Elizabeth says. "He thought that overcoat was just beautiful."

After catching up on family news, Ervin insisted upon treating his niece to dinner at a plush hotel dining room located across the street. "Before we went in the restaurant, Uncle Ervin decided he wanted to check into the hotel," Elizabeth says. "The desk clerk looked at him and said he'd have to pay in advance. Uncle Ervin was normally a very sweet and gentle person, but that made him mad. He started yelling and said, 'Why should I have to pay in advance? I'll settle my bill when I leave.'"

When the clerk held firm, the furious fiddler reached into the pockets of his garish overcoat and, as astonished guests looked on, began flinging large-denomination greenbacks around the lobby.

Still agitated at dinner, Ervin told a waiter that he intended to pay the tab for everyone in the restaurant. "There must have been a dozen other people in there," Elizabeth says. "And this was a very nice restaurant. I don't know how much money Uncle Ervin spent that night, but he was determined to prove something."

Later, when Elizabeth's car failed to start, Ervin told her to have "the best battery that money can buy" delivered and installed. "I was an independent person, and I said that it just needed a jump start," Elizabeth says. "Somebody had cables, and that's all it took. But I still remember how disappointed Uncle Ervin was that he couldn't buy me a battery."

Ervin's most prolific year as a songwriter was 1973, when he penned seven new tunes: *I'm Getting Gray Hair; I'm Glad I Didn't Fall for You; Please Doggies, Lead On; When My Baby Cries; North Carolina, I'm Coming Home; A New York Boy Gone Hillbilly*; and *Lonesome Ranger Blues*. All were published by MCA but, as far as can be determined, none were ever recorded.

These compositions, disparate through they may be, share common threads of loneliness, heartbreak, displacement, and downright resentment. For example, in *I'm Glad I Didn't Fall for You*, Ervin issues a chilling warning to an unfaithful lover: "If you think you're going to Heaven/On the level, babe/ I think you've got another thought/'Cause I've done prayed for the devil/To be there to head you off."

In *Lonesome Ranger Blues*, he contemplates heading west to find solace in death: "I'm a'heading straight/For the Lone Star State/With my good old jug of rye/When I'm dead I'll crave/Please dig my grave/Where the lonesome rangers die/Where the coyotes howl/I'm a lonesome ranger now."

Of course, this type of fatalism is endemic to country music, and easily contrived; yet, given Ervin's circumstances, it is likely that he was speaking from the heart.

That same year, Ervin took the bus to Greenville to visit Louallie. The trip warrants mentioning mainly because Louallie's guitar-playing brother, Virgil, made a crude but enchanting audiotape of a jam session that took place when the long-estranged couple dropped by to say hello. In the process, he captured the only recorded version of Ervin singing *Sweeter Than the Flowers*. The tape also reveals the old fiddler as his friends and family knew him: a masterful musician whose aimless rambling could be both baffling and maddening.

In addition to singing *Craven County Blues*, Ervin demonstrates his versatility by fiddling a bouncy *Alexander's Ragtime Band*, a toe-tapping *Old Joe Clark*, a melancholy *Stardust*, and a surprising series of tangos. His voice is ravaged—adding a touch of poignance to *Sweeter Than the Flowers*—but his fiddling is uniformly first-rate.

Louallie solos on the newly composed *Please Doggies, Lead On*, demonstrating her yodeling prowess on this formulaic cowboy ballad. Ervin then reaches back to vaudeville to resurrect the trick fiddling standard *Listen to the Mockingbird*, complete with bird whistle effects. Finally, with Virgil standing in for Gordon and Earl, the duo cuts loose on *Orange Blossom Special*, replicating even the silly banter of the 1953 DeLuxe release.

Yet, just as interesting as the music are the snatches of conversation. In discussing *Sweeter Than the Flowers*, Ervin demonstrates his naïve—even childlike—conception of money. "That song is now being sang by the great quartets of America," Ervin notes. "But we're making money on it, and we're mighty proud of that. In fact, the valuation of *Sweeter Than the Flowers* is now in the billions of dollars. That's how much that's already been made. The world is mighty proud to play my famous songs."

And, as was typical of Ervin, he refuses—or more accurately ignores—a request from Virgil to play the fiddle classic *Black Mountain Rag*. Instead, he launches into a rambling monologue about Fiddlin' John Carson, whom he claims to have met in Atlanta decades earlier. "I'm the only fiddle player that exists in the world that imitates [Carson]," Ervin states. Then, he and Virgil perform Carson's *The Little Old Log Cabin in the Lane*.

Ervin's longing for Louallie is painfully evident. He credits her with inspiring *Sweeter Than the Flowers*, saying, "I believe my dear wife, without a doubt, she enticed me to write it when we was together." He adds that *I'm Getting Gray Hair*— a heartbreaking plea for the return of an estranged loved one—was written about his doomed marriage. "This one is for Louallie," says Ervin. "I'm gonna make this song so famous, you'll be surprised. When [Louallie] retires from the world, the world will keep on loving this song about her." Nonplussed, Louallie lightens the mood and changes the subject by ribbing Ervin about Elon Smith, his "other girlfriend."

When asked by Virgil to speak into the microphone and tell the story of *Orange Blossom Special*, he manages to utter one relevant sentence before abruptly delivering an almost incomprehensible lament about death.

"Are we on the air now?" Ervin asks, surely aware that he is not speaking on the radio. "Hello, folks. We wrote the *Orange Blossom Special*. And we're so proud to be here in Virgil's home, havin' the time of our lives. You know, lots of people, so many people, have passed away up home. We hope everybody lives forever; we hope nobody won't never die."

"I AIN'T HAD A'HOLD of a fiddle for months," Ervin told a *Miami News* reporter in 1977. "An old boy like me can't do much. I'm a sugar diabetes baby, and I ain't got much of my strength left."

An accompanying photograph shows a frowning, toothless man wearing a battered fishing hat atop an unkempt mane of wiry gray hair. His bearded face is as cracked and creased as old leather, and his narrow eyes glare from beneath bushy, close-knit brows. This grim, grizzled character no longer even vaguely resembles the lovable moppet who had once charmed vaudeville, or the handsome young man who had once earned standing ovations at the Village Barn and the Royal Palm Club.

Yet, even a sadly depleted Ervin could manage to thrill audiences, as a reporter for *National Geographic* discovered. Rick Gore, dispatched by the magazine to report on the federal government's effort to convert Big Cypress Swamp into Big Cypress Nature Preserve, happened upon one of Ervin's Gator Hook performances while bravely sampling Loop Road nightlife, and described the scene in the magazine's August 1976 edition:

> The night starts slowly, until Joyce's [Joyce Willis,
> daughter of Gator Hook owner Jack Knight] group begins

to play and a mellow Gator Bill [Bill Schoelerman, a Pinecrest resident and expert frog-gigger] is crooning *Long Black Veil*.

Next, it's clogging time. The tempo of the music perks up, and I am drawn onto the floor by Sophie, a middle-aged woman with double taps on her shoes. "What kind of dance is this?" I gasp to Sophie as we tap, shuffle and spin across the floor. "It's part Irish jig, part Highland fling and part German somthin' that got all mixed up in the mountains of North Carolina. Out here, we call it the Everglades stomp."

A stub of a man now takes charge of the microphone, commanding instant attention with his backwoods twang. "I wrote this song for Momma," he intones. "She was swee-ee-ter than the flowers. The prettiest girl in all the world. There ain't nothin' too good for Momma."

The man is Ervin Rouse, composer of the classic *Orange Blossom Special*. He begins to wail: "Lookee yonder comin'...comin' down the railroad track...It's the *Orange Blossom Special*, bringin' my ba-ya-bee back."

And now, because the spirit has struck him, Ervin takes up his fiddle, and, sweet mercy, the crowd is entranced. Ervin soars, an old sorcerer concocting with his fiddle stick notes that strut and swagger, frenzied runs that sputter through your brain stem and make you want to call the hogs home.

Ervin perfected his technique during the Depression, when he and his three brothers packed into a car like Okies to play roadside bars around the country, passing their hats for nickels and dimes. "Once I played for thirty minutes continuous," he insists. "Eighty songs. I was wore down to a frazzle."

It was during his traveling days that Ervin turned out *Orange Blossom Special*, the royalties from which make him one of the Loop Road's wealthiest inhabitants. Nevertheless, his home, where he lives alone with his two dogs, Curly and Butterball, is ramshackle and dark. The walls are plastered with pictures of the country-music stars he once performed with.

"I don't think I could stay out here without my pictures," he says. "Been out here about ten years permanent now. A bunch of us hillbillies used to come here and hunt. This is all deer country. I'd never leave now. When you get out here,

something tells you to just relax, to kind of go along with
the country. 'Cause you cain't own it. And to be proud."

A remarkable color photograph accompanying Gore's article captures Ervin in
his element, standing before a microphone with his arms outstretched, clutching a
fiddle and a fishing hat in his meaty fist. He is wearing a battered Seminole Indian
jacket—perhaps the same one he wore for *The Johnny Cash Show* taping—over a
dingy white dress shirt; a wide, multi-colored tie is dangling loosely beneath his
stubbly jowls.

The image is, at first glance, a tragic one, revealing a shabby, battered man upon
whose face despair, disappointment, and a touch of madness have been indelibly
etched. Yet, it is also strangely triumphant; a celebration of music's transforming
power. At the Gator Hook, at least, hard-luck Ervin is akin to Acuff at the Ryman or
Sinatra at the Sands; commanding and in command.

Randy Wayne White also first encountered Ervin at the Gator Hook. "I was poking around Loop Road, and found this place," says White, who was then a columnist
for the *Fort Myers News-Press*. "A sign on the door said, 'No Guns or Knives.' It was
very rough, filled with gator poachers and all sorts of characters. I chewed tobacco
at the time, so I guess I fit in pretty well and everybody started buying me beers.
Then, after a while, I noticed an old man, sitting at a booth drinking a beer and
smoking a Pall Mall. Somebody told me it was Ervin Rouse, and said, 'Ervin, why
don't you play something?' Well, he played *Orange Blossom Special* a couple of
times over the course of the evening, and the last time he played it, there were tears
streaming down his face."

Intrigued, White introduced himself to the rumpled fiddler and inquired about his
connection to the song. "Ervin told me he had written it, but I thought, 'Yeah, sure,'"
White says. "Of course, I didn't dispute him in there. I just said something like, 'Oh,
that's great.' Later, I went into a music store and looked for the song on a record. And
sure enough, the author was listed as Ervin T. Rouse."

Unquestionably, Gator Hook patrons loved Ervin's music and accepted his eccentricities. Unfortunately, however, some unscrupulous hangers-on took advantage of
the fiddler's cluenessness. "It didn't take the vultures long to find out that Ervin had
some money," says Bear. "People would tell him sob stories and he'd write them
checks. There's no telling how much money he gave away."

In any case, as Ervin had noted in *National Geographic*, neither he nor anyone
else could own a piece of the Big Cypress and, as a result, his Gator Hook days
were drawing to a close. In 1974, the U.S. Congress had approved purchase of
more than a half-million acres—forty percent of the original swamp—to create the
Big Cypress National Preserve, thereby shielding this vast ecological wonderland
from development.

More than seventy thousand landowners, mostly absentee investors who had unwittingly purchased underwater lots, were obliged to sell, and most were pleased to do so. However, the handful of mavericks who actually lived on their property were enraged, and vigorously protested what they described as "a federal land grab."

Ultimately, however, Ervin and his neighbors were compelled to cooperate, although those who had constructed homes before 1971 were allowed to remain for their lifetimes via a leaseback provision. Ervin, then, could have continued using his Big Cypress acreage as a second home. Yet, he chose to leave the swamp behind in 1977, and rented an efficiency apartment attached to a small northwest Miami residence. "A lot of the people Ervin knew had moved after the land was bought," says Gene. "The Loop Road used to be a happenin' place, but it got to be where he was out there all by himself. I think he just got lonesome."

Soon the abandoned shacks had collapsed, and were swallowed whole by weeds and swamp grass. In 2002, a film crew from Boston-based Northern Light Productions went in search of Ervin's house while filming a documentary called *Orange Blossom Special: The Story of an American Anthem*. With the help of a park ranger, they found a pile of snake-infested rubble—and a minor treasure.

Lying on the ground near where the house had once stood was a battered mailbox. On one side the crudely painted but still vivid image of an orange glistened in the midday sun.

DURING THE LAST DECADE of his life, Ervin also attended country and bluegrass concerts in Miami, renewing acquaintances with old friends such as Lester Flatt, who headlined a 1973 bluegrass festival in Miami.

Lance LeRoy, Flatt's manager and agent, recalls Ervin's visit to Flatt's bus: "I remember that I had a hard time understanding him because of that heavy eastern North Carolina accent," LeRoy says. "He was a real fat man, and very scruffy. I seem to recall he had stains on his shirt that might have been tobacco juice. But he was very jolly, and his memory was very sharp. He and Lester rehashed old times, and they both seemed to enjoy their reunion."

At Gene's behest, Ervin later appeared as a featured performer at Miami's Pistol Range Park with Flatt and his post-Scruggs band, the Nashville Grass. "Of course, I also carried Ervin with me to my shows whenever he'd go," Gene says. "But along toward the end, he'd gotten to where he just couldn't perform."

As time passed and his health worsened, Ervin seemed increasingly prone to fits of melancholy. "One day he called me up and asked me to come get him," says Gene. "He wanted to ride out to Big Cypress and see his old place. So, I drove him. The little house was still there, and it still had some of his belongins' inside, but it was all overgrown. Well, Ervin just broke down and started cryin'."

Enroute back to the city, Gene comforted his forlorn friend by stopping at a roadside field and filching an armload of ripe tomatoes. "Ervin loved them things," Gene says. "He couldn't chew very well because he didn't have any teeth by then.

But he could sure eat tomatoes. We took a bunch back to my house, sliced 'em and salted 'em and had a good time."

White also dropped in from time to time, visiting Ervin and Earl in Alapatta. Because Earl seemed to be the only permanent resident of 3729 Northwest 20th Court—Mable and Guy had died in the early 1970s—White always assumed that the less personable elder brother actually owned the home. "Earl was grim and silent; he just looked pissed off all the time," recalls White. "But he seemed to follow Ervin's orders pretty well. I once asked Ervin if I could take a picture of him, and he said, 'Sure, but let me get my colorful [Seminole] jacket.' He loved that jacket. So, he told Earl to go rummaging through the dirty laundry and find it."

White also told his fiddling friend that he intended to write novels, and would like to use him in a cast of otherwise fictional characters. Recalls White: "Ervin said, 'Goddamn, Randy, that'd be great; I'd like it if you'd put me in one of your books!'" Perhaps with an eye toward how he might be portrayed, Ervin freely discussed his life and career with White, liberally mixing fantasy with fact. For example, he claimed to have sold *Orange Blossom Special* to RCA for three hundred dollars, and had therefore never received any royalties.

"I always thought he was impoverished," says White, who wrote a vivid passage in *The Man Who Invented Florida* describing his perception of Ervin's relationship with a tune "that had dominated him, dwarfed him and now had a life of its own:"

> They made the record, Ervin signed some papers, Earl pocketed a check for three hundred dollars and it was mostly all downhill after that.
>
> In the decades that followed, Ervin heard his song played on every late-night talk show by nearly every American country band. He heard it played on the radio. In bars, he heard it played on the jukebox. Once he turned on the public television station and there was a big orchestra playing it, up there in the goddamn city, New York. The sheet music was easy to find, too. All the music stores in Miami carried it, and that meant every music store in the country probably had it. Miami was such a modern place.
>
> Whenever Ervin got the chance, he would thumb through the bins of sheet music, or flip open the books until he found it: "*Orange Blossom Special*; music and lyrics, Ervin T. Rouse."
>
> His name was always right up there at the top, plain to read. Trouble was, nobody in the music stores believed it was him when he tried to tell them. Same with the country-music stars, when he wrote them letters, putting plenty of

postage so the envelopes would make it clear to Nashville. Same with the country radio stations when he'd call the special phone-in lines.

"You want to request *Orange Blossom Special*?"

"Nope. I wrote it. Just wanted you to know."

"Sure you did, partner, sure. That song's been around forever," they'd always say.

And Ervin would reply, "Man, I started young! What was I, seventeen, eighteen when I did it?" But they'd hang up before he had a chance to play the song for them over the phone. By the time he got the phone cradled so he could mount his fiddler under his chin and raise the bow, he'd hear click.

That song was so famous, nobody'd believe it was him that wrote it. But if they'd heard him play it, they'd have known. Nobody could play *Orange Blossom Special* like Ervin T. Rouse.

If Ervin often invented financial woes and exaggerated his lack of sophistication, at other times he displayed a naiveté regarding the world around him that could hardly have been fabricated. "One time, we were watching the sky after a space shuttle had been launched [from Cape Canaveral, some three hundred miles north]," White recalls. "Even down as far south as we were, you could see the plume of smoke. Ervin looked up at it and asked, 'When do they get back from the moon?' I said, 'Ervin, they're not going to the moon. They don't go to the moon in the space shuttle.' And he said, 'Hell yes, they do; that's where they go when they're up in them things.'"

Vassar Clements confirms that Ervin often seemed baffled by the simplest tasks. "I don't want to say this the wrong way, because Ervin was a genius at playing," Clements says. "But he was a man who didn't know a lot, and didn't care about a lot. I remember seeing him at a festival down in Florida where I was playing. He was carrying a ten thousand dollar royalty check for *Orange Blossom Special* in this old briefcase, and he walked up to a little booth and tried to buy a hot dog with that check. He didn't understand why you couldn't do that."

When White left the *News-Press* to focus on becoming a novelist, he told his replacement at the newspaper, Bob Morris, about Ervin. Morris, an avid hiker, had been to the Gator Hook before, while traversing a portion of the Florida Trail that passes near Pinecrest. "That was a hellish stretch," he recalls. "It took three days to hike three miles, so when you got off the trail, man, you were ready for a bar. And the Gator Hook was the only one anywhere around. You had to go there."

Eager to meet the character White had described, Morris returned to the bar in his capacity as a columnist. "I had been told that I was pretty likely to find [Ervin] at the Gator Hook," recalls Morris. "And he was there, playing his fiddle with some other bluegrass type musicians." The writer tried to engage Ervin in conversation, but quickly realized that his subject was "not in an interviewable condition." He later visited the old fiddler at his Alapatta home, and found him to be "disengaged; not rude or cantankerous, but just kind of oblivious. He answered questions, but he wasn't the colorful, funny spinner of tales that I had expected."

Probably, Ervin's lethargy was attributable to illness. "About all I can do is hum," he told Morris. "Got this diabetes, and it has my joints so stiff that I can barely hold up a fiddle, much less make it sound like anything. I'm one hell of a hummer, though."

In fact, uncontrolled diabetes, along with decades of alcohol abuse, had taken a terrible toll on Ervin's body. His kidneys and liver had begun to fail, and he had lost control of his bowels. Although he was scheduled for three dialysis treatments three times weekly, he often skipped the sessions, making his symptoms worse.

However, despite all appearances, Ervin was not destitute; *Orange Blossom Special* royalties alone had generated from twenty thousand to fifty thousand dollars annually since the mid-1960s, thereby providing a dependable if not a princely income. He could have afforded private nursing care, and even asked Gene how to go about locating a suitable assistant. "I told Ervin I'd ask around, but I didn't have any luck," Gene says. Apparently, it never occurred to either man that the telephone directory would have yielded dozens of leads.

In January 1981, Ervin's spirits were lifted by a reunion with John Hartford, Benny Martin, and Earl Scruggs when the musicians converged in Miami to perform at the Olympia Theater, a renovated movie palace of the type that Ervin had played as a young vaudevillian. "Benny and I had done a lot of talking about Ervin, and we wanted to see him," recalls Hartford. "So, before we came down, I called Gene and asked him if he could arrange it." Gene, sensing that his old friend's days were numbered, was only too happy to oblige. "I got Ervin cleaned up, and made sure he was wearin' decent clothes," he recalls. "Then I took him downtown and we went backstage. They were all tickled to see us, and we had a nice visit."

Following the show, Gene was scheduled to work at the Black Angus, where patrons received an unexpected treat: Hartford, Martin, and Scruggs tagged along, and performed alongside Gene and his combo. Ervin, however, was enfeebled and unsteady, and could only watch as his friends frolicked. Still, at the conclusion of the impromptu set, he gamely joined the musical cadre at Gene's home for a wee-hours jam session.

"John and Benny spent the night in John's bus, parked out in front of my house," says Gene. "Ervin finally went home, and said he was gonna have Gordy bring him back over in the morning. We were all gonna have breakfast, play some more music, and maybe go back to the Angus that night." But Ervin did not return, perhaps because he was exhausted, or perhaps because he was frustrated and embarrassed by his diminished skills.

In February 1981, Ervin's kidneys shut down. Comatose and toxic, he was transported via ambulance to Jackson Memorial Hospital. Yet, despite his grave condition, the uncooperative fiddler clawed futilely at the tubes cleansing his blood of poison and, in moments of lucidity, railed bitterly at the doctors and nurses who tended him.

Concurrently, hospital administrators contacted a not-for-profit agency called Dade County Jewish Family and Children's Services (JCFS), which provided guardianship programs for individuals deemed functionally incompetent. "Mr. Rouse was a hard-living man, and had always done things pretty much his way," recalls Frank Repensek, JCFS executive director. "He certainly was a man who valued his freedom. But, he had been skipping his dialysis treatments, and he had continued to drink despite his condition. So, given his history, doctors determined that he'd need twenty-four-hour supervision following his release, preferably in a nursing home. When he refused to follow that course, we got involved."

JCFS, now called The Guardianship Program of Dade County, investigated Ervin's situation and found no family members who were willing or able to assume responsibility for his care. The remaining siblings faced health and financial worries of their own, while Louallie and the children had rebuilt their lives in Maryland, and were understandably reluctant to take custody of a querulous, gravely ill man with whom they had little contact. "This is not at all unusual," says Repensek. "Sometimes, relocation simply isn't feasible. In this particular case, either a family member had to move to Florida, or Mr. Rouse had to move to Maryland. Neither of those things was going to happen."

So, with the family's consent, JCFS filed a Petition for Appointment of Guardian document with Judge Gene Williams of Florida's 11th Judicial Circuit. Privacy laws protect transcripts of the subsequent competency hearing, but the process appears to have been perfunctory. A court-appointed panel of psychologists, physicians, and social workers interviewed Ervin at the hospital, and testified that he suffered from a catch-all dysfunction called "organic brain syndrome," rendering him incapable of managing his affairs. Ervin did not attend the proceedings, nor did anyone speak on his behalf.

Consequently, on February 18, Judge Williams appointed JCFS as "guardian of the person and property of Ervin Rouse, incompetent, with full power to have the care, custody and control of said incompetent according to law, and to take possession of and to hold, for the benefit of said incompetent, all the property of said incompetent, and of the rents, income, issues and profits from it."

Then, JCFS placed Ervin in a Miami nursing home called Fair Haven, where he gradually gained strength thanks to aggressive medical intervention. Still, even Gene, who visited Ervin during his recuperation, was unsure how much his old friend understood about the precarious state of his health, and about the legal machinations that had left him in the custody of strangers. "By that time, Ervin was off his damn rocker," says Gene. "And I think he knew it. For sure, he knew he was in bad shape. Sometimes he'd say, 'Well, I don't give a damn what them people think.

Let 'em think I'm nuts.' Other times he'd make jokes about the situation, like, 'They're tryin' to say I'm crazy, but I'm crazy like a fox.'"

In at least one respect, Ervin had the bureaucrats snookered: they had consistently assumed that he was indigent, when in fact he had several hundred thousand dollars in cash and other assets. Just prior to his illness, he had received a royalty check from Asylum/Full Moon Records for more than thirty thousand dollars, all of which was attributable to the *Special's* inclusion on the multi-platinum *Urban Cowboy* soundtrack album. His home in Alapatta, although run-down and still occupied by relatives, was mortgage-free and valued at around fifty thousand dollars.

"Ervin used to brag that he hadn't ever been charged a penny for his medical care," Gene says. "I said, 'Ervin, you can't pull this off; eventually, they're gonna find out you've got money.'" As his legal guardian, JCFS did just that. "It was certainly a surprise when looked into Mr. Rouse's finances," understates Repensek.

But, after just a few months at Fair Haven, Ervin's health began to rapidly deteriorate, mandating his transfer back to Jackson Memorial. In addition to the effects of renal failure, diabetes had damaged circulation to his extremities, forcing doctors to amputate his ulcerous left leg below the knee. Shortly thereafter, he lapsed into a coma, lingering for days in a woozy dream state straddling life and death.

Daughter Eloise, rushing to Miami from her Maryland home, was concerned for her father's soul, and spent hours at his bedside, reading the Bible aloud. "Daddy always said he liked [televangelist] Jimmy Swaggart because he was a good performer," recalls Eloise. "I would like to have been able to talk to him, and to ask him questions [about his religious beliefs]. But he really couldn't communicate, so I read to him from the Bible, particularly John:14; 'In my Father's house are many mansions.' I wanted to comfort him, and he seemed to be listening."

As Ervin's condition steadily worsened, there was a telephone call from Johnny Cash, who prayed as the receiver rested near the failing fiddler's ear.

Ervin T. Rouse died on Thursday, July 9, 1981, at the age of sixty-four. Services were held at the Joseph Cofer Funeral Home in north Miami, and burial followed at Southern Memorial Park. The funeral was attended by about fifty mourners, including Louallie, the children, and the surviving Rouse siblings: Gordon, Earl, Hayward, and Gay (all but Gordon would be dead within three years).

As friends and family members filed past the open casket, they must have been somewhat taken aback to see Ervin wearing a dark suit and tie, his face smoothly shaved and his hair cut and combed. A magnificent floral arrangement in the shape of a train was displayed, and everyone concurred that the sender, Johnny Cash, had found an appropriate and original way to salute the man and his music.

"Gordon was just devastated," says Carrie. "Ervin was the dearest thing to his heart; in fact, to Gordon, Ervin even came before me."

Gene Christian arrived early, and found his old friend looking strangely at peace, if considerably better-groomed than usual. "I got to the funeral home before anybody else," Gene recalls. "I wandered around the different viewing rooms looking for Ervin, and finally I found him. I had some things I wanted to say to him, things that were just between him and me. We spent some private time together, and I told him goodbye."

"After everything is said, done and lied about, the fact is I wrote only a few pieces," Ervin had said in 1977. "A lot of songwriters will tell you big stories about the hundreds of songs they wrote. I wrote only a few, four or five maybe."

That self-deprecating tone was adopted in obituaries, which largely portrayed Ervin as a cranky old eccentric who had written—or co-written—one good tune a half-century before, and had spent the remainder of his life fiddling for tips in dingy dives. In fact, the *Miami Herald* described him as "frequently penniless."

In truth, Ervin T. Rouse had been a much more intriguing and complex man than the hillbilly caricature that he had helped to perpetuate, and his life, although marred by missteps and misfortune, had been full and exciting. "We were good-time Charlies," says Gene. "We did what we wanted to do, the way we wanted to do it."

Indeed, Ervin had traveled, performed, entertained, and composed at least one truly immortal song; he had overcome tragedy and poverty, and had been largely self-sufficient despite suffering from a form of mental illness that many find incapacitating.

This gifted but tormented free spirit might have been a better husband, father, brother, and friend; yet he was loved, even by those whom he had hurt. This, in and of itself, constitutes an honorable legacy.

"Ervin has never gotten his due as a musician," says Gene. "The few records that he made, they were pretty sorry. I even kidded with Ervin about it. I said, 'Where the hell did you all go to make them records, the dime store?' You just had to see him in person. There was nobody like him when it came to performin'. Plus, he was a good fella, and a dear friend. Not a day goes by that I don't miss him."

In the years following his brother's death, Gordon began to receive some of the recognition, if not the income, that had heretofore eluded him. During the campaign to have *Orange Blossom Special* named the official Florida state song, the last surviving Rouse brother and his wife found themselves in demand for newspaper interviews and television appearances. In April 1983, their travels brought them to Orlando, where Gordon was named an "honorary citizen" by Mayor Bill Frederick. Following the ceremony, Carrie was interviewed by *Orlando Sentinel* columnist Dean Johnson, who opined that *Old Folks at Home* was indeed a dreary little tune that ought to be replaced.

Then, while driving back to Miami along Florida's Turnpike, Gordon fell asleep at the wheel near Ft. Pierce, sending his Pontiac—with Carrie napping in the back seat—careening into a guardrail. "Rouse's Escape Called Miracle," read a headline in the *Sanford Herald*—and perhaps it was. Although the vehicle had flipped several times, mangling it beyond repair, neither Gordon nor Carrie had been seriously hurt.

Two months later, the couple traveled to Tallahassee to watch as the Florida Senate adopted a resolution saluting the Rouse Brothers "for their contribution to Florida by composing, recording and performing *Orange Blossom Special*, a song commemorating the train bearing that name." The document, which Gordon tearfully accepted during ceremonies on the Senate floor, reads as follows:

WHEREAS, Ervin Thomas Rouse Sr., deceased, and Ernest Gordon Rouse wrote and performed music extensively in the State of Florida and elsewhere as the Rouse Brothers, and

WHEREAS, the Rouse Brothers performed in such memorable arenas as the Olympia Theater, the Royal Palm Club, the Miami Biltmore and Wometco Theaters throughout the state, and

WHEREAS, in 1937 (sic) the Rouse Brothers wrote the song *Orange Blossom Special* in honor of the Seaboard Air Line railroad train called the Orange Blossom Special, and

WHEREAS, the Orange Blossom Special train ran from New York to West Palm Beach from 1925 until 1927, and from New York to Miami from 1927 until 1953, and

WHEREAS, the American Society of Composers, Authors and Publishers (ASCAP) named the song *Orange Blossom Special* as "the most played song (sic) in 1982," and

WHEREAS, the song *Orange Blossom Special* emphasizes the Florida citrus industry, one of the major industries of the state, and

WHEREAS, the Orange Blossom is the state flower, as designated by the 1909 Legislature, NOW THEREFORE,

Be it resolved by the Senate of the State of Florida: That the Florida Senate hereby recognizes and honors Ernest Gordon Rouse and the family of Ervin Thomas Rouse, Sr., for their contributions to the culture and popularity of the state by their musical performances, and especially by their composition, recording, and many performances of *Orange Blossom Special*. Be it further resolved that a copy of this resolution, with the seal of the Senate affixed, be presented to Ernest Gordon Rouse and the family of Ervin Thomas Rouse, Sr., as a tangible token of the sentiments expressed herein.

This is a true and correct copy of Senate Resolution No. 979, adopted by the Florida Senate on June 2, 1983. Curtis Peterson, President of the Senate.

In 1989, the *Special* won over an auditorium full of Baptist preachers just as easily as it had won over barrooms filled with carousers. During the Florida State Baptist Convention, held that year in Kissimmee, convention president Bill Billingsley, pastor of Sheridan Hills Baptist Church in Hollywood, found himself with time to fill when the proceedings unexpectedly ran ahead of schedule.

Billingsley turned to Bill Murk, an Illinois-based evangelist who had previously fiddled several sacred tunes for the gathering, and asked for some additional music. "If this weren't a Baptist meeting," joked Billingsley, "then I'd request *Orange Blossom Special*."

Coincidentally, seated next to Billingsley was Robert Knight, pastor of Stanton Memorial Church in Miami, who whispered to his colleague that the tune's co-composer, Gordon Rouse, was a member of his congregation. Billingsley, in turn, shared this revelation with attendees, and ruled that since a legitimate Baptist connection had been established, a performance of the *Special* would be entirely in order. Murk, of course, knew the song, and brought the delegates to their feet with his perhaps divinely inspired rendition.

In fact, Gordon and Carrie did attend Stanton Memorial, where Carrie was active in the Women's Missionary Union. But, while Carrie was officially a member, Gordon was not. Upon his return to Miami, Knight good-naturedly prodded Gordon, saying, "You've got me in all kinds of trouble. I just told the whole Florida Baptist Convention that you're a member of my church." Gordon and Knight shared a chuckle, but the discussion soon turned serious, with the musician and the minister discussing the particulars of Baptist theology. As a result, the following Sunday, Gordon came forward during the alter call at Stanton Memorial, saying that he wanted to become a member "to get the preacher off the hook." He was baptized in early 1991, and the offspring of a devout Methodist-turned-Jehovah's Witness rarely missed a service from that day forward.

In 1991, Gordon and Carrie attended a Charlie Daniels concert at the Ft. Lauderdale Swap Shop, a sprawling flea market featuring country entertainers performing alongside booths laden with knickknacks, automobile parts, tee-shirts, and used furniture. From the stage, the self-described "long-haired country boy" extolled the virtues of *Orange Blossom Special*, then asked seventy-seven-year-old Gordon to take a bow. The audience responded with a standing ovation, and remained on its feet as the rotund fiddler and his combo delivered a supercharged rendition of the famous tune. "Charlie plays the song closer to the way Ervin did it than anybody else," said Gordon, who was later besieged by autograph-seekers— including members of the Charlie Daniels Band.

Two years later, Gordon and Carrie were invited to Branson, Missouri, to dedicate the newly opened Orange Blossom Hotel. While visiting the country-music mecca, they were accorded red-carpet treatment at theaters operated by Box Car Willie and Japanese fiddler Souji Tobushi.

Box Car Willie, in fact, called Gordon to the stage and quipped, "Sir, if you wrote *Orange Blossom Special*, then you must be a very rich man." Frail Gordon, clearly savoring a moment in the limelight, related his version of how the *Special* was composed, praised his late brother's incomparable fiddling, and joined Box Car Willie on a shaky but affecting chorus of *Sweeter Than the Flowers*. During a performance the following day, Tobushi played the *Special* in Gordon's honor, and Carrie later told the *Branson Tri-Lakes Daily* that "Shoji is the only one I've heard play who, when I close my eyes, I think I hear Ervin."

From the stage, Johnny Cash also acknowledged Gordon during several Miami-area stops, as did Loretta Lynn and Willie Nelson. Gordon and Carrie were granted honorary lifetime memberships in the South Florida Bluegrass Association, and were frequently guests of honor at local bluegrass festivals. Although Gordon was by then too ill to perform, he graciously acknowledged the plaudits and the applause.

Yet, such accolades seemed strangely hollow without Ervin. Whether in public or in private, Gordon never failed to sing his brother's praises; and as his own health failed, he thought often of their tumultuous years together.

Near the end of his life, Gordon asked Carrie to drive him through Ervin's old Alapatta neighborhood, and the experience was both painful and cathartic. "The street had gotten bad," Carrie recalls. "There was trash everywhere, junk cars in the yards. Ervin's house was especially run down. It just got to Gordon somehow. Sitting there in the car, he started crying."

Gordon Rouse died on May 17, 1996, at the age of eighty. Services were held at Stanton Memorial, and burial followed at Southern Memorial Cemetery, near Ervin's plot. He was survived by Carrie, his wife of fifty-seven years, and was mourned by friends who recognized his quiet contribution to Ervin's legacy.

Later, his fellow bluegrass association members held a fundraiser to offset medical expenses, netting two hundred dollars.

"I didn't think I was ever supposed to do anything else but sing and play," Gordon had said in 1992. "Sometimes, you'd sweat blood, but it was so nice that I never did quit. We'd just keep on singing."

AS EVENING FALLS, LOCOMOTIVE NO. 172 and its thirteen flatcars rumble out of a trainyard in Taft, an unincorporated community south of Orlando named for the corpulent former President of the United States who had passed through—without stopping—in 1916.

The train is laden with Florida-grown fruits and vegetables—lettuce, tomatoes, celery and citrus—enroute to Wilmington, Delaware, and ultimately to grocery chains and corner markets in Boston, New York, Philadelphia, and other Northeastern cities. The 902-ton diesel hauls its tasty cargo six days weekly between November and July; seven days weekly during the peak season, May and June. All aboard the Orange Blossom Special, circa 1983.

The "new" Special had been unveiled with much fanfare; CSX Corporation, which had been formed in 1978 for the sole purpose of purchasing and merging Seaboard Coast Line Industries Inc. and Chessie System Inc., even brought Johnny Cash to Taft to dedicate the train's inaugural run.

With a top speed of seventy miles per hour, the Special may have remained "the fastest train on the line," but it was a freight train nonetheless, and a far cry from its glamorous namesake. Its purpose was to try and win back a significant share of the produce-shipping market—a business that truckers had come to dominate in the 1970s.

The Orange Blossom Special essentially vanished in 1990, when CSX ceased using names for its trains and adopted numerical identifiers. What had been the Special's namesake continued to operate, with the route extended northward to Kearny, New Jersey.

But the southbound line is today known as Number 173 between Kearney and Jacksonville, and as Number 177 between Jacksonville and Orlando. Northbound, the designations are Number 178 between Orlando and Jacksonville, and Number 174 between Jacksonville and Kearney. It is just another no-name freight train; no special cars, no special colors, no special mystique.

Yet, perhaps there are trains in Heaven. If so, the Special is surely racing through eternity, its posh dining car laden with fragrant cigars and good whiskey. Milling about, sharing laughs and swapping licks, would be Ervin, Chubby, and any number of departed fiddlers who were never able enjoy an earthbound journey.

The music would be so raucous that even the angels would put aside their harps to listen. Or, more likely, these winged pickers would join in, making a joyful noise indeed.

Afterword:
One More Ride

This book was originally published in 2002 as *Orange Blossom Boys: The Untold Story of Ervin T. Rouse, Chubby Wise and the Word's Most Famous Fiddle Tune*. The book you are now reading is a revised and updated version of that work.

Why tackle the topic again? Granted, *Orange Blossom Boys* sold well in its genre and attracted complimentary reviews. I assumed its publication meant that I was finished with this topic and ready to move on to something else. But as the book began to circulate, a number of Rouse and Wise associates previously unknown to me emerged with new stories and corrections to old ones. For example, Chubby's widow, Geneva, who had declined to be interviewed for the first edition, now wanted her side of the story told. In addition, new information about *The Johnny Cash Show* and Ervin's ill-fated appearance came to light, as did information about Cash and his relationship with the old fiddler.

At the same time, I was contacted by Boston-based Northern Light Productions. Owner Bestor Cram, an award-winning documentarian, wanted to make a film based on the *Orange Blossom Special* story and asked for my participation. The resulting work, *The Special: An American Anthem*, was screened at an array prestigious festivals around the country before being broadcast on PBS. That exposure, combined with the death of Johnny Cash, whose decidedly anti-bluegrass recording of *Orange Blossom Special* is probably the best-known, seemed to spark new interest in the topic.

One new contact led to another. Some previously closed doors opened. Before I knew it, I was revising *Orange Blossom Boys* and asking my publisher, Ron Middlebrook, to put it out there again. I am fortunate that Ron shares with me a passion for untold country music stories and forelorn musicians. He agreed that there was enough new information that another go-round, with a new title, was justified.

So if you have read the earlier version of this book, thank you. I hope you'll find enough new here to justify a second read. If you have not read *Orange Blossom Boys*, welcome aboard.

Randy Noles
March, 2007

Discography

Chubby Wise

Of the many solo fiddle albums Chubby Wise made for Stoneway Records, none are still in print. However, his last two albums, recorded for Pinecastle Records, are available on cassette tape and compact disc, as is his 1973 collaboration with Jerry Garcia:

- *Chubby Wise in Nashville* (Pinecastle Records, PRC-1031, 1994). Track list: *Fireball Mail, Trouble in Mind, Petal From a Faded Rose, Carroll County Blues, Georgianna Moon Waltz, If I Could Hear My Mother Pray Again, Waitin' On the Robert E. Lee, Cherokee Waltz, I'm Just Here To Get My Baby Out of Jail, Near the Cross, Daddy Blues, Down Yonder, Footprints in the Snow*. Solo fiddle.
- *Chubby Wise: An American Original* (Pinecastle Records, PRC-1041, 1995). Track list: *Cotton Eyed Joe, Green Valley Waltz, Bonaparte's Retreat, I Can't Stop Loving You, It's No Secret (What God Can Do), Under the Double Eagle, Little Liza Jane, The Sidewalk Waltz, I'm So Lonesome I Could Cry, Whispering Hope, Stones Rag, The Eighth of January*. Solo fiddle.
- *Chubby Wise and Mac Wiseman (The Original): Give Me My Smokies and The Tennessee Waltz* (Gilley's Records, 1982) Track list: *Give Me My Smokies and The Tennessee Waltz, Maiden's Prayer, The Waltz You Saved for Me, Wreck of the Old '97, The Prisoner's Song, Carroll County Blues, Mama Put My Little Shoes Away, Footprints in the Snow, Shackles and Chains, I Wonder How the Old Folks are at Home, Wabash Cannonball, Driftwood on the River, Catfish John, Lee Highway, Westphalia Waltz, Faded Love, It Rains Just the Same in Missouri, Faded Love, Pretty Little Widder, The Kind of Love, Mary Linda, Liberty, How Great Thou Art*.
- *The Good Ole Boys: Pistol Packin' Mama* (Round Records, RX-109/RX-LA597-G, 1976). Track list: *Ashes of Love; I'm Here To Get My Baby Out of Jail; Long Gone, Dim Lights, Thick Smoke; Deep Elem Blues; Pistol Packin' Mama; Banjo Signal; Toy Heart; Leave Well Enough Alone; Too Wise Special; On Top of Old Smokey; Barefoot Nelly; Don't You Hear Jerusalem Moan; Glendale Train*. Musicians include David Nelson (guitar/vocals), Frank Wakefield (mandolin/vocals), Don Reno (banjo/vocals), Pat Campbell (bass) and Chubby Wise (fiddle). Jerry Garcia, who does not play, is the producer.

Chubby's work with Bill Monroe can be enjoyed on two boxed sets: *The Music of Bill Monroe From 1936-1994* (MCA, 1994); and *The Essential Bill Monroe and His Blue Grass Boys: 1945-1949* (Sony/Columbia, 1989). Likewise, Chubby's work with Hank Snow is preserved on two boxed sets: *Hank Snow, The Singing Ranger: Volume 2* (Bear Family, 1990); and *Hank Snow: Thesaurus Transcriptions* (Bear Family, 1991). The latter includes the Rainbow Ranch Boys' version of *Orange Blossom Special*, with Chubby on the fiddle.

The Rouse Brothers

The only recording of the Rouse Brothers currently in print is their 1939 version of *Orange Blossom Special*, which appears on a Smithsonian Institution boxed set, *Classic Country Music*. In fact, their entire recorded output is minimal, and much of what they cut was never released.

On May 22, 1934, "The Three Floridians" (probably the Rouse Brothers) recorded four songs for ARC in New York City: *The Death of Young Stribling, My Family Circle, The Duval County Blues,* and *The Jacksonville Stomp*. None were released, and the master tapes have not been located. Therefore, because these recordings cannot be heard, it is impossible to definitively link the Rouse Brothers to the Three Floridians.

On June 3, 1936, "Earl Rouse and Brothers" (Gordon and Ervin) recorded eight songs for ARC in New York City. Two cuts were released: *I'm So Tired* backed by *Pedal Your Blues Away* (6-09-54), both Bob Miller compositions. Unreleased songs from the same session included *Please Let Me Walk With My Son, Are You Angry Little Darling, Some Old Day, Toll, Dixieland Echoes,* and *Under the Double Eagle*. The master tapes for these recordings are missing as well, meaning that the unreleased tunes are probably lost forever. Fortunately, however, *I'm So Tired* and *Pedal Your Blues Away* have been preserved in the archives of the Country Music Foundation.

On June 14, 1939, "The Rouse Brothers" (Ervin and Gordon only) returned to New York City to record six songs for Bluebird, all of which were released: *My Family Circle (Will the Circle Be Unbroken* backed by *Orange Blossom Special* (8218), *Bum Bum Blues* backed by *Craven County Blues* (8239), and *Some Old Day* backed by *Please Let Me Walk With My Son* (8197). Of these recordings, only *My Family Circle (Will the Circle Be Unbroken)* backed by *Orange Blossom Special*, and *Craven County Blues* backed by *Bum Bum Blues*, could be located.

In March, 1953, Bob Miller traveled to Miami and recorded two sides with "The Rouse Brothers" (Ervin, Earl, and an unidentified steel guitar player): *Loan Me a Buck* backed by a new version of *Orange Blossom Special*. The pairing was released on the Rockin' (514) and Deluxe (2004) labels, both subsidiaries of King Records.

Miller returned on October 23 that same year and recorded ten additional tunes with Ervin, Earl, and the anonymous steel man: *Home Brew Rag, Flop Eared Mule, Up Jumped the Devil, Mississippi Sawyer, Down Yonder, Under the Double Eagle, Jackson Schottische, Rubber Dolly, Arkansas Traveler,* and *Varsouviana*. Four of these cuts were released: *Home Brew Rag* backed by *Flop Eared Mule* (Deluxe 2019) and *Jackson Schottische* backed by *Rubber Dolly* (Deluxe 2007). Session notes appear to indicate that *Under the Double Eagle* was also released on Deluxe, but the B side is not indicated, nor is a release number shown. In any case, master tapes for this song, along with the other unreleased recordings from the 1953 sessions, have not been located. *Flop Eared Mule, Jackson Schottische, Home Brew Rag,* and *Rubber Dolly* survive on a handful of 78-rpm records.

Bibliography and Sources

Books

Allen, Bob (editor). *The Blackwell Guide to Recorded Country Music*. Blackwell Publishers, 1994

Altman, T.D. *Miami: City of the Future*. (Grove/Atlantic), 1987

Blum, Daniel. *A Pictorial History of the American Theater, 1860-1985*. Crown Publishers, 1986

Boorstin, Daniel J. *The Americans: The Democratic Experience*. Random House, 1973

Cash, Johnny. *Cash: The Autobiography*. HarperCollins, 1997

Collins, Ace. *The Stories Behind Country Music's All-Time Greatest 100 Songs*. Boulevard Books, 1996

Davidson, Marshall B. *Life in America*. Houghton Mifflin Company, 1951

Ewing, Tom. *The Bill Monroe Reader*. University of Illinois Press, 2000

Green, Doug. *Country Roots*. Hawthorn Books, 1976

Gunther, John. *Inside U.S.A*. Harper & Brothers, 1947

Horstman, Dorothy. *Sing Your Heart Out, Country Boy*. Country Music Foundation Press, (1975)

Kennedy, Stetson. *Palmetto Country*. Florida A&M University Press, 1942

Keuchel, Edward S. *History of Columbia County, Florida*. Sentry Press, 1996

Kennett, Lee. *G.I.: The American Soldier in World War II*. Warner Books, 1987

Kingsbury, Paul (editor). *Country: The Music and the Musicians*. Abbeville Press, 1988

Kingsbury, Paul (editor). *The Encyclopedia of Country Music*. Oxford University Press, 1998.

Jones, Margaret. *Patsy: The Life and Times of Patsy Cline*. HarperCollins, 1994

Lacey, Robert. *Ford: The Men and the Machine*. Little, Brown and Company, 1986

Malone, Bill C. *Country Music, USA*. University of Texas Press, 1968

Mehling, Harold. *The Most of Everything: The Story of Miami Beach*. Harcourt, Brace and Company, 1988

Meyer, Hazel. *The Gold In Tim Pan Alley*. Lippincott, 1958

Moore, Deborah Dash. *To the Golden Cities: Pursuing the American and Jewish Dream in Miami and L.A*. The Free Press, 1990

Morris, Roger. *Partners in Power: The Clintons and Their America*. Henry Holt and Company, 1993

Opdyke, John B. (editor) *Alachua County: A Sesquicentennial Tribute*. Alachua County Historical Commission, 1990

Philips, Stacy. *Hot Licks for Bluegrass Fiddle*. Oak Publications, 1984

Porterfield, Nolan. *Jimmie Rodgers: The Life and Times of America's Blue Yodler*. University of Illinois Press, 1979

Pugh, Ronnie. *Ernest Tubb: The Texas Troubadour*. Duke University Press, 1996

Rosenberg, Neil V. *Bluegrass: A History*. University of Illinois Press, 1985

Russell, Tony. *Country Music Records: A Discography*, 1921-1942. Country Music Foundation Press, 2006

Shelton, Robert. *The Country Music Story*. Castle Books, 1966

Shrady, Ted; Waldrop, Arthur. *Orange Blossom Special* (ACL/SCL Historical Society), 1996

Shorter, Edward. *A History of Psychiatry: From the Era of the Asylum to the Age of Prozac*. John Wiley and Sons, 1993

Smith, John L. *The Johnny Cash Discography*. Greenwood Press, 1985.

Smith, John L. *The Johnny Cash Discography: 1984-1993*. Greenwood Press, 1994

Smith, John L. *The Johnny Cash Record Catalogue*. Greenwood Press, 1994

Smith, Richard D. *Bluegrass: An Informal Guide*. A. Cappella Books, 1995

Smith, Richard D. *Can't You Hear Me Callin'—The Life of Bill Monroe*. Little, Brown, 2000

Snow, Hank. *The Hank Snow Story*. University of Illinois, 1994

Stockridge, Frank Parker; Perry, John Holliday. *So This Is Florida*. John H. Perry Publishing Company, 1926

Tichi, Cecclia. *High Lonesome: The American Culture of Country Music*. University of North Carolina Press, 1994

Tosches, Nick. *Country: The Twisted Roots of Rock 'n' Roll*. Da Capo Press, 1977, 1996

Tribe, Ivan. *The Stonemans: An Appalachian Family and the Music That Shaped Their Lives*. University of Illinois Press, 1993

Various, *The Encyclopedia of Popular Music*. Muze U.K., 1998

Watson, Alan D. *A History of New Bern and Craven County*. Tryon Palace Commission, 1987

Weigall, T.H. *Boom in Paradise*. Alfred H. King, 1929

Whitburn, Joel. *Top Country Singles, 1944-1988*. Record Research Inc., 1989

White, Randy Wayne. *The Man Who Invented Florida*. St. Martin's Press, 1993

Wolfe, Charles. *The Devil's Box: Masters of Southern Fiddling*. Vanderbilt University Press/Country Music Foundation Press, 1997

Wolfe, Charles. *A Good-Natured Riot: The Birth of the Grand Ole Opry*. Vanderbilt University Press/Country Music Foundation Press, 1999

Periodicals

Billboard, Bluegrass Unlimited, The Branson Tri-Lakes Daily, Country Music, Country Music People, Fiddler Magazine, The Florida Baptist Witness, Florida Times-Union, Jacksonville Magazine, The Journal of Country Music, The Lake City Reporter, Life, Miami Herald, Miami News, Miami New Times, New Bern Sun Journal, Nashville Banner, Nashville Tennessean, National Geographic, The Orlando Sentinel, The Rogers Affiliated Press Weekly News, The Sanford Herald, Sing Out, Smithsonian.

Organizations

Alachua County Historical Society; American Federation of Musicians; American Society of Composers, Authors and Publishers (ASCAP); Atlantic Coast Line and Seaboard Air Line Historical Society; Broadcast Music Incorporated (BMI); Collier County Sheriffs Department; Columbia County Historical Society; Columbia County Public Library; Country Music Foundation; Craven County Convention and Visitors Bureau; CSX Transportation; Hot Springs Historical Society; International Bluegrass Music Association (IBMA); Jacksonville Public Library; Lake City Community College; Library of Congress; MCA Music Publishing; Miami-Dade County Public Library; Orlando Public Library; Pinecastle Records; Rollins College; South Florida Bluegrass Association; St. Johns County Public Library; U.S. Army Medical Department Center and School, Wayne R. Austerman, Ph.D., command historian.

Audiotapes, Interviews, and Other Sources

For quotes from Chubby Wise, the author has used published sources as well as an unpublished transcript of a lengthy interview of the fiddler conducted By Joan Alderman, an Altha, Florida, schoolteacher. Other Wise quotes, as well as those from George Custer, were culled from audiotapes made by E. Vernon Douglas, Chief Judge of Florida's Third Judicial District. The author is also indebted to Philip Pacey, a librarian at the University of Lancashire in Preston, England, for access to his research on early railroad songs. Finally, thanks to Sally, Cody, and Luke.